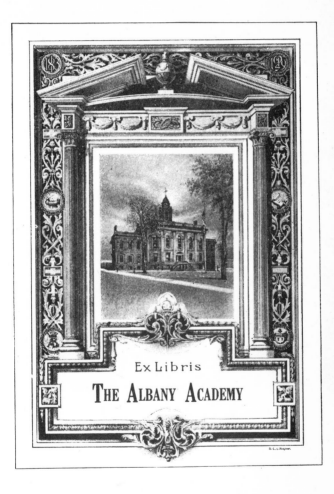

WOMEN AND MEN OF THE FRENCH RENAISSANCE

MARGUERITE DE VALOIS, REINE DE NAVARRE, SŒUR DE FRANÇOIS I

D'APRÈS CORNEILLE DE LYON

WOMEN AND MEN OF THE FRENCH RENAISSANCE

BY EDITH SICHEL

WITH NUMEROUS ILLUSTRATIONS

Mais les bons et louables esprits sont ceux...
qui osent avoir une passion, une admiration haute-
ment placée et qui la suivent.

SAINTE-BEUVE.

KENNIKAT PRESS
Port Washington, N. Y./London

WOMEN AND MEN OF THE FRENCH RENAISSANCE

First published in 1901
Reissued in 1970 by Kennikat Press
Library of Congress Catalog Card No: 74-110923
SBN 8046-0905-5

Manufactured by Taylor Publishing Company   Dallas, Texas

CONTENTS

BOOK I

THE FRENCH RENAISSANCE

BOOK II

MARGARET OF ANGOULÊME AND THE RENAISSANCE

BOOK III

RABELAIS AND HIS CONTEMPORARIES

CONTENTS

BOOK IV

END OF THE REIGN

LIST OF ILLUSTRATIONS

PREFACE

It has been difficult to find a title modest enough for a book which in no way claims to be a chronicle of events, political or military. It is merely a personal history—an effort to recall a few of the less-known figures that moved and had their being in France, in the first half of the sixteenth century.

My best thanks are due to Mr. J. G. Ritchie for the help he has given me in making my "Historical Summary"; and also to Mr. Henry Newbolt, editor of the "Monthly Review", for his kindness in allowing me to reprint part of Chapter XVII from an article ("The Religion of Rabelais") which appeared in the number of that periodical for December, 1900.

M. de Maulde's new book, "Les Femmes de la Renaissance," which (though written from a very different point of view) covers much the same period as my own, unfortunately appeared some time after I had written my volume—too late for me to profit by its store of information.

London, February 28th, 1901.

LIST OF WORKS CONSULTED

CONTEMPORARY

Lettres de Marguerite d'Angoulême.

Nouvelle Lettres de Marguerite d'Angoulême.

Les Marguerites de la Marguerite des Princesses: Poèmes de Marguerite d'Angouléme: FRANCK.

Nouvelles Poésies de Marguerite d'Angoulême: GÉNIN.

Poésies du Roi François I, de Louise de Savoie, Duchesse d'Angoulême, de Marguerite Reine de Navarre et Correspondance intime du Roi avec Diane de Poitiers et plusieurs autres dames de la Cour.

Lettres de Diane de Poitiers: GUIFFRY.

Lettres de Catherine de Médicis.

Oraison Funèbre sur Marguerite d'Angoulême: CHARLES DE SAINTE-MARTHE.

Le Tombeau de la Reine de Navarre.

Récit d'un Bourgeois de Paris du Seizième Siècle: edited by LALANNE.

Journal de Louise de Savoie.

Histoire de Louis XII: JEAN DE SAINT-GELAIS.

Histoire des Choses Mémorables: FLEURANGE.

Mémoires de Guillaume du Bellay.

Lettres de Jean du Bellay contained in l'Entrevue de François I et Henry VIII à Boulogne-sur-Mer: PÈRE HAMY.

Memoirs of Benvenuto Cellini.

Vie de Ronsard: BINET.

Histoire de Lyon: PARADIN.

Histoire de Notre Temps: PARADIN.

Histoire de Béarn et de Foix: OLHAGARAY.

Histoire Catholique: HILARION DE LA COSTE.

Dames Illustres: HILARION DE LA COSTE.

Dames Illustres: BRANTÔME.

Œuvres de Brantôme: Vol. VII.

Gargantua et Pantagruel: RABELAIS.

Epîtres de François Rabelais à Monseigneur l'Evêque de Maillezais.   Ecrites pendant son voyage d'Italie: RABELAIS.

L'Heptaméron: MARGUERITE D'ANGOULÊME.

Les Soupirs : OLIVIER DE MAGNY.

Œuvres poétiques de Louise Labê.

Le Débat de Folie et d'Amour: LOUISE LABÉ.

Œuvres poétiques de Clément Marot, de Pierre Ronsard, de Joachim du Bellay.

Œuvres Choisies de Ronsard: SAINTE-BEUVE.

Œuvres Choisies de Joachim du Bellay: BECQ DE FOUQUIÈRES.

Défense de la Poésie: JOACHIM DU BELLAY.

Cymbalum Mundi: BONAVENTURE DES PÉRIERS.

Le Second Enfer etc.: ETIENNE DOLET (Lyons, 1544).

Deux Dialogues de Platon, Philosophe divin et surnaturel, nouvellement traduite en langue française: ETIENNE DOLET.

L'Architecture: PHILIBERT DE L'ORME.

Poëtes Français depuis le Douzième Siècle jusquà Malesherbe.

BIOGRAPHICAL

Marguerite de Valois: LA COMTESSE D'HAUSSONVILLE.

Conférences sur Marguerite d'Angoulême: LURO.

Le Livre d'Etat de Marguerite d'Angoulême: LE COMTE DE LA FERRIÈRE.

Les Femmes des Valois: SAINT-AMAND.

Biographical Preface to "Lettres de Marguerite D'Angoulême: GÉNIN.

Biographical Preface to Les Marguerites de la Marguerite des Princesses: FRANCK

Trente Ans de Jeunesse: DE MAULDE LA CLAVIÈRE.

Life of Margaret of Angoulême: MARY ROBINSON.

Jeanne d'Albret: MISS FREER.

Le Château de Pau: LAGIÈZE.

Etudes sur François I: PAULIN PARIS.

Vie de Rabelais: FLEURY.

Vie de Rabelais: RENÉ MILLET.

Vie de Clément Marot (Biographical Preface to his works): HÉRICAULT.

Biographical Preface to the selected works of Joachim du Bellay · BECQ DE FOUQUIÈRES.

Vie de Louise Labé (Preface to Works) : BLANCHEMAIN.

Dictionnaires de Bayle; Chauffepié; La Croix du Maine; and Colletet.

Causeries de Lundi: SAINTE-BEUVE.

Collection Littéraire: KERALIO.

Vie de Clouet: BOUCHOT.

Vie de Philibert de l'Orme: VACHON.

Life of Etienne Dolet: CHRISTIE.

Caractères et Portraits: FEUGÈRE.

LITERARY AND CRITICAL

Tableau du Seizième Siècle: SAINTE-BEUVE.

Etudes Littéraires: BRUNETIÈRE.

Histoire de la Littérature française: RENÉ DOUMIC.

La Morale des Femmes: LEGOUVÉ.

Les Femmes de Brantôme: BOUCHOT.

HISTORICAL

Histoire de France (Vol. VII): HENRI MARTIN.

La Renaissance: MICHELET.

La Réforme: MICHELET.

The French Renaissance: MRS. PATTISON.

Pictures of the old French Court: CATHERINE BEARN.

Old Touraine: ANDREA COOK.

For Contemporary historical authorities see under "Contemporary".

AUTHOR'S NOTE.

With regard to the portrait described on p. 98, the author learns, too late to correct the text, that it is now ascribed to Corneille de Lyon, instead of to Clouet.

HISTORICAL SUMMARY
OF CONTEMPORARY EVENTS

LOUIS XIII
(1498—1515)

He married Anne de Bretagne after divorcing his first wife, the daughter of Louis XI. His Minister and right-hand man was Georges, Cardinal d'Amboise, a great financial reformer. The King had claims not only on Naples, but on Milan, in right of his grandmother, Valentine, heiress of the Visconti.

CONTEMPORARY SOVEREIGNS
LEO X, HENRY VII of England, FERDINAND THE CATHOLIC of Spain, the Emperor MAXIMILIAN.

1499—1500 The French took possession of Milan and, at the battle of Novara, made a prisoner of the Duke Ludovico Sforza, who was imprisoned for ten years in France and died at Loches. In concert with Ferdinand the Catholic of Spain, France then took
1503 Naples, but lost it again through Spanish treachery; the battle of Cerignola completed the French disasters. Louis retaliated by a fresh invasion both of Naples and of Spain. In Italy Bayard made his intrepid defence of the Bridge of Garigliano, but in vain: the French were defeated in both countries.
1506 Louis treated with Ferdinand. Meanwhile Venice, profiting by the troubles of the other States, acquired territory all round. By the exertions of Julius II
1508 (Raphael's Patron) the League of Cambrai was formed between Julius, Maximilian, Spain, and France. The

1509   French, led by Louis, took the initiative in attacking the Venetians; and defeated them at the battle of Agnadel. The Allies divided the Venetian domains.

1511   Having gained his ends against Venice, Julius II conspired with Ferdinand to drive France out of Italy, and made the Holy League between themselves, England, the Swiss and the Venetians. Gaston de Foix, the courageous young French general, was the spirit of the campaign; but he was killed at

1512   Ravenna, where the French were victorious. They were, notwithstanding, gradually expelled from Italy. Louis made another descent on the Milanese terri-

1513   tories and was defeated at the second battle of Novara. The complicated politics of this year resulted in his making peace with Henry VIII, Maximilian and Ferdinand, after the Battle of the Spurs, near Guinégate.

1514   Anne de Bretagne died on January 9th, and on August 7th, Louis made a second marriage with Mary Tudor, Henry VIII's sister.

1515   The King died.

FRANCIS I
(1515—1547)

Married (1) to Claude of France: (2) to Eleanor of Portugal.

CONTEMPORARY SOVEREIGNS

POPES LEO X; CLEMENT VII; and PAUL III.

HENRY VIII who came to the English throne in 1509.

CHARLES V of Austria and Spain, who was elected as Emperor in 1519.

1515   The King, discontented with Louis XII's treaties with Italy, resolved on a policy of aggression. He crossed the Alps at the head of his army, descended on Milan and won the battle of Marignan, routing the Swiss mercenaries. The fight resulted in the

	Treaty of Fribourg with the Swiss, and a Concordat
1516	with the Pope, Leo X.
1519	Imperial Election. Candidates: Charles V, Francis I, Henry VIII. Charles V was elected.
1520	Field of the Cloth of Gold. Francis failed to win over Henry VIII, who formed an alliance with the Emperor.
1521—1525	Charles V made war against the French. Francis was beaten on his three frontiers—those of Spain, Flanders and Italy. He was defeated at Pampluna and ended by losing Navarre. Also Milan, which revolted against the Governor, Lautrec, who was finally defeated at Bicocca (1522). The Constable
1523	of France deserted to the side of the Emperor and made a secret treaty with Charles and with Henry of England.
1524	Disasters for the French in Italy. Bayard was killed at Gattinara. The Constable invaded France and besieged Marseilles unsuccessfully. He was followed across the Alps by Francis, who engaged in the siege of Pavia, and was defeated and taken
1525	prisoner at the battle of that name.
1525—1526	The captivity of Francis in Spain. He made the Treaty of Madrid with Charles V, but never intended to keep it, and returned to France only to repudiate it.
1527	The Constable marched to Rome with an army of German adventurers and was killed as he scaled its walls. Rome was sacked and the Pope imprisoned.
1529	The Peace of Cambrai, or La Paix des Dames, was concluded: a Peace negotiated between the Emperor's aunt, Margaret of Austria, and Louise de Savoie, Francis' mother. There was no war for six years.
1529	The Collége de France was founded.
1531	Death of Louise de Savoie.
1533	Marriage of the Dauphin with Catherine de Médicis, niece of Clement VII.
1533—1535	Terrible persecution of the Protestants. It had begun before this, during the Regency of Louise

de Savoie, and there had been fresh outbursts after the King's return, notably in 1528.

Francis was tolerant, or not, as expediency demanded. Much depended on the Protestant German Princes, who allied themselves to him whenever they needed his protection against the Catholic Charles. But when Charles' policy inclined him to leniency towards them, the position was reversed.

1536   Hostilities resumed with the Emperor. Francis occupied Savoy and Piedmont. Charles invaded and ravaged Provence.

1538   He had to retreat and a truce was made at Nice.

1539   He visited Francis at Paris, but would not be won over.

1541—1544 New war between him and France. Francis cast about for allies and formed a league with Soliman the Magnificent, Sultan of Turkey—a pact which offended the other Powers. The Turks invaded Hungary, marched to the walls of Vienna and diverted the imperial forces. Francis won a great
1544   but fruitless victory at Cérisole, in Piedmont.

1544—1546 Henry VIII and Charles V invaded France, but they did not work well together and Charles made peace with France at Crépy.

Henry followed suit in 1546.

1547   Death of Francis I. Henry VIII died the same year; Charles V in 1556.

BOOK I

THE FRENCH RENAISSANCE

AUTHORITIES CONSULTED FOR CHAPTER I

Histoire des Choses Mémorables : FLEURANGE.

Récit d'un Bourgeois de Paris : edited by LALANNE.

Mémoires de Guillaume du Bellay.

l'Heptaméron : MARGUERITE D'ANGOULÊME.

Œuvres de Rabelais.

Etudes sur François I : PAULIN PARIS.

Les Femmes de Brantôme : BOUCHOT.

Tableau du Seizième Siècle : SAINTE-BEUVE.

La Renaissance (Histoire de France) : MICHELET.

Histoire de France : HENRI MARTIN.

Life of Etiènne Dolet : CHRISTIE.

La Morale des Femmes : LEGOUVÉ.

CHAPTER I

WHEN all is said and written the French Renaissance
with its impulse towards beauty and learning remains a
mystery—as inexplicable as youth: with its sudden craving
for poetry and knowledge, its religious doubts, its emotion.
The Renaissance is the youth of Western Nations, when
the impassioned mind beholds the world for the first time
in all its significance, when the senses are intensified and
the relations of things are changed.

The French Renaissance began with Charles VIII's return
from the wars in Italy at the end of the fifteenth century,
a hundred years later than the Italian Renaissance. Unlike
the latter, it was a movement springing rather from the
head than the imagination, and required the inspiring influence of some other country to arouse and to shape it. In
this, as in much else, France was not originative; and when
we examine the French Renaissance it is the essential French
qualities that we find there—the qualities which make and
mar the France of to-day. There is the gay philosophy
of common sense and daily life; the good humour and the
scepticism which come of living in the present; the graceful
imagination, never too great to be useful, which built the
delicious Châteaux of the Loire, planned their gardens and
adorned them with fantastic sculptures; which painted too

the portfolios of Court portraits, subtle interpretations of character and the main contribution of France to contemporary painting. Its national faculties are rather critical than creative, and so is its Renaissance.

But when we speak of the Renaissance we speak of an oceanic movement—of movement within movement. To handle it as a whole is a work too vast for limited space and powers; to describe one little corner of it is a task sufficiently difficult. Such is our restricted aim. The reign of Francis I covers the best period of the earlier Renaissance; and it is this reign and the years that immediately preceded it which fix our choice. Between 1490 and 1550 the modern world was born. Never was art, never was social life more significant than then.

Art and social life are, in a great measure, dependent upon women, who in a time like this are bound to play a prominent part. There was one woman of the day whose name has become identified with the French Renaissance— whose life is like a symbol of it. This was Margaret of Angoulême, sister of Francis I, his counsellor and closest friend. Her figure makes the natural centre of a record such as ours. Events and persons group themselves round her; she harmonizes while she dominates them.

To picture her generation it is needful to try and enter into its atmosphere and to watch the shifting scenes of the times. The Châteaux of the Loire, more than aught else, conjure before us the France of the day—the France that stood at the parting of the ways—between the old and the new. Sometimes exuberant fancy breaks in flower and hobgoblin over the sternness of the feudal towers; some-

times in a new building the slenderest battlements crown
an enchanted palace, like a delicate apology to the past;
sometimes a sixteenth-century wing, richly carved, is added
to an old fortress; or the past is altogether extinguished
in the sumptuous grace of the present.

Every one of them evokes visions. From the gates of
Blois and Chaumont there wind cavalcades, riding forth to
the hunt in the forest: the ladies on their jewelled horses,
some of them astride, dressed in green and scarlet and
little caps with plumes—the men in the slashes and diamonds
and golden taffeta of their day; or—when Chivalry was
revived for a Court game—in the suits of ancient knights,
well versed in Provençal ceremonies of the Courts of Love.
They are probably singing Marot's fashionable Psalms set
to popular tunes, as they amble along after the King, followed by a city of silken tents.

Or it is the moonlight wedding of the Duke of Urbino
at Amboise, "qui fut merveilleusement triomphante .... et
fut dansé et ballé le possible." Seventy-two damsels, disguised like Germans and Italians, accompany the minstrels
with tambourines; torches make a light as bright as day;
princes and peers are the dancers. The Pavane is the
measure they are treading, and they hold the hands
of laughing ladies whose dresses are stiff with gems: whose
manners are the strangest mixture of royal etiquette
and reckless easiness. They dance till morning—they
are never tired. All day they amuse themselves by watching from their marble balcony the siege of the mock city
that was built for the occasion; or by commenting on the
skill and prowess with which the Jeunesse dorée (François, Duc

d'Angoulême amongst them) outvie each other in their
serious sport.

Or the Court is moving from one Château to another,
with all the unimaginable difficulties then implied by a
journey. There were never less than three thousand people
in motion on the rough roads. In front go the "fourriers,"
to prepare lodgings for the King and his retinue in whatever town or village can be reached before nightfall; next
come cooks, pâtissiers, rôtissiers, to set up the banquet-
tables. Then follows the retinue itself: the glittering hedge
of horsemen, at once escort and distraction to the pale
beauties in mule-drawn litters. Their eyes are red from
fatigue: they jolt along behind silken curtains, too much
exhausted to listen to the bons-mots of their cavaliers. In
the centre of all comes the royal litter in which the King,
in white satin doublet, reposes on a white satin cushion.
Behind this train files an endless series of officials, fore-
stallers of every royal caprice. As they approach the village,
bells ring, the Curé runs out, followed by the ragged vil-
lagers, and hastens to greet the languid monarch. The
Court alights and disposes itself—chiefly in the peasants'
cottages. The State Chaperone, or Gouvernante, supervises
the Ladies' Hut and performs the duties of the roll-call.
When she goes over the names she generally finds that
two or three of her charges have escaped, in their stiff
brocades, to pursue fresh amourettes beyond her ken. Not
unfrequently some of the ladies are left behind in the hut,
ill from the effects of their journey, and they only join
their companions at their leisure—an easy matter when
expeditions sometimes lasted for several weeks.

Or it is the Army setting forth for Italy, the King again conspicuous, as gay in armour as in satin, with no more than a camp-bed for his needs.

War was, indeed, the only cure for the vices of peace. The noblemen's houses in those days were Aladdin's palaces —full of childish ingenuity of magnificence. The meals were a medley of artifice and barbarism. Ladies and gentlemen ate off one plate; tables were set out to look like green lawns, with live birds and flowers upon them. Scores of Varlets acted as standing candlesticks, and the trumpets alone put an end to the toasts. The great Gaston Phébus, Duke of Béarn and Foix, in Louis XII's reign, was kept in good temper between the courses by "*machines à surprise*" —a kind of show with a surprise in them. These "*surprises*" must have cost a fortune. One of them was a hollow mountain from which emerged babies dressed as savages, who danced an elaborate ballet. This may be puerile, but it is jovial. Inventive luxury belongs to early days: it has a lavish freshness about it as different as possible from the tired luxury of decadence.

These are Court scenes. The peasants and the middle-class had a life of their own. We may, if we please, witness a fantastic skirmish in the ample green valleys of the Loire, between the "Cake-bakers" and the "Vignerons." They have upset the Bakers' trays of "fouaces" as they carry them through the vineyards, up the hill to Chinon—perhaps to the Pâtissier Innocent who lives hard by Rabelais' home. Through the High Street clatters the Post, bringing news of the Italian wars to the Court at Blois. He has passed through many towns already, spreading his tidings in the

larger ones by the "Letters" that he carries: letters which
are printed and sold. Sometimes the news is brought North
by companies of perambulating merchants who are returning
from the fair at Lyons, the metropolis of the frontier.

Each town is a world in itself with its own character
unaffected by the rest. Paris ranks no higher than the
others in civilization, and is only distinguished as one of
the Court towns and the abode of the Parlement and the
Sorbonne. Lyons stands higher as a centre of literature, art,
trade, even of society; Bourges boasts the better University.
But there is life enough in the streets of Paris—and of other
towns too, for the matter of that—life that presents the
same strange union of old and new, of violence and polish.
Outside the Scholar-printer's shop a brawl rages and ends
in murder; inside, two authors in furred cloaks are discussing the nature of the soul. From the shadow of the Tour
de Nesle an assassin darts out at dusk to stab a rival or
an over-opulent colleague: he escapes promiscuously; next
day a petty thief is hanged in the Place de la Grève. In
the Place des Halles, the "Enfants Sans Souci" (a troop of
strolling-players) are acting a skit against the monks, loudly
applauded by students, loungers, and market-women; or else
they are joking and sparring with the rival company of
"les Basoches," in the winding alleys of the Marais.

Francis I spends a fortune every year on his pocket-
handkerchiefs, and one of his tailor's bills amounts to £15,600.
Upstart merchants follow suit, and brave it in costly silks.
At the same moment the King issues a Sumptuary Edict
forbidding the mercers to sell silk at all, except to the
Princes of the blood. But he does not disapprove of spend-

ing thousands on shows. Royal Birthdays, Royal Marriages, Royal Funerals must have lightened the Treasury considerably with their fancy dresses and processions, wax candles and draperies, black or scarlet. Every event is the signal for a pageant. In those days fairy cities, planned by the best artists and inhabited by Cupids, rose in a week to greet the King's return from his victories. Another time the monarch, torch in hand, heads a procession of copes and mitres to see a heretic burn; or a hooting crowd pursues another, who, wrapped in a sheet, is doing penance through the streets, until he at last prostrates himself on the " Parvis " of Paris—the great stone slab before Nôtre Dame.

Amidst all this changing and growing life, women are not the least noteworthy or the least puzzling figures. The whole Renaissance movement gave them great opportunities. The enthusiasm for beauty brought them into prominence. Art reproduced them in painting and sculpture. More than this, it furnished them with a field where their judgment was efficient and important, and gave them new topics of conversation. It may safely be said that their position in a country is one of the distinctest signs by which the state of its society can be judged. In France where the Arts became a social adornment, and the social art was foremost, they had peculiar advantages; and here, where social habits had been ripening long before the Renaissance, there is ample opportunity for watching the growth of their power.

Their relation to men is the chief index of their progress, and to trace the history of that relation is a fruitful theme for the philosopher. The Church helped their cause by its

worship of the Virgin, and invented Abbesses as well as
Saints—political women and philanthropists. Chivalry made
them prominent and surrounded them with a halo. With
the Courts of Love there gradually grew up a metaphysical
view of the passions, and every respectable lady had a
Platonic "Serviteur," as well as an ordinary husband. The
idea was often abused, but its primal beauty and sincerity
had their effect on daily life. Women began to be respected as a sex, not only in exceptional cases. At the
Court of the poet, Charles of Orleans, where nobody ever
ceased rhyming, the women rhymed with the best of them,
or honoured poetry by wearing their favourite ballades in
their girdles. This was in the middle of the fifteenth
century. The increased commercial intercourse with Italy,
followed by Charles VIII's conquests in that country, brought
new ideas into France; and the poetic conceptions of Dante's
Beatrice and Petrarch's Laura had their share in affecting
the current opinions about women. Chivalry and Feudalism
were dying before the unknown forces of modern civilization.
The change can be traced even in literary details. The
romantic term "Serviteur" is altered; it becomes "sûr et
parfaict Amy." A dispute began between the Court singers
of Sacred and of profane Love. It grew into a fashionable
feud—immortalized by Titian's picture. Soon after 1500,
the poetaster, Héroet, wrote a Platonic poem, "La parfaicte
Amye." It was answered by Marot's friend, La Borderie,
who, in his "Ange de Coeur," pleaded for profane Love;
while the more domestic Fontaine put in a word for the
legitimate joys of the hearth and published his poem of
"Contr' Amye." Love was regarded as an intellectual

exercise. It became a matter of breeding for every young
gentleman to have a Platonic mistress who formed his manners. She was chosen for him by his parents or guardians
without the faintest reference to his own wishes, or to any
warmer motive than that of education and parental interests
at Court. "Cette coutume avait telle force que ceux qui
ne la suivaient étaient regardés comme mal-appris et n'ayant
l'esprit capable d'honnête conversation," says a sixteenth-
century writer. His own mistress, he tells us, took care
to reprove him for all his mistakes. "Nulle autre personne
ne m'a tant aidé de m'introduire dans le monde." The
French alone understand how to combine convenience with
romance. This strange arrangement was probably part of
the conscious revival of chivalry under Francis—when chivalry was already a matter of history. Chivalric tales, chivalric dress, chivalric language, became the rage at Court.
The King often came down in the morning accoutred like
a knight of old. He even issued a royal decree that anyone who spoke a word in dishonour of a woman should be
hanged. The old terms of sentiment reappeared and mingled with the new Platonic phrases: the phrases so soon
assimilated by people of good tone from the rediscovered works
of Plato. Much of this, of course, was superficial; immorali-
ties abounded and morality was still regarded as heroic—
never as a matter of course. But though purisms of Love
are not virtue, they mean the existence of ideas more abstract than before. Even in the "Heptameron," which is
a tissue of gallantries, they come more than once to the
fore. The company of story-tellers is fond of reverting to
the subject. "By my faith," quoth the impatient Sir

Simontault, "if you had felt love's fire as others have done,
you would not thus turn it into a Platonic theory—good
for pen and paper, but not for use or practice " . . . . . " I
dare not even think my thought," answers the idealist,
Dagoucin, "for fear that my eyes may reveal it; for the more
closely I keep the flame covered, the greater groweth my
joy in knowing that I love perfectly." Precept and practice
too often live apart, and the morals of Dagoucin's contemporaries are one more proof of the platitude. It is difficult
to reconcile the refinement and the coarseness of Francis I's
generation. The current notions of Platonic friendship,
the fantastic conceits of intellect, came at the hour of emanci-
pation, together with the bold throwing off of asceticism,
with the unbridled spirits of holiday-making. Perhaps
this concurrence of strange influences may count for something in the curious state of morals that the age represents.
It is one thing to enter into its atmosphere, and another
to account for it. Yet without attempting the impossible,
it will not be unhelpful to continue our study of its women;
and, before proceeding to its history, to look a little more
closely at the ladies of the sixteenth century.

THE WOMEN OF THE FRENCH RENAISSANCE

AUTHORITIES CONSULTED FOR CHAPTER II

Part I

Nouvelles Poésies: MARGUERITE D'ANGOULÊME.

Histoire de Notre Temps: PARADIN.

Œuvres de Brantôme (Vol. VII).

Dames Illustres: BRANTÔME.

Dames Illustres: HILARION DE LA COSTE.

l'Heptaméron: MARGUERITE D'ANGOULÊME.

Œuvres de Rabelais.

Le Château de Pau: LAGIÈZE.

Marguerite de Valois: LA COMTESSE D'HAUSSONVILLE.

Les Femmes de Brantôme: BOUCHOT.

Collection Littéraire: KERALIO.

La Morale des Femmes: LEGOUVÉ.

La Vie de Philibert de l'Orme: VACHON.

Trente Ans de Jeunesse: DE MAULDE LA CLAVIÈRE.

Part II

Histoire de Louis XII: JEAN DE ST.-GELAIS.

Appendix to l'Heptaméron.

Histoire des Choses Mémorables: FLEURANGE.

Trente Ans de Jeunesse: DE MAULDE LA CLAVIÈRE.

Pictures of the old French Court: CATHERINE BEARN.

Les Femmes de Brantôme: BOUCHOT.

Marguerite de Valois: LA COMTESSE D'HAUSSONVILLE.

CHAPTER II

I

THESE women of the Renaissance are, indeed, a bewildering psychological problem. The confusion of contrasts presented by them becomes overpowering, and so does their manifold energy. In the same person, often almost at the same moment, we find the noblest conduct and the lowest morals, the Stoic and the Epicurean, the Bacchante and the Student, learning and puerility, side by side. The King's sister Margaret, scholar, poet, and sage, builds up the pillars of the Temple in her Allegory from the tomes of Plato as well as from those of the New Testament. She promulgates an advanced naturalism and discusses metaphysics with the Reformers. Yet when her maid-in-waiting lies dying, she stands at her bedside in a mood more enquiring than sorrowful, and watches for the passing of the soul. It comes up (she has heard) by the throat and so out at the lips; and it is generally speedy, except in the case of the swan whose long neck causes some delay. The union of matter-of-factness and imagination reminds us of what we see in children. Curiosity was the dominant appetite of the day and begot infinite credulity: and this at a time when good sense was shaking the foundations of the Church, as well amongst

women as amongst men.   Like children, too, the ladies loved
adventure.   They indulged in all manner of delicious escapades—graceful, fantastic, reckless, such as turn the world
into a Shakspeare comedy.   If we want to enjoy their histories we must approach them as fairy tales—as the chronicles of an enchanted palace that knows nothing of moral
responsibility.   Then, perhaps, for a moment we too shall be
infected and shall, like them, "partir d'un bon éclat de
rire" at their jolly casuistry, successful lying, and Shrove
Tuesday amenities.

The sudden Pagan enthusiasm for the forces of Nature,
resulting from newly quickened senses and newly studied
classics, had far-reaching effects on morals.   Every age
chooses a special virtue to admire and a special vice to
abhor, and hypocrisy was the bugbear of the sixteenth
century.   Frankness and spontaniety were its idols.   Nature
was to them the secret school-master who, says Margaret,
"teaches other lessons than those of the school-master at
school."   Brantôme follows suit: "Nature," he writes, "is
very perfect, and if we follow such a good captain, we can
never stray from the safe road."   Unfortunately, neither he
nor his contemporaries hesitated to "follow."   He applied
his theories and severely censured any censure of morals.
Our Edward III came off very badly in his opinion for his
imprisonment of his mother, Isabella, on account of her
relations with Mortimer.   "Such a little crime"—he regret-
fully exclaims—"little I call it, because it is natural."   It
requires a delicate and steady discrimination to draw the
line between Nature and Licence, and delicacy was not the
strong point of the sixteenth century.

Contemporary literature gives us the lowest idea of the Mid-Renaissance women, from Francis I's accession onwards. If we believe Brantôme and the " Heptameron," our two great sources of information, we shall conclude that they had but one occupation, that of gallantry.   In both these authorities the monotony of such a subject becomes nauseous.   But they cannot be regarded as altogether veracious.   The "Heptameron" is a Court record of Court scandals, and Brantôme is also a Court biographer, with a love of impropriety.   They must not be read without many side-glances at history. Great immorality there was, but it was sometimes exaggerated, and we must remember that the incredibly gross language and topics of the day did not always mean what they implied.   Elaborate Platonic loves adopted the phrases and images of profaner passions and, however innocent or pedantic, created false impressions.   Polite society encouraged the discussion of every subject between men and women.   Modesty of speech was an insult to Nature, and if a thing existed it was worthy to be talked about.   Perhaps it followed that the only prevailing idea of fun was associated with gallantry —a tradition natural to the France of all times.   No story was considered amusing in which someone did not deceive someone else about a love-affair.

Contemporary records, then, are not libellous.   They are only untrue in making gallantry the exclusive occupation of their heroines, instead of one amongst many.   It has often been urged that the revolt from asceticism—the slackening of spiritual authority—was the reason of their moral laxity. It arose quite as much, perhaps more, from their prodigal vitality : the vitality of women whose heyday was also the

heyday of the world. Everything is fresh to them. Here
again they are like children—on a fine day—who leap because they cannot keep still: their emotions are no more
than an outlet for their superfluous energy. It found many
others in which they indulged as keenly—riding, shooting,
practical jokes, or hunting, nothing came amiss to them.
If we are to believe Brantôme, a poor nobleman died of a
broken heart because, whenever he tried to speak of his
passion, his lady-love would only talk of the chase. She
never thought of anything but stags and hounds; and at
last, after many futile wishes to turn into a dog, as his only
chance of happiness, he gave up the game and expired.

Soldiering was another vent for their forces. Among the
poorer classes it was followed as a lucrative profession. In
the wars against the Emperor Maximilian, in Guienne, a
certain Captain Dunois, pressed for time and money, formed
a brigade of 350 girls to construct fortifications; he paid
them at the rate of 1 franc 80 centimes a day—hardly more
than half the wages of the cheapest workman. At another
place he used the same means to get the towers pierced
with cannon-holes, and the walls and drawbridges repaired,
all in one short month. If the lowly pursued arms for gain,
the rich pursued them for glory. A contemporary writer
tells us that ladies had been made both Captains and Generals; and in his wars in Picardy Francis thanked the women
for the military service they had given them. One day,
during the siege of La Rochelle, in his son's reign, the dis-
couraged enemy lifted their eyes to the fort so successfully
held against them, and saw emerging on the battlements a
regiment of white-robed ladies. This was the Protestant gar-

rison that had conducted the defence. Their white uniforms
are a feminine touch. They said they were for clean ness:
who shall say that they were not for coquetry also? Perhaps they wished to form a contrast to their sisters of Italy
—the troop of Signoras who "looked like a moving opal"
when their captains drilled them in the Piazza of Siena. But
neither in France nor in Italy did manoeuvres ever degenerate
into ballets, and wherever women were soldiers real work
was accomplished.

There were, in fact, very few things which the women of
those days did not attempt. There was a feminine architect,
employed on the Tuileries (she bore the appropriate name of
Mademoiselle du Perron); and Cathérine de Médicis herself
imposed her own plans on the builders of her palace. But
the typical Renaissance lady did not devote herself to one
art: she achieved a good deal of everything. Universality
was her badge, and all she touched she did creditably—
generally with brilliance. Admirable Crichtons in the feminine gender abounded. Madame de Retz, for instance,
in the latter half of the century, remains a monument of
activity. She had ten children; she educated them herself;
she became a great scholar; she gave herself up to the arts;
she amused herself with many lovers; she cheered the Court
by her jokes; she led forth her troops in the King's name
against her own son, who had joined the Ligue against the
throne; she routed him completely: and all this with a face
that was not even beautiful. No doubt she also ministered
to starving dependents. Great ladies then acknowledged
responsibilities towards the poor as a matter of course, and
organized charity is by no means the invention of our own

times. The bad and the good—King's mistresses and high-hearted spinsters—seem to have divided its duties. The great Diane de Poitiers was the Dorcas of her almshouses at Anet. Old maids formed convent schools, often in the teeth of opposition. [1] In the sixteenth century there was but one Ursuline school; in the middle of the seventeenth there were three hundred and ten.

Letters even more than philanthropy were the general resource of able women. The pursuit of the classics was no longer exceptional, but an ordinary element of feminine education; and Brantôme complains that the customary schoolroom reading of Virgil and Ovid frequently corrupted the imagination of young girls. There were many erudite rhymers—there were many agreeable Minervas. More than one princess figured among their ranks and helped to make literature fashionable. Anne de Bretagne, though she could not read Latin, liked nothing better than to talk about Livy and to have learned works dedicated to her. Margaret

[1] There was Mademoiselle Sainte-Beuve, who took a lodging opposite the school she had built, from which she could watch her "bees," as she called them. The children were so fond of her that for a year after her death, they laid her plate at their table and begged that a picture of her at her window might be painted.

There was also Mademoiselle Saintonge, who was opposed by her father and stoned by the children of the town for her intention of founding a school. Undaunted she left her home and, followed by five little girls, she moved into a garret, though she had no money either for food or firing. Ten years afterwards she was leading a procession through the streets to honour the opening of her big new Convent-school.

of Angoulême had the real love of the Muses and was
capable of sacrifice for their sake. So was her niece, Margaret
of Savoy, the gracious friend of poets. There was also their
cousin, Renée of Ferrara, daughter of Louis XII—a sumptuous young scholar with Protestant leanings, divided between
Olympus and Geneva. They wrote, they learned, they listened. Literature and art were *de bon ton*. Every grandee
had a crowd of poetasters dependent on his purse-strings,
and the most modest government official felt himself bound
to become a patron or an author. The Poetry of those days
was no strain upon feeling or imagination. Metrical expression of fictitious sentiments was all that was required,
and elegance covered a multitude of sins.

The swarm of contemporary minor poetesses is only to be
outdone by the swarm of minor poets in our own day.
Louise Labé whose lyre had a human chord—Margaret of
Angoulême who could be both tender and graceful—are the
only ones that detach themselves from the rest. An amiable
host has been drowned in the kindly waves of oblivion.
Now and then an expert tries to revive one or two of them,
but the task is hardly worth the pains, and next to nothing
can be known about them. There was a mystic sonneteer,
Madame d'Entragues, in Louis XII's reign : there was a
Viscountess who wrote plays (she seems to have existed at
all times), and translated the Precepts of Socrates. There
were sometimes whole families of mothers and daughters—
Cathérines, Antoinettes, Dianes and Lucrèces—who pursued
an indefatigable course of high-minded verse. [1]

---

[1] The famous Mademoiselle de Gournai, Montaigne's friend, is
outside the period we are considering. His Essays were not

There exists a curious letter from one lady of Lyons[1] to another, exhorting women to study. It shows us that their Cause was well known in 1555. "I can," she writes, "do no more than implore virtuous ladies to raise their minds a little above their distaffs and their spindles. It is for them to rouse themselves and to show the world that, even if we were not born to command, we should not be despised as companions (whether in public or in private) of those who *are* born to rule: to rule and to be obeyed." The hour has now struck, continues this votary of her rights, when man can no longer shackle the "honest liberty which her sex has so long yearned for . . . .", when women are to prove how deeply men have hitherto wronged them. They must equal if not surpass them in intellectual achievement; they must make for real possessions rather than for rings and chains —rather than for self-tormenting passions which, unlike knowledge, leave nothing behind them but a "cheating of the Past"—the shadows of pain and delusion.

Had we a magician's wand, it would be a pleasant feat to conjure the writer of this letter into the middle of the English life of to-day. She would probably lose no time in surprise, but agitate at once for the Suffrage. As it is, we can but hope that she has found congenial company in the Elysian Fields of Blue-stockings: that even now she is conversing with Mrs. Carter and Miss Seward, or perhaps with Hannah More herself.

published till 1595. Her friendship with him is more of a classic than her long-winded mythological novel, or any of her literary achievements.

[1] Louise Labé.

Whether women are creative or not is a question often debated. The sixteenth century, like other centuries, seems to point to an answer in the negative. It is surely curious that a time which produced so many poetesses should have left us so little that counts. Not one of them reached the front rank : nearly all were the priestesses of coteries. But they had begun to discover where their strength lay. Conversation—most interpretative of arts—had already claimed Frenchwomen for its own, and as soon as Society existed their quick sympathies found a field there. A Princess of Naples, whom Brantôme knew, apologized to a great French nobleman for the dull entertainment she was giving him. Her ladies, said she, had not the Frenchwomen's gift for "causerie." And it is this "gift for causerie" which has always distinguished them ; which belonged then, as it belongs now, to every Frenchwoman of whatever class—to the average as well as to the gifted.

The Hôtel Rambouillet in the next century was not evolved from nothing. We can trace its ancestry in Renaissance days, and the Courts of literary princesses were, perhaps, the first Salons. Poetesses followed their example. The ladies of the "Heptameron" fence adroitly over abstruse topics—"parlant autant par passion que par raison"; the men reply to them as equals. The ordinary ladies of those days had, indeed, enough practice in conversation. They received visits from their beaux while they were dressing and undressing. Their nightgowns were jewelled, their bedrooms hung with silk. Their morning began in bed with their maid's arrival and the choice of their dress for the day —or the hour. Then came the ceremony of the bath in

an oval silver basin, and the ceremony of putting on the little
fairy slippers, and the ceremony of dressing the hair—
elaborately intertwined with pearls. When they went out they
wore diminutive masks to shield their complexions from the
sun. Like ladies of times less remote their great object was
not to be bored: for "Dulness is an incurable malady,"
says the young widow in the "Heptameron." They had
many distractions every day, and the first and the last were
the services of the Church. They do not seem to have been
very strict about them, for the goodly company of story-
tellers in Margaret's book got so much interested in their
story-telling that they kept the Monks waiting for more
than an hour for Vespers. The next evening when they
tried to be punctual they found the church empty; the
festive brothers had hidden behind a hedge to listen to the
stories that could so pervert their congregation.

It was the fashion to tell this kind of "Nouvelle" not
only in the pleasant meadows, but also in the drawing-rooms
of the Châteaux. Sometimes the pretty narrators varied
them by making acrostics and *jeux de mots*. Now it was
with their tongues, now with their needles. They stitched
devices for their friends and lovers. A big "S" embroidered
on a scarf stood for "Largesse"—an "S" barred by an
arrow for "Fermesse." When they were tired of their
tambour-frames they took to their viols and their lutes; or
they had singing lessons from the fashionable master, Albert
de Rippe; or they gossiped about the Court Chapel master,
Josquin des Prés, and his musical theory of the "Verbe Coloré"
and the stories he told them of the Vatican Choir. When
they were tired of all other occupations they sent for their

Fool, or their Folle, (there was a Folle who was as famous
as Triboulet,[1]) and laughed at the crudest of sallies.   They
believed all that was told them with an undiscriminating
curiosity and everything seemed equally true—the account
of a wizard who could recreate Venice Beauties, or facts
about the fauna of the Indies.   Any man who chose to spin
yarns was an authority, and even a grave historian accepted
a traveller's tale of magic on the rather vague word of a
gentleman who (he heard) had been appointed "Captain of
a place called Peru."

We should not probably have understood their speech.
If you did not wish to be vulgar, you must use "s" for
"r," aad "e" for "a"—saying "Pasis" for Paris, "méri"
for *mari* and the like.   And they had euphuisms of deport-
ment as well as of tongue.   In the lame Anne de Bretagne's
day every self-respecting woman had a limp; in that of her
successor, Mary Tudor, all the ladies of rank were cold in
manner, à l'Anglaise.   Strangest of all was their religion:
a curious medley of orthodox piety and of Paganism, which
made them careful in observance and very careless in appli-
cation.   Conviction of sin goes counter to the French tradition of common-sense and of gaiety.   These ladies held many
weapons ready against it: Penance and Absolution, or the
new-fangled doctrine of Predestination and Grace.   Many of
them leaned towards the Reformation, when Reformation
still meant nothing more schismatic than the reform of the
Roman Church.   They read the Bible for the first time and
found it a surprising new literature.   They drew from it

[1] Jeanne Sevin.

illustrations for every circumstance in life—even for their
jokes—without any sense of irreverence. From their birth
to their death they were surprising. Queens and Princesses
were bound to die conventionally and to say an effective
last word, but their inferiors were seldom edifying on their
deathbeds. Sometimes they remained philosophical. Brantôme's niece was a scientific Précieuse who understood her
own pulse and left her body to be dissected. Madame de
la Rochefoucauld was nobler. Her Confessor tried to console
her by preaching the worthlessness of life: "I am still in
the verdure of life," she replied, "and I love living. Nevertheless I will welcome death as if I were ugly and abject."
But the majority were like the merry Mademoiselle de
Limeuil who died at Court. During her illness, "jamais le
bec ne lui cessa.... car elle était fort grande parleuse."
"'Julien,' she said to her favourite Varlet, a sweet player of
instruments, 'Julien, take your violin, and until you see
that I am dead, (for I am passing away,) go on playing
"The Defeat of the Swiss" to me as well as you can, and
when you come to the words "All is lost", play the phrase
four or five times over, as piteously as possible.' He did
so—and when he came to 'All is lost', she said the words
twice—and turning to the other side of the bed: 'All *is*
lost, with that chord,' quoth she, and thus she died.... Voilà,"
ends her chronicler, "une mort joyeuse et plaisante." [1]

Joyousness and pleasantness were essential qualities in the
eyes of King Francis. Sadness he regarded as a capital
offence. No lady without happy spirits and happy looks

[1] Brantôme, Vol. IX.

was admitted into his Petite Bande, the inner circle of
goddesses who had to accompany him wherever he went.
They hunted with him in the forest; their table was next
his at dinner; they had the same dishes as he did, and after
the banquet they amused him by their sallies. Their dresses
toned with the hangings of the rooms they sat in, and their
outdoor clothes were dyed to match the ever changing
colours of the royal regiment. Francis chose their gowns
himself and it was he who paid for them—indeed, he did the
same for all the ladies of his court. We get entertaining
impressions about their figures from the royal memoranda
of the yards of stuff that were purchased. Ten ells was
the average quantity—eleven ells for a stout nymph—but
a certain Madame de Canaples needed as much as sixteen.
The King's favourite dresses were of gooseberry-coloured
satin, or of reddish-purple velvet with white lining and
silver sleeves. The Petite Bande was always more sumptuous than the rest. Beauty was not so much a condition
of membership as what we should now call style, and wit
was indispensable. One of its leading women, Cathérine de
Médicis, the dowerless bride of the Dauphin, was to our
modern ideas decidedly plain; but her figure was distinguished, so was her mind; and Francis, quick to detect
power in others, had the skill to take her under his wing
and to use her brain.

The Petite Bande, consisting of women and a King, was
bound to become more or less of a political agency. Cathérine was made for such a circle. In the next reign she had
her own Battalion—"The Flying Squadron," as she called
it—and herself supervised her ladies' lovers. But by that

time intrigue was a science, and to govern a Kingdom by intrigue was part of a Queen's education. Cathérine was no exception. She was only one of a dynasty: the dynasty of Renaissance Stateswomen.

II

Political women were, in fact, becoming daily more prominent. They were by no means an unmitigated blessing, and the sharp-tongued amongst them were known as "les Marquises de Malebouche." One of these went so far as to try and interfere at the Etats de Blois (the parliamentary council) and was reproved for her daring by King Louis XII. But she was at no loss for a retort. "In the times," she said, "when lords and princes went to the Crusades and achieved great feats, there was nothing for us poor women to do but to pray and watch, and fast and make vows, so that God might give them a prosperous voyage and a safe return. But now-a-days, when we see that they accomplish no more than we do, it is quite right for us to talk about everything. For why on earth should we pray God for them, considering they are no better than ourselves?"

The first eminent political woman, in the modern sense of the word, was Anne de Beaujeu, a person of masterful vitality, the favourite daughter and confidant of Louis XI and the guardian of her brother, Charles VIII. She arranged her ward's state business, married him to Anne de Bretagne, restrained his extravagant desires for Italian Empire and, by her French policy of good sense, assured prosperity in his kingdom. Had he in later years yielded to her opposition, he would never have set forth on his fantastic campaign in Italy, and things would have been better for himself and for France. She was a strong masculine woman of the same kind as her contemporary, Margaret of Austria, but a less important personality; the latter, as Charles V's aunt and Regent of the Netherlands, had a wider field for her energies. Anne de Beaujeu was never tired of scheming. When she was no longer her brother's guardian, she held a court of her own where she plotted and intrigued to her brain's content; and perhaps her greatest triumph was the marriage of her only daughter to the Constable Montpensier, the greatest nobleman in France.

Anne de Bretagne, the wife successively of Charles VIII and Louis XII, was of a different type. She was essentially the provincial Frenchwoman, and might, for all the difference of century, have stepped straight out of one of Balzac's novels. She was also a schemer and a woman of affairs, but both affairs and schemes were confined in a narrow circle. Plain of countenance, sincerely pious, bigoted, charitable, prudish and rather pedantic, with a mild taste for learning, she liked luxury in her dress and surroundings and spent largely on works of art: more from a middle-class belief in a palatial establishment than from any real love of beauty. She was full of a fussy kindliness, readiest to show itself to the people of Brittany; indeed, she was always a Bretonne first and a Frenchwoman afterwards. Had she lived to-day, she would have belonged to countless committees, and Associations for befriending young girls. As it was, she must have had enough to do with the philanthropy then in favour: endowing schools and convents, providing poor girls with a *dot* and a trousseau, or needy scholars with a place at Court.

All these ends were actively promoted by her second husband, Louis XII, who was a singular mixture of parsimony and charity. He was stingy about household expenses and amusements; but he spent large sums in relieving distress and often denied himself personal comforts in order to lessen the taxes. His life he fashioned upon Marcus Aurelius: he was always reading him, and his reforming government was the outcome of his studies. But though he deserved to be called the Father of his people, he allowed himself the luxury of hobbies. He had his garden and his library.

"Ptolemée Philadelphe," as men called him after another princely book-lover, filled his shelves with choice volumes. [1] He patronized poets and painters and showed his preference for such as were characteristic Frenchmen. But he loved haggling more than what he haggled for, and nothing put him into a better temper than driving a bargain over a work of art.

With Anne's wishes he never interfered. He had been in love with her during her first marriage, and his faithful affection for her, as well as hers for him, is a refreshing little oasis of respectability amid increasing scandals. Her dominant passion was marriage-making. She pursued it with such religious ardour that the Pope presented her with an " Autel portatif"—a travelling altar —at which she was licensed to bless marriages at any

---

[1] They afterwards went to Paris and formed the kernel of the Bibliothèque Nationale.

moment. The union of her daughter Claude with Charles
V became the fixed idea of her existence. She preferred
any prince to Francis, whose mother she cordially detested. This affair was the only subject on which she
sparred with her husband. He shilly-shallied between his
love for his wife, and his own wish for Francis—his Heir-
Apparent—whom Claude eventually married after the death
of her mother.

Short of matrimony, Anne acknowledged no tender relations, even in play. Her Court was very strict—over-severe,
thought some—and amongst them Anne Boleyn, whose French
mother had secured her a place there. Petulant at the
Queen's restrictions, she left her in a fit of temper and took
refuge with the King's sister, Margaret of Angoulême. [1] Less
spoiled ladies were obliged to subject themselves to the
Queen's code of etiquette. It was customary for those of
high rank to have, each of them, a private duenna, a
"Maîtresse," also of high birth; but the ordinary maids-of-
honour were under the direction of a Gouvernante who appears
never to have left them. Under Anne de Bretagne's rule,
no man, except their Confessor, was ever allowed to approach
them unless it was in her royal presence. Otherwise they
saw no one but old ladies and each other, and had few
resources beside pious books and tambour-frames. Caution
cut its own throat. Confessors made love and had to be
expelled. One of them lost his head and preached on the

[1] Anne Boleyn remained in this position for some time after
the Field of the Cloth of Gold, when Henry VIII first saw her
amidst Margaret's ladies, and perhaps, even then, marked her for
his own.

tender passion, much to the scandal of the Queen and the congregation.

There was, in the next age, a reaction against all this severity. A distaste for a quiet life seems a generic quality, common to the half of womankind and no more peculiar to the nineteenth than the sixteenth century. The Hearth, for which their sex is made, seldom contents them, and they carry their nervous energies elsewhere. State busybodies, as we said, were on the increase, and the meddlesome lady of Blois had her rivals. By Cathérine de Médicis' day, they seem to have become a public nuisance. "Political women," she said, "behaved as if they possessed the lion's share of the world, and were going to inherit it..... It was not as if, like men, they gave the sweat of their brows to the work of life—not they. They allowed themselves a good time, gossiping in the chimney corner, very comfortable in their easy-chairs—or else on their cushions and couches..... And so they go on chattering at their ease about the world and the condition of France, as if it were they who did everything."

Among the buzzing swarm of dilettantes, however, there rises up here and there a more impressive figure—especially earlier in the century, before State-affairs became the fashion. Like painters, like poets, political ladies had their "School": Margaret of Austria and Anne de Beaujeu their pupils. Such was Louise de Savoie, mother of King Francis and of his sister, Margaret. She was a real stateswoman, who played a dominant part and took things seriously. Her politics were always personal, often passionate, and sometimes wicked —but they were not frivolous. She re-adjusted the balance

by her morals, in which frivolity formed a conspicuous element. It is the first years of her Court and of her
children's lives that we shall presently proceed to chronicle.
But we can hardly understand them without at least knowing
something of the intellectual atmosphere that surrounded
them. And before going farther, it may be well to cast a
glance in that direction.

AUTHORITIES CONSULTED FOR CHAPTER III

Histoire de France (Vol. VIII): MARTIN.

La Renaissance: MICHELET.

La Réforme: MICHELET.

Récit d'un Bourgeois de Paris: edited by LALANNE.

Dictionnaire Historique: BAYLE.

Life of Etienne Dolet: CHRISTIE.

Caractères et Portraits: FEUGÈRE.

Etudes sur François I: PAULIN PARIS.

Etudes Littéraires: BRUNETIÈRE.

Les Marguerites de la Princesse des Marguerites: MARGUERITE D'ANGOULÊME (with Biographical Preface by FRANCK).

Conférences sur Marguerite d'Angoulême: LURO.

CHAPTER III

I

THE SCHOLARS OF THE RENAISSANCE

THE Scholars of the Renaissance fill a unique position. Never before or since has scholarship occupied the place it did at that time. It was a newly-found country in which each man was discovering and exploring for himself, untrammelled by the etiquette of the Schools—working by the light of morning, after long groping amid the shadows of scholasticism. Clearness had not stiffened into pedantry, discussion had not crystallized into rules; it was still a keen quest after truth, undertaken by no dust-stained wayfarers, but by strong hopeful men in the fulness of their youth. They did not seek a goddess of cold pure marble, but a living mistress—an intense romance : the rómance lay uppermost for them. Erasmus could never get through the chapters on old Age and Friendship in his Cicero without pausing to kiss the page. "Many truly are to be ranked among the Saints," he writes, "who do not find a place in our lists of them." Classical style was then—as it still is in a few individuals—a sixth sense, an aesthetic appetite. There was a poet of the time who every year burned a copy of Martial as a sacrifice to Catullus—the object of his worship. Another man of letters—a great Scholar—stretched on a

bed of suffering, said that his one consolation in his misery
had been the style of a letter that a friend wrote to him
in Latin. His contemporary, Cardinal Bembo, went farther
still, and in spite of his red hat, implored young men not
to read St. Paul for fear it should injure their style.

Enthusiasm was not the only quality which set this generation apart in the annals of scholarship. The Scholars of the
sixteenth century throughout Europe were a race—a nation
—with their own language, their own unwritten laws. They
corresponded with each other all over the world, though
comparatively few of them ever met in person. They shared
in spirit each other's labours, imparting every fresh result of
research. Such energy involved endless penmanship. Erasmus
generally wrote twenty, and received forty letters a day.
Sometimes the desire to see a great Scholar (the commentator of some obscure Latin passage—the interpreter of
some subtle inflexion of gender) would inflame the breast of
his correspondent, and he crossed the seas to visit him.
The houses of Budé in Paris, and of Julius Cæsar Scaliger
in Verona, were always full of such guests. It was thus that
Erasmus went to see Sir Thomas More, drawn to him also
by the magnetism of kindred ideas; thus that a Paduan
writer describes—only, sad to say, in imagination—the visit
of More to Villovanus, and their long midsummer days of
dialectic in the meadows round Padua.

Great movements, whether or not the result of law, always
seem like miracle. If the moment is ripe, the right men and
the right events spring up at its call. When time and
chance meet there is an electric shock, and design and accident play into one another's hands. It is as if Fate had

written a drama and compelled actors and scenery to fall in with her purposes. Such an epoch was the Renaissance. Writers have sought for its antecedents; they have accounted for it in a dozen ways. Yet when they have done their best, the enigma is unanswered: the mystery of birth remains impregnable. All that they can achieve is to throw light, not on the origin of the Renaissance, but on the conditions which made its existence possible. Those conditions are by now too well-known and have been too often discussed to need re-stating in these pages. The subject is too vast, the task too big for us.

But apart from general causes there are secondary ones, different in each country according to its individual history. France was no exception. The wars of three successive monarchs—Charles VIII, Louis XII, and Francis I—with Italy had done an immense amount in spreading Italian art, Italian literature, Italian standards of beauty. If the royal busybodies worked sad mischief by always meddling, whether called for or not, with the politics of Milan, of Venice, or of Florence, they also did a great deal of good. The constant relations between the two peoples had widened the field of commerce; and Italian merchants as well as Italian artists settled in French towns. Besides this, the influence of Italian churchmen—many of them patrons of learning—the cosmopolitan nature of the Médicis Popes, the universal correspondence of Scholars in all lands: all these facts had their share in bringing about the great result. So had such Court marriages as that of the Princess Renée with the Duke of Ferrara, or that of the Dauphin with Cathérine de Médicis. Side facts too have their importance. The general appointment of resident Ambassadors instead of special Envoys, was not without significance. It spoke of a Europe bound together, instead of isolated nations; of intercourse in times of peace, no less than in times of war.

The analysis of these elements belongs, we repeat, to more solid pens; it is the work of philosophic historians. And the same may be said of the first distinguished spirits concerned therein. The Abélards, the Roger Bacons cannot be dismissed in a few pages. We must be content to accept the state of things as we find it in France at the end of the fifteenth, the beginning of the sixteenth century. Still all-prevailing stood out the great Conservative forces: the Sorbonne—or Faculty of Theologians—a court of judgment for learning, for creed, and for discussion; its foster-child, the University; and the equally narrow Parlement—the assembly which registered the royal decrees. If it refused to do so, the King was impotent, unless he chose to act arbitrarily; a power which made it an important political factor, though it very seldom dared to exercise it. The influence both of Parlement and of Sorbonne is astounding to read of. The fear inspired by the Sorbonne, even occasionally in the King, was almost like a superstition. It had acquired a divine right, a papacy of its own, which no one had contested; it could summon a Princess to appear at its bar; it was practically the omnipotent censor of all the thought and literature of the Kingdom.

Against these troops of bigotry, there mustered an ever-growing band of rebels. The more spiritual among them took refuge in Mysticism, which afterwards exercised no small influence on the Reformation; the more intellectual became men of science—rational philosophers—and made the centre of the Renaissance. Between the hostile camps stood the Court—generously inclining to the new order, but in credulous fear of the old one.

To grasp the extent of the Sorbonne's power we must remember its hold over the University. It had in its hands the education of youth. This education was of the most pedantic. Methods were regarded as all-important, and for-mulæ were more thought of than the matter formulated. The ordinary scholastic training given at the Universities consisted in learning the seven "Liberal Arts", after master-ing which a student took his "oath of scholarship", received his Scholar's Diploma and was allowed to hold public philo-sophical disputations with the Schoolmen. We need only turn to Rabelais' "Gargantua" if we wish to realise the absurd hair-splittings which constituted these debates, and the endless ingenuity and waste of mental force which went to them. They were a kind of intellectual gymnastics which induced activity of brain at the expense of thought, and all the secondary qualities were given a first place. Nothing was true but that which could be proved—and proved by the Schoolmen's methods—an opinion fatal to the interests of Truth. Skill in proof became the one thing needful, and the Sorbonne a Citadel of the densest casuistry. There were various groups among the disputers. Some, however fallacious, were at least grave in intention; others degenerated into absurdity. There were the Nominalists and Realists— or Aristotelians and Platonists; or the set that spent their time discussing how many negations go to make an affirma-tive; or the "Cornifucians"—the "makers of horned argu-ments"—who sat and cavilled as to whether, if a donkey

were led in a leash to market, it was the cord, or the
holder of the cord that actually led him : a question over
which there was a feud which divided men into camps.
Such burlesque instances of pedantry were probably rare,
but the stories of these hair-splitting pundits remain as a
measure of man's power to take himself seriously. They
did not then appear preposterous, except to the few ; the
average person accepted them with the rest of his normal life.

It was, as usual, in Italy that these fallacious processes
were most effectively superseded. That strange race, the
Cardinals of the Renaissance, gave the final blow to the
Italian Schoolmen and new life to the Scholars. Academic
ideals were not upheld by men such as Cardinal Bembo,
who only took to the study of the Scriptures after he
became a Cardinal, and favoured the book of Pomponazzi
against the immortality of the soul : a work condemned by
the Inquisition and burned at Venice. This typical prelate
spent his time between his garden and library, his medals
and antiquities, his Roman palace and his Paduan Villa ;
and busied himself with the fresh developments of philosophy.
Aristotle, disfigured by the Schoolmen, had hitherto been
their prophet and their bulwark. Men now began to read
him for themselves, and in Italy the Aristotelians divided
into two parties, centering in the school of Aristotle at Padua.
On the one hand was the Pantheistic party, counting among
them the Christian Cardinal Sadoleto ; on the other, was
the band of the Materialists, to which the Pagan Bembo
belonged. Casuistry gave way to real debate ; hair-splitting
to dialectics ; and not in Italy alone. She gave impetus to
the movement, but other nations vied with her. Even

before Bembo's day there had been a handful of men—a
scanty advance-guard—in France.

Tho first of its members had been students of the dead
languages. Greek and Hebrew were considered the tongues
of heresy; they were hated and forbidden by the Sorbonne,
which practically permitted nothing but ecclesiastical Latin.
The knowledge of Greek meant a knowledge of the New
Testament, and led to an undesirable study of the Scriptures.
Preachers declaimed against it in their sermons. "A new
language has been discovered"—so said a monk from the
pulpit—"It is called Greek. Beware of it with caution.
It is a language which gives birth to every heresy." As
for an acquaintance with Hebrew, it implied a possible
return to Judaism and must be fought tooth and nail. The
mal-treatment of the Jews in those days was persistent,
especially in Germany, where the Dominicans of Cologne
persecuted them. The courageous German Scholar, Reuchlin,
happily a friend of Maximilian's, made himself their Apolo-
gist and saved many from the flames. He had long been
a deeply versed reader of the Kabala and the Talmud.
Hebrew philosophy, he said, was higher than the Greek
and anterior to it. One of his disciples[1] went beyond him
and maintained that he found both St. Paul and Plato
in them. Reuchlin was practically the founder of the
rising school of Hebraists which had such a following in
France, and figured not unfrequently in the records of
religious tolerance as well as in those of learning. Postel,
Vatable, Paul Paradis, were its first French pupils of

---

[1] Pico della Mirandola.

importance: lesser lights than Reuchlin, but none the less
noble learners.

Vatable became a student, a bold critic of the Psalms
and Proverbs; Paradis, the teacher of Margaret of Angoulême.
Postel was more interesting. He was a traveller in the
East, an Orientalist; a visionary who dreamed of beholding
"l'Antique Orient"—"of seeing re-established the unity of
the primitive world." He nearly lost his reason in the
contemplation of his vast ideal. Yet he was not unaided.
The King honoured him, and received him wayworn from
his travels; Margaret delighted in helping him. But, like
other dreamers, he left little behind him. Perhaps his best
epitaph is his favourite saying in the Kabala—" Death is
the kiss of God"—a poet's summary of a poet's ambitions.

There is something pathetic in the idea of these men,
all mature and some of them old; grave and stately in
their furred robes, yet as little children where knowledge
was concerned; humble, reverent, aglow with curiosity. All
were alike banded together in opposition to ignorance and
the Schoolmen. Most of them followed the classics for the
pure love of learning; a few pursued them as a literary
channel for their own ideas, or as a medium of satire against
the Monks. Such men formed the germ of a national literature and, by their neat sarcasms, helped on the work of
Reform in ways that they did not realise. If the Reformation sprang from a conviction of sin, the Renaissance resulted from a conviction of folly; and satire offered a field
in which both movements could be blended.

But the most important tribe of the great Scholar race
was the growing tribe of the Printers, who then wielded a

power never since possessed by them. They constituted a kind of tribunal of scholarship, criticising, discriminating, pronouncing. Not only the "Correctors," drawn from all nations, but every man employed in the printing business had to be a scholar of refinement. It was not then as now, when editors of the classics are innumerable; all these men were editors for the first time, revising newly-discovered manuscripts—which formed their main stock-in-trade. The word "trade" confronts us as with a lie and should be replaced by Art. We of to-day can hardly imagine the tender and reverent care with which these sixteenth-century publishers handled the pages they were printing, chose their paper and their type, measured their margins, spelled out their readings. Each volume was a work of love and beauty, brooded over, dreamed of, as if it were an artist's creation; and half the secret of their exquisite productions was the number of studious men employed upon them.

The Free Press at Bâle, one of the most famous of its kind, could soon count a considerable number of rivals—foremost among them the great Paris firm of the Estienne family. Their house boasted three printers, Scholars of distinction, each representing a separate generation: Henri, the founder and the friend of Budé, doing his best work in 1500; Robert, his son, with whom we have most to do; and Henri the second, grandson of the first, whose masterpieces belong to a later period. Henri the elder had published Latin classics; Robert Estienne was practically the first man in France to print both Greek and Hebrew, and besides this he was an eminent Latin grammarian. The Estiennes had plenty of material. In the last thirty years of the fifteenth century the accurate knowledge of the Latin tongue had rapidly progressed, and Greek was beginning to make more way. A translation of Virgil into French appeared in 1470, and one of Homer in 1488. They were followed by a volume of Plato, in 1512, a birthday in the history of the world. It was published by the House of Estienne almost at the same time as Lefèbre's translation of St. Paul. Twelve years earlier they had brought out Erasmus' "Adagia," which had created a sensation throughout France; and this, together with their later publications, was enough to mark them as pillars of the Renaissance. Their shop in the Rue St. Jean de Beauvais—like many other printers' shops— made a kind of club for Scholars, who met there to discuss doubtful passages or new discoveries. Here came Budaeus and Doletus to gossip about Cicero—or to talk scandal about critics' emendations. Here the poetasters resorted to ask about the sale of their works. Nor were more distinguished guests wanting. The grandees of the Court were to be found there, spurred by idle curiosity; or Margaret of Angoulême, moved by her zeal for knowledge; or the King himself, who was kept waiting in the shop while Robert Estienne finished the correction of a precious proof which he would leave to none but himself.

Robert Estienne married a Scholar's daughter, and the household, children and all, spoke nothing but Latin. This arrangement was no pedantic affectation, but a needful means of intercourse, as the polyglot assembly of the "Correctors" lived with the family and Latin was the only common tongue possible to everyone. One wonders if they forgot their French and whether the daughters' suitors (were they the ten Correctors?) were obliged to make love to them in Latin. Years afterwards the son, Henri, wrote a letter to *his* boy, describing the grandfather's household. "Your grandfather," he said, "understood everything that was said in Latin, as well as if it had been French; and your Aunt Catherine, far from needing an interpreter to help her, expressed herself so well in the same tongue, that her meaning was clear to everyone. The very servants grew accustomed to Latin and ended by using it. But what, above all, contributed to make this practice general was that my brothers and myself, from the moment that we first began to lisp, would never have dared to use any other language in the presence of my father and his Correctors."

The Estiennes were for years a very prosperous family. Stimulated by the King's protection and the growing opportunities for knowledge, the father, Robert, worked hard at philology; wrote his "Trésor de la langue Latine, [1] an erudite dictionary which still holds good; published successive editions of the Scriptures with comments in Greek, Latin and Hebrew; and set up in a pattern Greek type— "les Grecs du roi"—ordered by the King, and still the delight of Connoisseurs in the Imprimerie Royale.

The classics were the most popular and acknowledged of all studies, but the New Learning by no means confined itself to them. Bent on enlightenment, it propagated every kind of knowledge, renovating and transforming, and founded new schools of thought in all directions. The general tendency was to substitute a national for a scholastic ideal;

---

[1] Stephani Thesaurus.

to replace hypothesis by science. In Medicine, the old unscientific physicians were superseded by the rising generation :
students who based their conclusions upon fact and experiment, instead of forcing them to fit a preconceived theory. [1]
The doctors of that day were also philosophers; the anato-
mists, the surgical lecturers, abounded in shrewd observation of the mind as well as the modern notions of hygiene.
In history, too, there was an effort to find a sequence, to form-
ulate the laws that govern its revolutions, to trace the influence of climate upon its course. [2]   Even the Law had its dreamers of dreams—legal dreams of revised codes.   Nothing was
dull to these fervent learners, and then, when all things
were possible, there was no soil so dry that it did not bring
forth flowers. [3] Astronomy, geography, mathematics, travel,
were illumined by the names of daring votaries—Progressives
as we should call them—famous for a moment and forgotten
for centuries : men who would have been content to serve
their mistress, Knowledge, for no better wages than an occasional smile.

There was, however, one typical scholar about whom there
clung none of this pathos.   He was famous, he was prosperous, in his own day.   Fate contrived that he should present
that rare contrast—an interesting life and a smooth career.
This was Guillaume Budé—known as Budaeus—Greek scholar,
King's librarian, "Maître des Requêtes," "Prévôt des Mar-

---

[1] Ambroise Paré, the King's physician; Vesale of Brussels;
Cop, Charles V's doctor; Rabelais, Dubois Servet and others.

[2] Bodin was the chief historian of this school.

[3] The great lawyers of the day were Arnoult du Ferrier,
Cujas and Dumoulin.

chands," the friend of Margaret : her friend and her colleague
in their great educational scheme, the Collége de France,
from which their two names are inseparable.

II

"It is Philology," once wrote Budé, "that has so long
been my companion, my associate, my mistress, bound to
me by every tie of close affection.... But I have been
forced to loosen the bonds of a love so devouring....
that I found it destructive to my health." This passage
might stand for his motto. Impassioned intellect, absorbing
heart and soul, made the sum of the man. It kept him
alive, it consumed him. He sacrificed all he had to it.
But he showed no signs of it in boyhood ; his force was
reserved for maturity. Budé was born at Paris in 1467.
His family was good and he had the education of a gentleman. He was sent to study Jurisprudence at the University
of Orleans, but he was insufficiently prepared for his training there and, after three years, he returned—knowing
nothing. He went home to his father's Château and devoted
himself to sport and the distractions of a country-life. He
was in no wise remarkable, unless it were for his keenness.
A few years passed in this way. Then—with no ostensible
cause for it—he underwent a conversion : an intellectual
conversion, no less enduring than it was sudden. He hunted
no more, gave up all pleasure, and shut himself up to study
with an almost violent concentration. His only regret was
the need for eating and sleeping which robbed him of so
much time. He found leisure to marry, however, with his

library safely in the background. Even on his wedding-day
he disappeared for three hours, and escaped to his deserted
books. Happily his wife was no sporting lady, never content
without hawk or hounds, but a sensible helpmate who looked
out his books and found the passages he wanted. She would
have had a bad time otherwise, and warnings about health,
or worldly exhortations fell upon deaf ears.

He had had no real master; he was not any man's disciple.
A few stray lessons here and there were all the help he got.
Yet his solitary labours had raised him to such a point that
there was nobody in France who could compete with him in
knowledge of all kinds. Greek was already the chief object
of his pursuit. He had once had twenty lessons from the
Greek, Lascaris. He had also, at great cost, bribed a
Lacedemonian, "Hieronymus", a new comer to Paris, to
read Homer aloud to him; but as "Hieronymus" did not
himself understand what he was reading, he was not of
much use to his pupil. Budé's own continuous studies were
more than enough. He began his career in print by a
translation of Plutarch, and succeeded from the outset in
steering clear of the Sorbonne.

All through his life Budé was that *rara avis*, a prudent
enthusiast. He kept well with orthodox and heterodox—
and though this was not his most lovable attainment, it
was not the least of the services he rendered to the cause
of learning. And however cautious he was, he did not fail
in sincerity. Meanwhile his reputation was growing in high
places. Charles VIII invited him to Court, but died before
he could advance him. Louis XII, however, did not forget
him, but twice sent him on State errands to Italy, and

made him one of his Secretaries. When Francis I succeeded
to the throne, he followed the example of his predecessor
and despatched him on an embassy to Rome. But Budé
still resisted all temptation: he did not wish for a Court
life, and he had no important meeting with the King until
1520. Francis was at Ardres, for the Field of the Cloth
of Gold, when he summoned Budé, then fifty-three years
old, to come to him. Whether he was prompted by pleasure
in his talk (he loved to hear him debate), or a wish for his
presence as the representative of learning, it is difficult to
say, but this occasion was a fresh starting-point in Budé's
fortunes. Honours flowed in upon him. He was made royal
Librarian and Maître des Requêtes; the Hôtel de Ville
elected him Provost of the Merchants of Paris. The only
hitches in his course were his quarrels with the corrupt
Chancellor, Duprat, bigot and money-maker, the fact of
whose presence still kept him from the Court unless his
office compelled him to attend there. He only came thither
of his own free will when his friend, Poyer, became Chancellor in his turn and often demanded his companionship.
After that he became a constant guest at the King's palaces,
though nothing made him relax the austerity of his toils.

Intellectual asceticism is almost as ingrained as intellectual
aestheticism. Though Budé might have staked his virtue to
possess a choice edition of Plato, it cost him nothing to
abstain from easy living. As he always refused to be painted,
we can picture him as we like—probably a pale, hawk-eyed,
thin-lipped man, in a furred cap and mantle—a fit subject
for a Holbein. His reputation as a Greek Scholar was ever
on the increase. He translated Greek authors; he edited;

he emended. Who they were, and what he did to them, is of little moment now save to experts; but it was enough then to make his name ring through Europe. His correspondence with other Scholars was bewildering in its bulk. As age crept upon him, he found he could not write so many letters: "for they are," he said pathetically, "by way of being an amusement; they ought to be written with a young sprightliness, and with vitality of style." Many of his correspondents addressed him without knowing him; Rabelais was one of them; Dolet was another. His intercourse with Erasmus was not so agreeable. They had begun by being very good friends and Budé had asked the King to invite Erasmus to Court. But something that the latter had said or done had offended the French scholar. He would never quote him after that, and he often criticised, without naming him. Their feud at last broke out in a storm of vituperative letters. Budé, it must be owned, was less polite than Erasmus. This was in character. Whatever he was as a Scholar, Budé was not popular as a man. He bore a general character for haughtiness. "This great person," says Bayle, "was more feared than loved in the Republic of Letters. It seems to me that this is no perfection, but rather a sign that he was proud and impatient, and armed himself at all points against such as criticized him." He might have added "against such as differed from him." There was a certain Venetian scholar who long lived in terror, because he was generally considered to disagree with Budé and dreaded the possible consequences. There was mystery about a mortal who was clothed in all the panoply of success, and yet had not lifted a finger to get it for himself.

He had all this time been faithful to his "Mistress Philology." He had two wives—so he wrote after twelve years of marriage—the one bore him girls and boys, and the other, Philology, bore him books. His only grief seems to have been that the books were not as numerous as the children, eleven of whom filled his house. But he consoled himself by reflecting that he would be able to make up the deficiency. At home as abroad, he was an instance of a perfectly happy, if perfectly selfish person.

It was when he was over sixty that he, with Margaret of Angoulême and the King, organized the Collége de France. But before we look further at their scheme, it is well to forestall events and finish the sketch of a career that was rapidly drawing to its close. In 1540, he had accompanied Francis for change of air to Normandy. Taken suddenly ill with fever, Budé made haste to return to his home, and it was here that, surrounded by his family, he died at seventy-three. He left the chilliest and most lucid directions about his funeral. He was to be buried by night, because otherwise there would be "too much weeping and too many screams from little children"—his numerous grandsons and granddaughters. "I wish to be carried to earth by night," he had written, "without any sort of ceremony, or more than one or two torches..... For I can never approve of the practice of gloomy rites and of funeral pomps, and I forbid their celebration in my honour....."

This deviation from custom was in itself enough to rouse suspicion of heresy. The impression was confirmed by the action of his widow, who returned to Geneva and there made open profession of Protestantism—swayed, as all thought,

by his wishes. Some of her children followed her example,
and one of his sons became Professor of Hebrew in the
town, and translated the Psalms into Latin. The man who
had escaped the stigma in his life was looked at askance
after death. The Schoolmen buzzed round his memory, but
they had not solid evidence for their charges. His writings
show no more innovating tendency than a wish for the reform of Rome. In his "Transitu Hellenismi ad Christian-
ismum," which, in 1535, he dedicated to the King, he frankly
recommends the old religion; he even praises Francis for
leading the expiatory procession which followed on the affair
of the Placards and the Reformers' insults to the Mass.
That he did so is a blot on his name, but the rudeness
and violence of the Protestants had irritated his fastidious
temper. We must, in justice, remember that it was not
always intolerance which caused opposition to the new religion. The crudeness, the bad manners of its votaries were
offensive to good taste, and exasperated intellectual men
who cared little about doctrine. In this, as in all else,
Budé was entirely the recluse—the Scholar who dreaded all
commotion.

The Collége de France remained as his best monument—
a memorial of his intercourse with the King. An account
of its institution must necessarily take us far into the reign
of Francis, and yet such a sketch belongs to any general
survey of the French Renaissance and finds its right place
in connection with the name of Budé.

III

Classics, philosophy, science, could have found no happier patron than Francis I—the Sorbonne no more unpromising monarch. He was full of meteoric gifts and coruscating energies. His life in Paris was a restless one. He went "quasi tous les jours faire des mommons en masque, et habits dissimulés et inconnus"—returning from his escapades to discuss Plautus and Virgil, or to scheme for the bold dissemination of the study of Greek in his Kingdom. As to other votaries of the Renaissance, Greek was a magic word to him. But there was no form of knowledge that did not appeal to him, and he helped and was helped by the burst of learning that followed his accession. The question of education interested him, and anyone with something to say on the matter found at least a hearing from him. Discrimination was not the gift of his day, and he had not the power of distinguishing real talent from the plausible brilliance of charlatans. Sincere charlatans belong to enthusiastic times, and "faddists" are not confined to the nineteenth, or the twentieth century. We hear of a certain Camillo da Forti, philosopher-poet, who came from Italy to Paris with a scheme to set before the King. He would teach him Greek and Latin in three months. It was the easiest thing in the world. He had made a great amphitheatre—it had taken him forty years to perfect it. It had tier upon tier of drawers, and they represented memory. Each tier was divided and sub-divided into various branches of knowledge; each drawer was labelled with a different intellectual quality. How any man was to learn by it, it

is difficult to understand; but his victims believed in this
solemn toy quite as earnestly as he did. The King listened
and approved: indeed his acceptance of the scheme seems
sufficient proof of his simplicity.

Fortunately, he indulged in graver and more practical
plans and, spurred on by his youth and his love of chivalry,
he made himself the Crusader of the Renaissance. As early
as 1517, or '18, he had begun to dream of a new College,
and when he was wounded in the wars of 1521, he vowed
on his sick-bed to build one. It was to hold six thousand
scholars and to stand in the place now occupied by the
Institut. Budé resolved that this first idea should be the
germ, not of a mere College, but of another and a real
University: no stronghold of dogma, no servile shadow of
the Sorbonne, but the beating heart of intellectual life
from which knowledge should circulate throughout the Kingdom of France. This was not an easy undertaking. It
was not that enlightenment had as yet become synonymous
with heresy, political or religious; but to raise such an
institution meant the opposition of the Sorbonne and the
Parlement—of all the Conservative powers which hedged in
royal authority: to make, as it were, a family quarrel, with
disagreeable results. Budé, however, had a strong ally in the
fascinating man of letters, the Cardinal Jean du Bellay, and
both found a willing instrument in the King's sister, Margaret. This was work to the liking of a princess who spent
a large proportion of her income in endowing poor students
and keeping them at College. She waited for eight years
before her hopes were fulfilled, but she never relaxed her
efforts. At last the moment seemed ripe.

In the year 1529, the Treaty of Cambrai was ratified and brought peace in the wars between Francis and Charles V. Security reigned, and the French King was glad to seize the opportunity to indulge his favourite passion for building. At this particular time he also had cause for private irritation with the Sorbonne and, always the creature of impulse, was by no means unwilling to play it a bad turn. So when Budé diplomatically suggested the erection, not of a formidable University, but of a modest little "Collége universataire," to consist of two Chairs for Greek and Hebrew—and when Margaret added her persuasions—he gave an easy consent. Even after this, it was to her that the College and the choice of the Professors was really due. The impressionable King loved the beginning of a scheme rather than its completion. He cared much more to talk with experts upon all subjects, whether art, war or wisdom, than to master any one of them. Amateur that he was, he enjoyed visiting houses of learning, or artists in their studios with his "Mignonne"—so he called his sister; but when it came to choosing the right person for the right place, it was she who took the lead without letting him suspect it.

She never performed this office better than for the Collége de France, helped as she was by the counsel of such men as Budé, Erasmus, Pierre Duchatel, the King's Reader, and Guillaume Petit, the enlightened Bishop of Senlis, her own and her brother's Confessor. In 1530, the Professorships had increased from two to five. The Greek Chairs were occupied by Toussaint, the friend of Erasmus, and by Danés, a nobleman of Paris; the Hebrew ones by Vatable, Paul Paradis, and one of Margaret's Italian protégés. Gradually the scheme grew larger. Postel, the Eastern dreamer, rested from his travels in a Chair for Arabic and Chaldaic, which Royalty had created for him. Philosophy, Medicine, Mathematics, Letters, were all nobly represented. By the year 1545, the five Professorships had become eleven.

The College had now assumed important proportions—had taken its place as the first intellectual influence in the Kingdom. The King had affiliated to it the Estiennes' Printing business—henceforward known as the Imprimerie Royale: a faithful colleague in the work of sowing knowledge. The Sorbonne was not likely to forget that the Estiennes had published Lefèbre d'Etaples' translation of the New Testament, besides other heretical works. They looked upon the Firm with suspicion and their fears proved only too well founded. At this glorious moment, when Reformers, Scholars, Poets, Wits, and Men of Science still made common cause, with the King as their leader; when Reformers meant nothing more startling than a Broad Church of Rome, it naturally followed that the College became a nucleus for Liberals in religion as well as for scholarly innovators. Lefèbre d'Etaples was the centre of this Broad Church party. He, Farel, and Berquin—who was destined to such fierce persecution—were its most radical members; but Budé, Toussaint, Julius Cæsar Scaliger, Petit, Marot, and the Estienne family, were no less of the group: foreshadowing the Gallicans of later days and untiringly opposed to the spirit of scholasticism.

The Sorbonne, meanwhile, had not been idle. It had rushed to arms under the command of its pitiless leader, Noël Béda, a fanatic Schoolman of great reputation among

his contemporaries. Fortune seemed to favour the theologians. They were backed by the sympathy of University
and Parlement, and warmly supported by the foremost
statesman of the day, the Chancellor Duprat, who hated
learning and Reform. In spite of all, the Sorbonne was for
once impotent. In vain it re-iterated that Greek was the
language of heresy, Hebrew of Judaism; in vain it condemned the proposition that Scripture could not be properly
understood without the study of both languages; and in
vain it pronounced St. Jerome's Latin version infallible.
On this occasion the Parlement itself dared not actively
espouse such verdicts against the College of the King. In
a last effort to vie with its rival, the ancient University
even tried to decant a little new wine into its old bottles;
but it lost any possible chance of popularity by closing the
public University Lectures, its chief link with the outside
world.

AUTHORITIES CONSULTED FOR CHAPTER IV

The French Renaissance: Mrs. PATTISON.
Vie de Clouet: BOUCHOT.
La Renaissance: MICHELET.
Etudes sur François I: PAULIN PARIS.
Etudes Littéraires: BRUNETIÈRE.

CHAPTER IV

IF we turn from the progress of Knowledge to that of the Arts, there is much to arrest us. Architecture is the one which flourished most vigorously in France, and is perhaps most characteristic of the French genius. A practical rather than an ideal art, it exists to make beauty available and, as it were, to domesticate it. The French Renaissance, as we have already said, was not creative—and it is worthy of remark that imaginative painting, the Art which lives on Ideas, hardly existed in the France of that period. The School of St. Martin at Tours furnished names now remembered by none but Scholars; and Jean Perréal (de Paris), the exquisite Fouquet, and the less exquisite Cousin, are the only well-known creators of subject-pictures in the fifteenth and sixteenth centuries. Painting was practically represented by portraits—the galleries of lords and ladies left us by the Clouets, by Corneille de Lyons, later on by Dumoustier. It is the same with the beautiful sculpture of the time. The names of famous sculptors are, we shall see, more frequent than those of the painters, but it is portrait-sculpture in which they excel: noble busts and full-length figures, on tombs and elsewhere. Or else it is in decorative carvings—delicious reliefs of nymphs and fauns, interwoven with birds and beasts and flowers—dainty devices—epigrams in stone,

as sparkling in their wit as the bons-mots of the eighteenth
century. Even the more poetic statues, like Jean Goujon's
famous Diana, are, if not modelled from reigning beauties,
at least a compliment in their honour.

In Literature we come across much the same tendencies.
The French poetry of the sixteenth century, whether from the
airy Marot, or the light-footed haunters of classic groves,
Ronsard and Du Bellay, seldom, if ever, goes deep. It seems
to be cut in marble, and moves us by beauty of form rather
than of thought; by the singer's exquisite sense of fitness,
not by his feeling. His poems have little to do with the
soul. As often as not they are nothing more than an
arrested kiss, blown on a poet's finger-tips to a lady who
passes in a moment—or a sigh of sentiment breathed near
a forest-fountain. As for prose, even Rabelais, the bold
thinker, was essentially a critic of life, interpreting rather
than inventing ideas: a Master of Satire, in itself a social
art and then, as ever, an outlet for French writers.

This grace and wit, these powers of portraiture and of
criticism—met with in every art of the French Renaissance
—are typical French qualities. They are often surprisingly
like those of ancient Rome. A sixteenth-century bust of a
Frenchwoman might pass for the head of a Faustina, or a
Livia. A Horace and a Juvenal would have easily naturalized
themselves as Frenchmen. Intellectual tastes, matter-of-
factness, sparkling precision and a delicate sense of form,
are alike the characteristics of ancient Rome and of the
Paris of all times. They show a social rather than an
originative genius; the critical gift of the interpreter, and
not the shaping fancy of the poet. And this, if we may say

so, is what makes the Renaissance in France a smaller movement than the Renaissance in other countries.

Nations, like persons, remain themselves. They go through
the same phases as each other and are all alike modified
by them; yet every one keeps its own particular character.
Certain qualities are common to all: in each romance reigns,
and thought is an emotion instead of a process. But beyond
this, the Renaissance of different countries varies as much
as the youth of different individuals.

In Italy passion and imagination made it into a superb
banquet of art and knowledge, a triumphal procession of
beauty. In Germany, the philosophical element was stronger
than the beautiful. Albrecht Dürer is an intellectual painter,
so is Lucas Kranach; and they interest the mind when they
do not charm the eye. Writers of profound erudition like
Reuchlin, intellectual fencers like Ulrich von Hutten, get
their strength from ideas; and the Reformation itself, though
mainly a moral movement, was closely bound up with the
conception of mental liberty. In England, our painting and
sculpture were done for us by other countries, and our
aesthetic qualities were, as usual, behindhand;[1] but our will
and purpose found scope in the one great art that gives
expression to them—the Drama—that singular meeting-
ground of beauty and moral force. They found vent too
in poetry: not the crystalline songs of the French poets, but
the lyrics and sonnets of deep feeling, impossible to divorce
from the spiritual side of life. The France of the Renaissance followed its social genius, and delighted in building

[1] Tudor architecture was really a development of Gothic art
and cannot be reckoned as belonging to the Renaissance.

dwelling-places : no overpowering palaces, but palace homes
suited to the needs of every-day intercourse.

Francis I was the typical Frenchman, both in his strong
points and his weak ones.   He was an amateur—in the
literal sense of the word.   He loved all the arts, but building was his grand passion, satisfying his restless energies as
well as his sumptuous tastes.   He wandered over the land
like a magic Sower, and Châteaux sprang up in his steps,
embosomed in green lawns and river gardens.   Here he
raised a fairy palace—there he altered, or added—leaving
behind him a new wing, or an airy tower; some web of
stonework or spiral staircase, which the Prince and builder,
in their outburst of fancy, delighted to fashion in the shape
of shell and flower-cup.   Such were the fantastic Château
of Chenonceaux, and the smaller and dreamier Azay-le-
Rideau, which hangs Naiad-like over the waters of the
Vienne; such the new buildings at Blois (added to those
already there), a triumph of Renaissance splendour, breaking
into midsummer wealth of marble fruit and blossom; or the
huge incoherent mass of Chambord, more magnificent than
beautiful, in which the king's boastfulness seems almost to
have overreached itself.   Loveliest of all must have been
the Château de Madrid, or Longchamps, covered with the
work of Girolamo de la Robbia: the enchanted castle buried
in the Bois de Boulogne, and destroyed in the days of the
French Revolution.

The interior of these Châteaux matched the rest of them.
They are rich in prodigal fancy and no two designs on wall
or ceiling repeat each other.   The display of dancing Cupids,
each with a different instrument of music—the curling mer-

Device of Queen Claude.
(Wife of Francis I.)
From the Palace of Blois.

F. p. 62.

maidens and swaying lotus-flowers—fill us with surprise at
so much joy in living. It is as if the world were keeping
holiday at Nature's return to her rights. Carven witticisms
abound; the devices of court and nobles make a history in
epigram. There is' the princely salamander of Francis, surrounded by flames; its motto is "Nutrisco et extinguo"—I
feed on it and I extinguish it—and it means, we are surprised to hear, that the King nourished good by destroying
evil. Posterity may comment as it pleases. Or there are
the bristling porcupine of Louis XII and the ermine of
Anne de Bretagne. Here is Queen Claude's sweet swan,
with a sword thrust through its heart; there Louise de
Savoie's four wings in the shape of Time's sickle, tied by a
cord to show that she could not fly: a Pagan emblem of
Destiny. There are plenty of quips for us to choose from.
They are quite indifferently placed, whether in the private
Chapel, or in my Lady's Chamber. The face of the little
jester with the padlock on his lips, looking out from the
fireplace in the rich merchant's house at Bourges, tells us
that Wit means Silence; the dainty Love chasing a salamander, in a niche of the Chambord staircase, is a Courtier's
summary of the King's existence.

The walls are hung with tapestries, paintings, embroideries.
Cynical subjects are fashionable: cavalcades of Fools—Love's
Fools, Time's Fools, Money's Fools—or Pageants of Love
woven in subtle colours, such as we still see in the Beauvais
tapestries at Chaumont. Here are Boccaccian gallantries—
lovers with lutes, and ladies robed in blue and green and
rose-colour, seated on fresh banks of flowers; near them a
jester and a viol player, with death's-heads peering from

their pockets; or a lovely youth beating old age with a crutch; here an iris, there a snail or a bird: and presiding over all, the Angel of Love, with wings of flame and feet lightly poised on air.

The ornamentation of the Châteaux was the last stage in their creation. The buildings themselves, though they seemed to spring up by magic, had, like all good art, a long and worthy pedigree. There were two periods in Renaissance architecture in France—each influencing the other; the first lasted from about 1450 to 1515, and centered in Touraine; the second centered in Paris and lasted from 1515 to 1589, the date of Henri IV's accession. The second of these does not yet concern us. The first began with the work of the Franc-maçons, the noble army of nameless men who built for building's sake and left no histories behind them. The school of Touraine arose as its mother school, that of Burgundy, decayed. The Burgundian school was, in its turn, the child of Flanders, and almost entirely Flemish in its nature. It was left to the young school of Touraine to create a French art which, from the first, announced a distinct character. It was directly influenced by the Italians, lying as it did on a road much used by travellers from Italy to Paris, or to England. It sent its artists to Italy and they enriched it by their experience. But although it was never transformed by the Italians, it was modified, and assimilated such qualities as suited it. Transmuting late Gothic, it replaced redundant ornament by Renaissance traceries; it laid its hand on feudal castles and turned them into courtly homes. The energy and fancy that had built and beautified the churches now found scope in decorating the Hôtels of ambitious merchants and citizens. Fortified towers lost their warlike look, battlements turned into cornices, moats were changed to fish-ponds and terraces, rooms grew larger and more numerous, and servants no longer slept in cellars. Architecture might be taken as the epitome of social history. With Francis I appear secret chambers and secret staircases: redolent of intrigue and social complications. In the Château de Madrid such rooms were even made between the two ceilings over the great Hall, that the King might watch in person all that went on there. In his time also the *garde-robe* began to encroach upon space—small wonder in the court of a monarch who required all his courtiers to have thirty suits of clothes, so that he might never suffer from monotony.

As time progressed, names of individual artists began to stand forth and to be remembered, but they were still few and far between. There is Pierre Nepveu, called le Trinqueau, who worked at Blois and completed Chambord; or Bastien François, who is supposed to have built Azay-le-Rideau; or his great-uncle, Michel Colombe, who belonged in spirit to the second period, but lived in the first.

Colombe is perhaps best known as a sculptor. Beginning his artist-life at Dijon, he was trained by the old Flemish masters, but his work very early showed a French character of its own. Later on he is supposed to have gone to Italy. At all events he had Italians working under him, and a Tuscan grace breathes from his marble creations, fusing harmoniously with the grace of France. He began his career under Louis XI, working through the reigns of Charles VIII, and of Louis XII, who gave him a commission at Tours. Here he was settled by 1473, and here he worked at the Cathedral. His nephews, Bastien and Martin le François, helped him. Fountains for rich citizens, sculpture for Châteaux, tombs for nobles and their ladies, came from his unwearied hand. He had a good many pupils. He was, indeed, the only French sculptor to found a School of his own—the School of Tours.

Under his chisel there grew up, in the forest of Bourg-en-Bresse, the marble Church of Brou—the shrine of married love, built to perpetuate the grief of the Duchess Margaret for the beautiful Duke Philibert de Savoie. He was killed one day out hunting, and she, Margaret of Austria, gave herself up to his memory and ordered Michel Colombe to raise a chapel for his tomb. It was to be a chapel with room for his mother's resting-place, and her own when her time should come. On one side he made her an Oratory, where, while the tomb was being built, she often prayed—using it as her living-room, that she might still hold daily converse with the dead. It remains there with stone fireplace and jewelled window, its silent Altar keeping watch over the great tombs. In the centre lies the warrior Philibert at full length, his hair cut square over his forehead. At his head and feet, and at either side, stand stately marble children, tender sentinels of his sleep; one holds his helmet, one his gauntlet, another, at his head, is weeping. His face is turned to the figure of his wife on the left, his praying hands to the right—towards the tranquil form of his mother on her couch of stone. Below, surrounded by birds and flowers, is stretched, according to the fashion of the

The Tomb of Duke Philibert de Savoie in the Church of Brou.

F. p. 66.

times, his "gisant", or naked figure, to show him in death
as the upper figure shows him in life. Margaret's tomb is
smaller, but no less regal. Above, she lies with queenly
robe and diadem; below, with the face of a statesman,
masculine, almost rugged—her figure covered from head to
foot by the glory of her hair; and her resting-place is
crowned by a canopy of richly wrought niches, each of
them filled by courtly saints or long-haired Virgins,
who seem, like maids of honour, to wait for her last
waking.

The work was finished in 1471, when Michel Colombe
must have been near eighty; it was his last creation—the
last creation also of the earlier and purer Renaissance. Rich
yet austere, simple yet fantastic, it stands as an epitome
of contemporary sculpture, and as such it is fitting to be
dwelt upon.

There were other big sculptors at Tours beside Michel
Colombe and his School. Jean Juste and his son were
famous enough in their day. Jean made the poetic tomb
of Charles VIII's boy and girl in the Cathedral of Tours;
and that of Louis XII and Anne de Bretagne, which were
carried to Saint Denis: works more naïf, perhaps more
touching, than those of Michel Colombe, but not so typical
of the full splendour of the Renaissance.

Of the painters of this period we know little more than
of the sculptors. Tours, the town of spires, the city of
St. Martin and the Painters, "the heart of the garden of
France" (as Rabelais called Touraine), was in these earlier
days the centre of art. It was also the place of royal
residence, and its glory only waned when, later in his reign,

Francis I moved the Court to Paris. The two rival Schools
of painting, those of Tours and Paris, were then united.
The School of Tours was the older, beginning as early as
the ninth century; it was probably instituted on the foun-
dation of St. Martin of Tours, to whose Collegiate Chapter
so many illuminations belong. Its nameless pupils, like the
Franc-maçons, served to found a robust national school.
Like them they were affected by Italy, like them they
subdued its qualities to the needs of France. Italian influence was shown in colour and detail, never in spirit.
Poetry disappeared, prose, rich and dainty, took its place.
The School of Paris, on the other hand, corresponded to
the sculptors' School at Dijon and was under the power of
Burgundian traditions. But here again French character
holds its own, and French gaiety modifies Flemish severity.

A good many names of painters are mentioned in French
records of the fifteenth, even of the sixteenth, century. Their
work has completely disappeared, devoured by the wars of
religion, or the Puritan Reformers. Of the names that
remain, the greatest belong to Tours. In this city was
born, between 1415 and 1420, Jean Fouquet, the friend
and executor of Agnés Sorel, possibly also the maker of
her lovely tomb at Loches. He went from Tours to Rome,
where we find him about 1440, painting (by the order
of his master Filarete) a portrait of Pope Eugenius IV.
He returned to his native town and, after that, his career
is only to be traced through State account-books. If men
had but realized how much of history—how very much of
artists' biography—is founded on accounts, perhaps they
would have kept them more fully. The name of Fouquet

Figure from the Tomb of Margaret of Austria
in the Church of Brou.

F. p. 68.

is mentioned in the statement of Charles VIII's funeral expenses, when a messenger is paid "40 sols" for carrying the cast of the dead King's face to "Foulquet le peintre." It occurs again in connection with pageants—canopy-paintings for the King of Portugal's entry into Tours—a Livy for Pierre de Beaujeu—a Book of Hours for Charles of Orleans' widow, who paid his travelling expenses when he came to visit her at Blois. He was Court painter for the last ten years of his life, and he died about 1480. His reputation was great enough to inspire the poetasters of the day, though perhaps they were easily inspired. One of Charles VIII's officers, writing from Italy, describes a palace so glorious that "even Foulquet could not paint it." A few of his portraits remain, besides the fine picture of Charles VII's Secretary in the Louvre, but his best works were his illustrations—each a gem of light and colour. Livy, Josephus, Virgil, Boccaccio, Froissart, and Books of Hours, came from his master-hand; loveliest of all the Book of Hours which he did for Etienne Chevalier: scenes from the Life of Christ and the Saints, now to be seen in part at Chantilly.

His successor in fame proceeded from the School of Paris —"Jean Perréal dit de Paris," artist, decorator, glass painter. "Jean de Paris, nous nous fions en vous et tout notre honneur gît en vous; nous vous le remettons et promettons que nous vous contenterons bien"—so spake the Corporation of Lyons, when they entrusted him with the decorations of the city for the Entry of Charles VIII. He must have been in good odour, for the next year his property was exempted from taxes by the King's orders, and he was afterwards made Painter Laureate and Court Surgeon, though happily he never practised his surgery. In 1504, he was taken into the pay of Margaret of Austria, but he still belonged to the French Court and was made "Garde de la Vaisselle" to Anne de Bretagne. He led a charming, vagabond existence. Louis XII took him with him on his Italian campaign, and sent him to London to supervise the trousseau of his Tudor bride, "pour aider à dresser ledict appareil à la mode de France." Millinery then was an art, and the dresses that shine in the old pictures were often planned by the artists who painted them. The last mention of Perréal occurs about 1527, when he must have been an old man. His busy brush has left very little behind it: the Madonna in the Louvre, neat and brilliant, and the wonderful "Bible Historiée," now at Corpus Christi College, Oxford—the homelier, less fantastic pendant of Fouquet's work at Chantilly.

The career of Jean de Paris brings us to the Clouets, one of whom was the greatest artist of the French Renaissance; the most delicate portrait painter France has ever possessed. There were four of them, and the youngest, François, was the most illustrious. The first, Jean, mentioned by Marot, did decorative work at Brussels for Charles the Bold; the second, also Jean, the friend of Marot's father, was Court painter to Francis I, and was known by the nickname of Janet, or Jehannot. So was his son, the great François. Hence the fourth Clouet, in the service of Margaret of Angoulême and alluded to as "le frère de Janet," may have been either his uncle, or his brother. Him we can dismiss. It was only Jean the second and his son who achieved distinction.

Jean lived his early life at Tours, where he married a

goldsmith's daughter and where his son François was born. He left it in 1523, to take up his office at Court, and lived between Paris and Fontainebleau on a salary of five pounds a year, besides what he made by his separate works. This was considered a good income. Painters at that time ranked higher and received more than men of letters; their travelling expenses were paid as well as their wages, and François Clouet, also painter-in-general to the Valois, even had a suit of mourning thrown in.

This youngest Clouet climbed high on the Court ladder. He was the friend of the lordly Ronsard, and the Poet wrote sonnets to the Painter. Clouet must have been beloved by the throng of ladies whom his hand so exquisitely immortalized. "He surpassed all his fellows in his lovely portraying of Nature," says one of his contemporaries, and the galaxy of his drawings and paintings does not contradict the saying. Who that has seen them has not felt the spell of his scintillating pencil? Who has not marvelled at his power of lucidity? there is no other word for it. Now it is a portfolio of drawings, strong of line, faint in colour, living in charm. Now again a painting in oils: the little head of a princess, keen, delicate, simple though bejewelled; or the full-length figure of a Duke in black velvet—either of them springing in bold relief from a deep blue, or a fresh green background.

The work of the father, Jean Clouet, comes, at its best, very near to that of the son, and critics have often failed to identify the elder man's pictures. The portrait in the Louvre, of Francis I in white satin against red damask, is supposed to be his, and so is that of the same King in the

Uffizi. François Clouet's Elizabeth of Austria and Henri II in the Louvre, his boy at Hampton Court, his Dauphin at Antwerp, his Castle Howard drawings, now at Chantilly, are all too much known to need comment. The man was unceasingly active, and lived into the reign of the last Valois. He did anything that came to his hand. He decorated coffers, he painted pageants, he struck coins, he made effigies of each monarch as he died. His own death must have been about 1584—a date which carries us beyond our scope and into the second half of the French Renaissance.

To this period of time, when the Italian painters migrated to France, when the architects Lescot and de l'Orme fought with their Italian rivals, much of François Clouet's work belongs. But only as far as date is concerned. In spirit he was wholly unaffected by them, and the most French of French artists. The same may be said of his follower, Corneille de Lyon (celebrated by Brantôme), who painted Cathérine de Médicis and her ladies.

The minor arts, too, had been increasing. Famous in those days—the earlier days of Clouet—were the names of the glass-painters, Cousin and Pinaigrier. The work of both men is nearly all destroyed, and of Pinaigrier little is known save that he laboured at the windows of Chartres Cathedral. But Jean Cousin was great in his generation: serious yet versatile, a painter, an engraver, and a writer on perspective. He painted the windows in the Cathedral of Sens and was famed for his pictures in oils, though none but a few connoisseurs now turn their eyes to his last Judgment on the walls of the Louvre—the composition of one who knew the work of Michael Angelo. Suspected of being a

Huguenot, he was none the less a disciple of the Mid-Renaissance; his Sibyl, still existing on a window at Sens, and the name of his picture in that city, "Eve, the first Pandora," seem to express his complex aim. But, like so many others, he has passed into that twilight country between oblivion and remembrance, where none but experts enter, and his life is investigated by few except the satellites of Museums.

Below men such as these came the crowd of artistic artificers—goldsmiths, gem-cutters, enamellers and potters, who reached their apotheosis in the next reign, with the advent of Bernard Palissy and Léonard Limousin. The perfection of secondary arts, the extravagance of detail, were the signs of decadence. The French Renaissance carried in itself the germ of its own destruction. Its worship of nature turned into an immoral materialism; its exaltation of humanity into individualism and the destruction of society; while the love of beauty, which had illumined its golden age, ended by separating form from idea and hastening its downward course. [1] We need some reason to account for the ill effects of such noble inclinations, and it is not far to seek. Nature-worship, beauty-worship, knowledge of man—each of these forces was isolated and impotent, for lack of the quality which binds them all together. The sense of reverence was wanting in France. It was its absence in the heart of the people which ruined the French Reformation; its absence which devastated Freedom and spoiled the French Revolution; its absence which weakens the life of the France of

---

[1] Brunetière: Histoire Littéraire.

to-day. Had the French of the sixteenth century added reverence to their other powers, their art would have struck a deeper and more moving note, their wisdom have had a wider and more enduring effect. With this one thing necessary they might have become the Chosen Nation—the Nation elected to achieve the union of old and new; of truth and criticism; of faith and reason.

BOOK II

MARGARET OF ANGOULÊME AND THE RENAISSANCE

AUTHORITIES CONSULTED FOR CHAPTER V

Journal de Louise de Savoie.

Poésies de François I, et de Louise de Savoie:
CHAMPOLLION-FIGEAC.

Histoire de Louis XII: JEAN DE SAINT-GELAIS.

Histoire des Choses Mémorables: FLEURANGE.

Lettres de Marguerite d'Angoulême (Biographical Preface):
GÉNIN.

l'Heptaméron: MARGUERITE D'ANGOULÊME.

Oraison Funèbre sur Marguerite d'Angoulême:
SAINTE-MARTHE.

Bayle's Dictionnaire Historique.

Histoire de France: HENRI MARTIN.

Trente Ans de Jeunesse: DE MAULDE LA CLAVIÈRE.

Marguerite de Valois: LA COMTESSE D'HAUSSONVILLE.

Pictures of the old French Court: CATHERINE BEARN.

Louise de Savoie, marié en 148, a Charles d'Orléans comte d'Angoulême

MADAME·LA·RÉGENTE·

Louise de Savoie, Madame la Régente.
Cabinet des Estampes de la Bibliothèque Nationale ;
d'après Jean Clouet.

F. p. 76.

CHAPTER V

(1492—1515)

THE COURT OF LOUISE DE SAVOIE

ART and Learning found no impotent ally in Louise de Savoie, Countess of Angoulême, and in her son and daughter; and Scholars and Artists found a pleasant home in the Court of her young days: the Court that she governed so gaily. Louise de Savoie began her career early in life. Born in 1476, she was the child of the Sieur de Bresse and Marguerite de Bourbon, who both died in her early childhood. She was left in the care of her aunt, the powerful Anne de Beaujeu, who led her the hard life of a poor relation at Court, and allowed her scant indulgence beyond eighty francs at the New Year, with which to buy herself a crimson satin dress for state occasions. Her birth, however, ensured a brilliant marriage. Louise had, at two years old, been affianced to the Comte d'Angoulême, her senior by many years and a peer of royal blood. Anne de Beaujeu, determined not to lose such a match, re-opened negotiations with him eight years later. The Count was at that moment deeply in love with a certain Jeanne de Polignac, and it took two years to persuade him to marry Louise; but he did so at last, on condition that he might bring his mistress to live at Court.

This was not the best training for a girl of twelve, strong of mind, none too soft by nature, very pleasure-loving, very ambitious. Ambition was, indeed, the most serious trait in her character, and, in the absence of worthier passions, often served to dignify it.

In 1492, her daughter Margaret was born. Various relations objected to her name as out of the family tradition, and suggested that Louise or Charlotte would be more suitable; but Margaret she remained—"La Marguerite des Marguerites"—"la perle des Valois." Her birth was followed by that of Francis in 1494, and, not long after this, the husband of Louise died. Much against her will, it was decided that her cousin Louis d'Orléans (afterwards Louis XII) should have a share in the guardianship of her children, but though he might have claimed some authority in her household, at first he allowed her to do much as she liked. The real potentates in her palace were Octavien de St.-Gelais and his brother, Jean, her Valet, who had a strange ascendency over her and entirely regulated her home life. Closer relations were suspected between them. Valets in that day filled a unique position. They were a combination of attendant, secretary and "amuser," raised socially from menial associations to a kind of convenient equality. It gave them every opportunity for a free and easy friendship, and it did not prevent their being thrown away at pleasure. The conditions of the post, with its generous salary, made it an excellent sinecure for Poets and Scholars. Swift in Sir William Temple's house—the seventeenth-century Chaplain—is the nearest approach to the Valet of the Renaissance. Jean de St.-Gelais, however, was not famous for his learning. Where intellect was concerned, Louise was more swayed by his brother, Octavien, afterwards Bishop of Angoulême: "a Boccaccian poet," a cleric who translated Ovid, an author whose works were as heavy as his life was light.

This man was the embodiment of his day. He represented one party in the strange literary movement that enlivened the last years of the fifteenth century—the rivalry between the old Classical and the new Boccaccian influences. The French, with their strange mixture of levity, romance and materialism, speedily took to Boccaccio. [1] He ruled the world of fashion, and with it Louise de Savoie and her Court at Cognac and at Amboise. Poems, pageants, manners, morals, were all alike Boccaccian. The Church followed suit and produced Boccaccian prelates. Octavien de St.-Gelais was the first among them, and his works are an index of his character. Fed on Ovid, he wrote viciously till promotion came in sight, when mythological Romance gave way to stilted Allegory. He is with Virgil in Hades. Sensuality beckons him to follow her to heaven; he ends by listening to Prudence, in the shape of a Bishopric. Later, when he was still more respectable, he made a translation of Virgil and presented it to Louis, who liked to be thought a judge of the classics. With such a man at her right hand, with poets and patrons of this kind all round her, it would

---

[1] There was, it is true, an ante-Italian poet called Bouchet, who aimed at founding a national literature. But he was easily overcome by the fashionable Boccaccian poet, Jean Lemaire, whom Louise de Savoie protected. Lemaire was the author of "L'amant vert," a heavy poem in praise of Margaret of Austria, into whose service he eventually passed.

have been surprising had Louise de Savoie, their disciple and their mistress, been other than she was. Herself an accomplished verse-writer of their dull school, she composed "Epistles" like the rest of them.

The last ten years of the fifteenth century represent a period of decadence: a time when there was a universal taste for the unwholesome and abnormal; when the old order had practically ended, the new not yet begun. Any kind of decadence is harmful, but perhaps none is so objectionable as that which borrows the form, the license, the detail, of classical scholarship, without its chiselled beauty and sense of the exquisite. There is no more arid art then the endless elaborate verses, the pedantic improprieties and futile erudition, that existed just before the Renaissance. The decadence of every age is perhaps interesting, or at least intelligible, to itself; and to us, who are also going through a decadent period, the shapes that it takes seem, not less silly, but less tedious than those of the Past. In our case French influence takes the place that Italian did then; and, if we carry the analogy farther, we may find some hope in it. Boccaccio suggested modern ideas as well as a lax morality. Amidst the corruption there lived the germ of the new life: the Renaissance, in short, came from Italy. This last decade of the fifteenth century was like the Autumn. Decay met the eye on every side; but the dead leaves went to enrich the soil and to foster the growth of the young seeds hidden in the earth.

The decadence did not confine itself to literature. Religion was degenerate and, like the poetry of the day, possessed more form than substance. The professors of a dry or a false creed always mistake credulity for belief, and superstition is the piety of the materialist—a stop-gap for faith. Louise was a Pedant in observance, as well as a Boccaccian in morals : as sincerely distraught at missing a Mass as she was at giving up a gallant. Her Astrologer—something of a Scholar—was the only person who dared to point out her discrepancies. One day she had reproved him for speaking against the priests. " Ah!" he broke out, " while people scold me for telling the truth, they are recommending women and girls to read the novels of Boccaccio .... a school of depravity. They do not attempt, these severe critics, to read such works in secret. They gloat over them, translate them, popularize them. They seem to think they are fulfilling an Apostolic Mission—even when they are Princes of the Church, like the Bishop of Angoulême."

The same Astrologer complained that she asked him for too many horoscopes. Superstitious she was to any extent. Sorcery and prophecy were important realities to her and to all her contemporaries. There lived at Tours a holy man, patronized by royalty. Anne de Beaujeu and Anne de Bretagne repaired to him that his prayers might obtain a child for them, and attributed their daughters to his services. Louise, in a fit of envy, went also to consult him. This lucky prophet promised her a son who should be King, and, when he died, she rewarded him by getting him canonized. It seems rather an empty honour that his body was exhumed in her presence and that she held his hand through the ceremony, although she had a horror of death. She could never bear the mention of the word. When she heard it, " Mais oui," she would say, " nous savons bien que nous devons mourir," and the subject was at once dismissed. The material side of life was all that she wanted.

It was in vain that Louis XII tried to re-marry her—first to the Duke Hercules of Este, then to Ferdinand, the brother of Charles V, last to Henry VII of England, who originally applied for the hand of her eight-year-old daughter. Louise was obdurate; a husband would have complicated (he would not have prevented) her gallantries; and she wanted to be everything to her children. Her maternal feeling was the one real feeling about her—a fierce instinct too often suggesting the tigress. There were few virtues and no vices that she would not have dared in its name, and the fact that her son was heir to the crown was not without its glamour. From the first she always had her children about her; they slept in her room and she watched their every moment. This was not done without difficulty. Louis d'Orléans, as was said, acted with her as their guardian. He began by being very friendly to her. When he came to the throne he was still unmarried and he treated her children as his own. He begged them to come to him at Chinon and at Blois; he gave his best rooms to their mother; he spent hours in romping with the boy—to all appearances his heir. He wanted family life, and to them he turned for it. But in a few days his mood suddenly changed, he became suspicious of Louise—cold, tyrannical. He charged his trusty soldier, the Maréchal de Gié, with the supervision of her and her family. He would have robbed her of her right of guardianship, had not the Maréchal prevented it. The scandal with her Valet, St.-Gelais, was probably the cause. The next event was his dismissal—at Gié's instigation—and the lady's departure for Amboise. Here she was ordered to remain under the eye of the man she chose to regard as her foe. In reality he was more her friend than most people, though his friendship often coincided with his interests and he expressed his kindness roughly. As for the King, she never forgave him, and her feelings were not softened by his marriage with Anne de Bretagne, the provincial bourgeoise, born to disagree with the light and courtly Countess of Angoulême. Matters grew worse after the birth of Anne's daughter, Claude. The King and Gié destined her for Francis, as a solution of the vexed question of succession. This enraged Louise, who had other views about his marriage.

A set battle began between her and Gié. She lived in constant fear of her children being taken from her, and even arranged that their levée should take place alone with her in her room. The customary maids of honour would surely be the King's accomplices. When Gié's representative waited outside her bedroom door to take the young Count to Mass, she refused to let the child go and complained to Louis. She had no opportunity to avenge her wrongs at the moment, but she made herself disagreeable whenever she could. She rejected Gié's son as a playmate for her own, in return for which Gié forbade Francis to sleep in her room. This was short-sighted on his part, for, as he was to learn to his cost, she forgot nothing and practised endless patience in waiting for her revenge. Meanwhile she came off victorious and kept the children with her.

Her boy's smallest doings are chronicled in her journal. "This day of the Conversion of St. Paul, January 25th,

1501, about two hours after noon," she writes, "my King, my Lord, my Cæsar and my son, was run away with, close by Amboise, on a palfrey given him by the Maréchal de Gié, and so great was the danger that those who were preseut thought it irremediable. But God, the Protector of widows, foreseeing the future, would not forsake me, knowing that if an accident had so suddenly robbed me of my love, I should have been too miserable to endure it."

Her idea of moral training was to win her children's hearts for herself; but within these limits she was as educational as Miss Edgeworth. On her own hearth—a Renaissance hearth—she was a model of the domestic virtues. At first she taught her boy and girl herself (she made a great point of verse-writing), but later she employed tutors. They were all very careful to invoke her as Wisdom and Prudence and Beauty. There is a characteristic picture of her at about this date as the Fountain of all Good—with minor streams of Justice and Knowledge flowing from her son and her daughter. If this was what she expected from her pedagogues, no wonder that they were dull. The only remarkable man among them was Christophe Longueuil, a Parisian lawyer, who boldly preferred France to Italy and taught Francis French history instead of Roman. He had to meet a tempest from his colleagues, not to be wondered at if we glance at the Prince's earlier lessons. His history copy-book, when he was just ten, is still to be seen: full of badly scrawled jumbles of stray facts about miscellaneous people— Adam, Semiramis, Sardanapalus, Alexander, and Constantine —with a list of the French kings. This was not much of an improvement on his mother's library, and if morals are affected by literature, his own, in after days, were by no means inconsistent.

He first went to Court when he was eight, and at this tender age he begins to be mentioned in the ambassadors' despatches. "My son," Louise writes in her diary, "went away from Amboise to become a courtier and left me all alone." At home he practised every sort of manly exercise. He was brought up with other little Messieurs : Montpensier, Montmorency and Chabot, the great soldiers, the greatest sailor, of later times. But his chief playmate was Fleurange—"le Jeune Aventureux"—who has recorded the outset of his own journey in the world and the boyish life of his century. His words still breathe a vigorous quaintness.

"Now History saith that when le Jeune Aventureux was eight or nine years old and dwelling in the house of Monsieur his father at Sedan—this young man, seeing that he was of an age to ride a little horse and having read in his time divers books concerning adventurous knights of a past day, and also having heard tell of their exploits, took counsel with himself that he would go see the world, and repair to the Court of the French King, Louis XII, who was then the greatest Prince in Christendom. (His father, persuaded by his mother, gave him three gentlemen as companions and he set forth). . . . Le Jeune Aventureux, being come to Blois, sent forward one Tourneville to announce his arrival to the King—who was well pleased and bade him rest and refresh himself till the morrow, after which he called him to his presence. 'My son,' quoth he, 'you are very welcome ; you are too young to serve me, and therefore do I send you to Monsieur d'Angoulême at Amboise, since he is of your age, and I think that you will get on well together.' To which le Jeune Aventureux made answer: 'I will go whithersoever you shall command me; yet am I old enough to serve you and to go to the wars if you desire it.' Then spake his liege: 'My friend, your courage is good, but I should be afraid that your legs would fail you on the road; all the same I promise that you shall go, and when I start I will send you tidings.' And the King sent him thence to the Queen and her ladies, who made marvellous good cheer for him."

The next day he reached Amboise, where Louise of Savoy (or Angoulême) held her court, and where "he found a lodging between the two bridges, at the sign of Saint Barbara." Mother and son gave him a royal welcome, and "ledit Sieur d'Angoulême and le Jeune Aventureux, being almost of the same age and height, were speedily good comrades one with another, and whoever lacked good counsel would soon have found it betwixt these two gentlemen."

It is refreshing to find these minute dignitaries having their childish quarrels. When the King came to visit them, sailing down the Loire in his barge, they went to meet him in their litter. But as it had only one "Trou" as exit, a quarrel arose as to who should have precedence: "for that le Jeune Aventureux, who had arrived but two days before, thought himself as great a Lord as my Lord of Angoulême." We can fancy them on the green lawns that hang over the river, leaping, running, tilting, bombarding mimic castles, or playing with little arrows at "tuer à la serpentine." "I think," says Fleurange, when he sums up his young master's

Le Seigneur de Sedan et de Fleurange.
(Portraits des Personnages français les plus illustres
du XVIième siècle, avec Notices par P. G. J. Niel).

F. p. 86.

childhood, "that never was a Prince who had more various pastimes than my Lord; nor was any fed with better doctrines than those which his mother gave him."

In all his doings and most of his studies Francis had one sure and admiring participator—his sister Margaret. He was a signal instance of a man too much surrounded by affectionate women. To his mother he always represented the drama of existence; and to Margaret its romance. Hers was a complicated being—subtly compounded of emotion and intellect; but the first impression that she made on those who saw her was that of a loving human creature. She was born smiling, says an old chronicler, and held out her little hand to each comer—"a sure and certain sign of a generous disposition." "The Spirit of God," he adds, "soon began to manifest itself in her. It showed in her eyes and her countenance, her gait and her speech, indeed in all her actions." Her nature was rather intense than passionate: to concentrate lavish affection on a few people was all that she demanded. In these early days she poured it forth on her brother and mother—"Notre Trinité," as she liked to call the group. "A perfect Triangle," she says, "of which I pray that I may become the smallest angle of an angle."

The idea of Three, so popular among the Schoolmen, had a fascination for her mind, which was always addicted to mysticism. A kind of metaphysical theology was, from her girlhood onwards, her favourite study. At first she shared her brother's tutor; later she had one to herself. She soon outstripped Francis in scholarship, learned Spanish, Italian, Greek and Latin at an early age, and studied Hebrew with

the great teacher, Paul Paradis. Her mother loved her
daughter with less enchantment, but almost as much as she
loved her son. She prized the girl's gifts and made the
most of them. She surrounded her with long-robed Scholars
and gave her philosophers for servants. Does this mean
that they read out Aristotle to her instead of bringing in
the dinner? Perhaps it was the best way to teach their
mistress to practise their precepts. At twelve Margaret
visited the Court, where she graduated in the art of conversation and watched over her little brother: somewhat
anxiously, perhaps, for his resplendent tastes already showed
themselves. "Ce garçon là me gâtera tout," the King said
one day after seeing him. The good economical Father of
his People knew that his heir-apparent had no taste for
civic virtues.

In 1505, the great Cardinal d'Amboise, the King's right
hand in reform and in finance, was appointed the prince's
"governor." He exercised an influence over him the reverse
of that of his mother. Had the Cardinal stayed longer
with him, it is possible that his chameleon character might
have been set in another mould. It seems prophetic that
the rival influence to Amboise was Triboulet, the King's
favourite fool, a creature of infinite wit, who always dined
with Louis at his table. To be between Minister and Fool
was a characteristic position for Francis I. We can see the
boy in his cloth of gold, with his sunny smile, bandying
quips with the Court Jester, or playing wild jokes upon the
Court Beauties.

Louise of Savoy must have hated—and probably respected—Amboise; but the drama of her life at this period was

a domestic one, and consisted in her relations with Anne
de Bretagne. The two women were, we repeat, the opposite
of one another: the Queen provincial, plain and respectable;
the Countess urban, exquisite and immoral. The recurrent
question of the heirship caused constant jealousy between
them. The birth of Claude was harmless—the Salic law
had settled that—but Louise lived in perpetual dread that
a royal son would be born. Their quarrels were public
property. "The Queen," says an old chronicler, "thwarted
her in all her affairs," "et ne fut jamais heure que ces
deux maisons ne fussent toujours en pique." There were
forever false hopes about the Queen—ill-concealed spite on
the part of Louise—hopes ending in smoke at Blois—open
rejoicings at Amboise. When at last the Countess' fears
were realized, there is an almost savage joy in the entry
she makes in her journal. "His birth" (she writes on
October 24th, 1502) "will not hinder the exaltation of my
Cæsar; for the infant was born dead."

As the years went on and the Queen's expectations
diminished, a fresh irritation was created by the idea of the
two children's marriage. The King planned it while both
were still babies, as an obvious way of settling the succession
and satisfying his affections. Anne de Bretagne, the great
matchmaker, was against it, having decided to marry her
daughter to Charles V. Louise was also strongly opposed
to the marriage with Claude, and on this point the two
women were in unison—like all foes, agreeing only in opposition. Meanwhile the good-natured King played fast and
loose with both sides. The astute Anne left him no peace
and made him sign a document ratifying Claude's marriage

with Charles V. At the same moment, behind her back, he was making arrangements for the match with Francis. He slily assured her that he knew the plottings of Louise, but that "he was resolved not to marry his mice, except to the rats of his barn." "Really," replied the Queen with some sourness, "to hear you, one would think that all the mothers were conspiring for the unhappiness of their daughters." Louis was annoyed at her persistence, and "told her that, at the Creation, God had given horns to hinds as well as to stags, but finding they wanted to govern everybody, he took them away as a punishment."

It was not till Anne's death that the marriage of Francis with Claude actually took place. For his own ends, the Maréchal de Gié was the King's right hand in the matter, and the fact did not endear him the more to the Countess of Angoulême.

But her moment for revenge had come—a revenge which was typical of her character and of her century. The Procès de Gié, so famous in its time, was a tissue of scandals. The Marshal was accused of treason and corruption on a number of false charges. These charges were trumped up by Louise. She was helped by three of Gié's creatures whom she had suborned—and they, in their turn, sheltered themselves behind the Queen. Unfortunately Gié had made an enemy of Anne. He thought her a provincial, whose object was to aggrandize Brittany, and she was not unwilling to pay him out. She backed Louise who, like the engineer she was, mined and undermined, fabricated lies, and got false witnesses for the asking. In the course of Gié's defence he said he had ever been the friend of Louise; and her hatred of him, he declared, was due to his dismissal of St.-Gelais. No wonder that, after months of appealing and quarrelling, he was found guilty. The King all this time was lying dangerously ill, and could not defend his old comrade. The Marshal was deprived of his honours and banished for five years. Louise was avenged and freed from his supervision.

As Francis grew older, he lorded it over his family. They called him their Cæsar and only loved him the better for it. Cæsar was precocious, and at fifteen he began to be sentimental. His first flame was the pensive Anne de Graville, who dreamed over her lute and her Petrarch at Angoulême. The young Prince, butterfly-like, poised for a moment on this flower and then flitted on. All the world was his garden where to choose. He went to Paris. He had boon-companions. Together, masked and disguised, they roamed every night through the streets of the city "faire des mommons." They entered promiscuous houses—they attended balls at their discretion. At one such a dance, Francis (he was then about twenty) met Madame Dishomme, the sparkling young wife of a rich and elderly lawyer. He consulted the lawyer professionally; he got access to the lady. The flirtation was longer than his first one. We can still see the old advocate, standing somewhat pompously in his black robe lined with marten, a wax taper in each hand, bowing the Prince upstairs and bidding his wife do her best to entertain him. It is all like a brilliant, objectionable little comedy, with no sounder moral than "he who laughs the last, laughs the longest." Contemporaries merely regarded it as one of the thousand luxuries then considered needful for the golden youth of Princes—like the £17,500 that Francis spent yearly on jewels.

In 1514, Anne de Bretagne died suddenly at Blois. Louise and her son held open rejoicings at the event, after which the Heir-apparent bought a handsome suit of black satin mourning. The King alone grieved for his wife and begged that the grave might be made large enough for two: "Car devant que soit l'an passé, je serai avec elle." In spite of all this, he rallied to make a fresh effort and to push his favourite plan. That same year Francis and Claude, both in black, were married at St. Germain: he unwilling, and she submissive. His only wedding gifts to her were a four-post bed and a counterpane. There were no trumpets or feastings, "pas un ombre de drap d'or, ou de soie." Louise was not present, and after dinner the bridegroom went a-hunting in the park as usual—a wedding-day which seemed an epitome of the poor little bride's existence. She was sweet-looking, but unimpressive, and rather lame like her mother; and she made no demur about retiring to Blois directly after her marriage. Her lord remained in Paris to finish the Dishomme episode, and was only persuaded by his urgent friends to return to her for a short time in July.

His lax morals—like those of his parents—did not affect his filial relations, and he was almost as romantic a son as Louise was a mother. The year before his wedding, with great difficulty he posted home to Cognac for the joy of spending New Year's Day with her; later still she mentions in her journal that she has been very ill with gout and "my son sat up with me all the night." Her feeling for

him derived a new splendour from the proximity of his
crown. For some years past it had almost become a certainty
and she had allowed her fantastic ambition to travel beyond
it. She dreamed of nothing less for him than the Empire
of the East; she already saw him a second Alexander the
Great. To the Western world, India and the East were
still a fairy-land—an Aladdin's cave where everything was
possible. The commerce with India, hitherto monopolized
by the Venetians, opened up dreamy vistas of boundless
speculation. Travellers had it all their own way; their
fabulous tales of molten gold, millionaire Mermen, and solvent
Sirens, were believed by Kings as well as by peasants, and
show how credulous these refined sceptics could be. A
monk called Thénaud came to live at Louise's Court and,
in 1509, wrote a "History of Marguerite de France." He
established the descent of French Royalty in direct line
from a son of Japheths', and proved it to be the only survival
of the great Dynasties of Assyria, Persia, Greece and Rome.
Francis, he said, was "born for great things—to govern the
world, and not to see after a little province." Two years
afterwards, in 1511, Louis accepted the Sultan's offer of the
monopoly of safe-conducts to Palestine, and sent an embassy
to Cairo, which Thénaud was permitted to join. This was
at the instigation of Louise. He was to go by Jerusalem
to Persia, and to interview the Sophi on Francis' behalf.
Then he was to travel to India to study "the Indian route"
(as popular a theme as the North-West Passage), and so to
perfect the scheme of the French Prince's Eastern Empire.
Accompanied by Margaret's Secretary, he reached Cairo,
Sinai, Jerusalem, and even contrived to enter the service of

a Persian Princess; but he could not get into Persia, and
failed in his final purpose.

From all these visions Louise was suddenly awakened by
a rude shock. At the end of 1514, Louis XII, far from
filling the second place in the tomb that he had ordered
for his wife, announced his intention of marrying again.
His choice had fallen on the eighteen-year-old Mary Tudor,
sister of Henry VIII. Louis sent his first painter, Jean de
Paris, to London, to paint her portrait and to plan her
trousseau. He prepared gorgeous pageants to greet her and
himself went in state to receive her at Calais. Francis,
Margaret, and a superb retinue accompanied him : no expense,
no emotion was spared. Louise of Savoy was checkmated,
and by no means agreeable on the occasion. " Le 22 Sep-
tembre, 1514," is her spiteful entry in her journal, " le roi
Louis XII, fort antique et débile, (the King was no more
than fifty-two) sortit de Paris, pour aller au devant de sa
jeune femme, la reine Marie."

" Le 9 Octobre, 1514, furent les amoureuses noces de
Louis XII, roi de France, et de Marie d'Angleterre; et furent
épousés a dix heures du matin."

Henry VIII, who had, as we know, a high standard of
wifely conduct, sent the King a letter with his sister, expressing his hopes that her capricious character would not
harm conjugal peace. "Et ainsi," he added, in painstaking
French, "lui donnâmes avisement et conseil avant son dé-
partement et ne faisons aucun doûte, l'un jour plus que
l'autre, ne la trouvez telle qu'elle ne doit être envers vous."
The "Avisement" had no further result than the complete
bewitching of the poor old King. He now dined at noor

instead of eight in the morning, went to bed at midnight instead of six, "fit gentil compagnon avec sa femme"—and was rewarded by falling ill. His wife consoled him by romances, which she sang while he lay in his bed.

She was a good-natured woman, light of heart, light of head, light of morals, and this was a defect which stood Louise and her son in good stead. Mary Tudor had brought over in her train an English noble, Charles Brandon, Duke of Suffolk, with whom she was suspected to have more than friendly relations—a fact which, once proved, would deprive her of queenly rights and prevent any child of hers from being acknowledged as heir. Mother and son set spies upon her at every turn; Francis (who found a flirtation with Mary a necessary part of the manœuvres) commanded his wife never to leave the Queen's side by day; another trustworthy lady slept in her room at night. The King's death, on January 1st, 1515, not three months after his marriage, put a sudden end to their plottings. Mary Tudor went through the ordeal then prescribed by royal etiquette for royal widows—to lie in bed for six weeks in a dark room only lit by candles—after which she arose, married the Duke of Suffolk, and returned to England.

There was now no obstacle between Francis and the throne; his mother's joy reached its zenith; and, at twenty-one years of age, he became King of France.

AUTHORITIES CONSULTED FOR CHAPTER VI

Récit d'un Bourgeois de Paris: edited by LALANNE.

Dames Illustres: BRANTÔME.

Dames Illustres: HILARION DE LA COSTE.

l'Heptaméron: MARGUERITE D'ANGOULÊME.

Histoire de Béarn et de Foix; OLHAGARAY.

Oraison Funèbre sur Maguerite d'Angoulême:
                                    SAINTE-MARTHE.

Biographical Preface to Œuvres Choisies de Marot:
                                    HÉRICAULT.

Etudes sur François I: PAULIN PARIS.

Femmes des Valois: ST. AMAND.

Lettres de Marguerite d'Angoulême (Biographical
                          Preface): GÉNIN.

Marguerite de Valois: LA COMTESSE D'HAUSSONVILLE.

Conférences sur Marguerite d'Angoulême: LURO.

Trente Ans de Jeunesse: DE MAULDE LA CLAVIÈRE.

CHAPTER VI

(1500—1515)

MARGARET OF ANGOULÊME

"LA Marguerite des Marguerites" had meanwhile been growing into womanhood. Her title was no mere compliment inspired by courtiers' flattery. When we have allowed for the due proportion of sycophancy, we are still surprised by the unanimity of the old chroniclers about her and by the sense of originality that their portraits of her leave with us. Early in life she chose as her crest a big daisy, with the motto, "Non inferiora secutus," [1] "en signe" (says Brantôme) "qu'elle dirigeait et tendait toutes ses actions, pensées, volontés, et affections à ce grand soleil d'en haut, qui était Dieu"; and her "great sun," as we know, was a light of the mind as well as of virtue, its rays falling on the pages both of Plato and the Bible. She was well called "l'élixir des Valois." She possessed their intellect without its coldness; their love of beauty without its voluptuousness; their urbanity without its treacherous lightness; their kindness without its instability. She was ever hospitable to ideas, whatever camp they came from, and the smiling baby holding out her hand to each comer was the fitting symbol of all her thoughts. This hospitality of mind, this maternal charity, made her, as time went on, the refuge of the

[1] "Not following the lower."

Reformers. She claimed the wounded and distressed as her own, protecting them at her private peril with a steadfast chivalry. "Your royal Margaret"—says one of the pedagogue poets, who had no expectations from her to bias his words —"has always been the road and the path of those who have lost their way: the door at which they may knock. She does not wait for them to approach, but calls them to her by the kindness of her countenance, and runs to meet them like the father of the Prodigal Son."

Margaret's sweetness was tempered by her humour—a quality rare among the women of four hundred years ago. Humour, which is supposed to foster a critical spirit, can afford to laugh where the many would condemn, and is quite as conducive to leniency as to satire. No really indulgent spirit judges, indeed, without it. It is expressed in Margaret's countenance. Beautiful she was not, in spite of all that courtiers wrote about her; but her face was original and characteristic. There seems to be no picture of her as a girl; nothing authentic of earlier date than Clouet's portrait, [1] taken when she was about forty. This is the less to be regretted, because the woman painted there must always have been much the same—of a type that is probably better-looking in middle-age than in youth. She is essentially a Valois; she has the long nose of her royal brother, his small eyes and heavy half-shut lids, with their mysterious look; but the brow is straighter and wider, the jaw square and strong, and the mouth—an index of character—firm, calm, benign, yet gently satirical: the lower lip rather full and sensitive, restrained as it were by the upper, which is cri-

[1] In the Gallery at Chantilly.

tical and austere. The hair, hidden beneath a close-fitting black hood, is of a lightish brown; the head is well set on a long neck; and the fine right hand caresses a little spaniel. The whole leaves an impression of mingled gentleness and power—of mysticism and common-sense—of suffering sensitiveness and wise serenity—the impression of a woman born for many experiences.

They began early. We know that at eight years old she was wooed by Henry VII. Rather later Louis offered her, with a splendid dowry, to Arthur Prince of Wales; but for the moment England was cold to France and preferred Catherine of Aragon. That Princess was fated to stand in the way of Margaret's marriage. Prince Henry was next proposed for her, then Ferdinand of Calabria. Both were Catherine's suitors; both rejected Margaret. Catherine, worse luck for her, was forced to marry her brother-in-law. Margaret was well delivered from him. Not long after this, when she was twelve, Henry VII resumed his courtship, unabashed by the fact that his son had preceded him. This is the first occasion on which Margaret begins to reveal herself. She flatly refused to accept him. What, she cried, they wanted to carry her off to a distant country where a foreign tongue was talked, and to marry her to a King? and what a King! old, decrepit! Francis was to be a king one day; could she not find a husband young, rich and noble, without crossing the seas?

Her heart, half child's, half woman's, had already had its bird-like flutterings—had for the last three years been innocently occupied by two of her playmates—the little Duc d'Alençon and Gaston de Foix, son of the superb Gaston Phébus, Duke of Béarn. Destined to fall at Ravenna in the flower of youth, Gaston died, as he lived, in the odour of romance. Fiery, gentle, chivalric, even in boyhood he inspired a serious feeling in Margaret's breast. Her mother encouraged it and asked him a great deal to Amboise. While their loves were still but at the spring, there entered upon the scene Guillaume Gouffier de Bonnivet, who had been one of Charles VIII's pages. He first met Margaret on the green terraces and in the long low chambers of the Château of Chaumont; then at Tours, where he seems to have told her of his new-born love. He followed up these meetings by making endless stratagems to see her. One of these was his marriage with an ugly friend, an old playmate, of hers, Bonaventura du Puy du Fou, who was constantly at the Amboise Court. Margaret seems to have confided to him her attachment to Gaston, and, not long after, he was obliged to go off to the wars. During his two years' absence his feeling grew in intensity. He kept up a busy correspondence with his wife, who made constant mention of her mistress, and Margaret herself often sent him a line in her own writing. He returned—melancholy, preoccupied: so much so, that one of the Court ladies guessed his secret. Perhaps this determined him; at any rate he took the bold step of confessing his passion to Margaret, one day when they were alone together, leaning out of the palace window. She reproved him gently; she said that she was not angry, that she trusted to his honour. But she could not prevent a certain embarrassment in her manner towards him, and it ended by driving him into voluntary exile.

She wrote and begged him to return. He came. Louise favoured his strange suit, and even seems to have talked of

a "mariage à l'étranger." All smiled on his fortunes when
the wars again claimed him, and he was taken prisoner.
During his confinement, Margaret, then seventeen, was married
to the Duc d'Alençon. She had wept many tears, she had
wasted away, all for love of the faithless Gaston, who had
gone out into the world. She left Amboise for the Château
of Alençon: her heart more solitary and susceptible, more
thankful for a constant devotion, than ever before. When
Bonnivet returned, she steeled herself to meet him by watching his arrival, unseen, from an upper window which over-
looked the courtyard, so that she might, as she said, "find
him again" without meeting him in person. When that
meeting did take place it was in the presence of others,
and she embraced him calmly; but, privately, she promised
herself all the consolations of friendship. Unfortunately his
wife, who had accompanied Margaret to Alençon, died at
this moment and his only pretext for remaining at Court
was gone. He fell ill and Margaret nursed him herself.
This was, perhaps, unwise, for her pity so far overcame her
that once, while tending him, she clasped him in her arms
and broke down all his resolutions. He again made advan-
ces and she again repelled them, quietly but firmly. He
told her that her fickle Gaston had not deserved her—that
her husband was unworthy of her; and she replied with
frankness that she did not like her bridegroom, that Gaston
loved another—but that from him, Bonnivet, she had expected friendship, and where was it? He begged her forgiveness, but she remained sceptical and they separated. No
sooner had he gone than her fortitude vanished; she yielded
to her feelings and cried all day. Louise discovered her

secret, pressed him to her heart, and promised she would make Margaret write to him. A few letters reached him, so cold that they caused him to despair. There was nothing for it but for him to go away, and he succeeded in getting an appointment about the King's person.

One day Louise had a sudden letter to announce his coming and ask her to receive him late that night. Knowing his real wishes and bent on furthering them—without for a moment imagining that Margaret could object—she sent her to her room to prepare for his arrival. Her daughter pretended to obey; but instead of doing so, she went to her private chapel, prostrated herself in prayer, and taking up a large stone, belaboured her face with it till it bled. Her mother, finding her in this condition, wasted no time in comment, but carefully bandaged her wound and sent her to her lover. In spite of her protests, in spite of all her disfigurements, he pressed his suit fervently, till at last she called for Louise—not, we may hope, without a touch of malicious pleasure. Louise, in her stage character of mother, was obliged to appear, and embarrassed excuses ensued. But when he had once gone, she scolded her child severely for "hating all that she loved." She took the high tone of the injured elder and refused to speak to her for days: the only estrangement they had. [1]

The whole of this strange story, and the sequel of Bonnivet's brazen adventures (as told, hardly veiled, in the "Heptameron") are so topsy-turvy that, at the end of them, we

---

[1] The identification of the personages in this story—told in the "Heptameron"—is due to the researches of M. De Maulde la Clavière as given in "Trente Ans de Jeunesse."

ourselves feel astray and seem to be walking head-downwards in a kind of moral Antipodes. We have no map, no clue to this outlandish country, the inhabitants of which do such unimaginable things. Yet Margaret could still weep for Bonnivet when he fell on the field of Pavia.

Her marriage with the Duc d'Alençon was a marriage of convenience—Francis' convenience. The Duke and he were both heirs of Marie d'Armagnac, and the wedding settled their rival claims. It took place in 1509. The bridegroom, somewhat insignificant in looks and in character, was at first distasteful, then a subject of indifference to Margaret. But he gave her a Court of her own and the position she needed. Before we go farther, it is well to pause and look at her now: already a woman in the plenitude of her experience; conscious of her tastes and half conscious of her aims.

She was not yet the stateswoman that she afterwards became—more from circumstances than predilection. But a liberal thinker, a mystic theologian, and a guardian of the arts, she was from the beginning. Nature had given her these tastes, and she needed no experience to develop them. As a woman of letters her position at that moment was unique, for she cared for ideas more than for verbiage or for scholarship. Ideas alone satisfied her, whether they came from Plato or from Calvin, from Marot or Erasmus. And the idea on which she based all the others was tolerance: a warm tolerance, a large charity, born both of heart and of head. This quality inclined her from the first towards the Reformers; it made her the refuge of such different men as the fanatic Calvin and the free-thinking Dolet; the object

of Erasmus' admiration; the patient listener to the truth,
however unpalatable; until Reformation no longer meant
reformed Rome, but assumed the garb of heresy and frightened her sensitive conscience. In Margaret, till that happened, the supposed enemies, Renaissance and Reformation,
were made one. If the persecuted Calvin was harboured at
her Court, Rabelais also dedicated to her the third book of
his "Gargantua et Pantagruel." Artist and early Christian
met in her: the artist whom we know from the "Heptameron," with her love of rich brocades and flowery meadows
and the golden idleness of summer; the early Christian, who,
after first youth, wore plain black garments, shared her goods
with the poor, and taught them the love of God.

A distinguished French critic[1] says that "she was less
remarkable in her actions than her intentions," and that in
the two great objects of her life she failed. She wanted to
establish a reformed Church—free from persecution—and she
wished to see her brother the Prince of enlightenment; to
place him "at the head of Civilization, of Reform and of
Learning, of Mercy and of Freedom." In both aims she
missed her mark. Her failure was chiefly due to the fact
that, womanlike, her purposes were bound up with the
thought of other people. Moderate as she was, she would
never have gone the whole length of the Reformers; but
even had she followed them farther than she did, it would
have opened an impassable gulf between her and those she
loved. As to her plans for Francis, it was only for his
sake that she desired their fulfilment, and she could not

---

[1] St. Amand: Femmes des Valois.

reckon on him as she could do on herself. She schemed for the man as she imagined him—as he might have been—not for the man as he was. Altruism such as this, which sweetens private life, contains the germ of weakness when it is used in public matters; and the qualities that made her a good woman marred her as a worker for the world. The strong person cares for himself on the road he has marked out as his own; and had she done so, had she put Causes before persons, she might have had more effect and have left a clearer mark upon history.

In the early years of his reign, while Francis was under her influence, he became something of what she took him to be. He resembled her greatly on the intellectual side: in his love of letters and of art, his perception of what was true in thought, and his fine amenity of temper. When he was with her and stimulated by her faith in him, it was these qualities that came foremost, and it was no wonder that she believed in the realization of her dreams. Inspired by her, he established the Collége de France with its band of advanced Scholars; he favoured Reform and those who wished to purify the Church; he helped needy talent, encouraged all that was beautiful, and gathered round him men of parts from every civilized country. Unfortunately he was impressionable in other directions; he could well have said with Shakespeare—

> "Two loves I have of comfort and despair
> Which, like two spirits, do suggest me still."

In his case "the worser spirit" was his mother. If in some ways he resembled his sister, in others he was like Louise.

He had inherited her light temperament, to which good faith meant little or nothing; her narrowness of vision; her bigotry, when bigotry suited self-interest. He had also latent in him her power of cruelty, though his youth and his spirits long concealed it. One can imagine the vivid charm of so many conflicting elements; the fascination of one who at this moment was a lotos-eating Prince of the East; at that a soldier on a hard camp-bed. He must, too, have possessed a large share of magnetism—the inexplicable quality which explains the inexplicable. It alone accounts for the real enthusiastic love that he got from all sorts and conditions of men, apart from hyperbolic expression or courtly servility. He had, we gather, a large Shakespearian sweetness—a lavish courage which appealed to the crowd—the sunny splendour and careless profusion of a June day. These were the gifts that made him the idol of his army, and the boon-companion of scholars as of soldiers; of little children as of ambitious beauties.

His Court opened with a slight but characteristic episode which shows him to us in all the sumptuous pride of his youth. A wild boar had been let loose for sport in the courtyard of the palace where he was staying. Angered in some unforeseen way, it rushed at the barricaded gallery, crowded with guests, broke down the defences and, passing all the other people by, made straight for Francis. He might have fled into the Queen's room at his back, but he stood coolly facing the beast "comme s'il eût vu venir à lui une demoiselle." Bidding everyone else stand behind him, he took his sword and stabbed the animal so that it stumbled back to the courtyard and died. There is a kind of superb boastfulness about the deed that brings him before us more vividly than many weightier events.

More important, and more significant of his best qualities, was the part he played at Marignan—the battle which opened the campaign against the Pope with which he began his reign. There, on the Lombard plain, he stands a man among his men, generous and jovial—sharing their hardships —eating his scant meal astride a cannon—weary and stained with the blood of his foes—cheering the flagging—humble in the face of his great victory, as he kneels to his blameless Bayard and begs him to knight his Monarch. Seeing him thus at work, away from banquets and from women, it is easier to understand the loud acclaims of his contemporaries; and we ourselves, for a moment, are almost dazzled by the glamour.

AUTHORITIES CONSULTED FOR CHAPTER VII

Poésies du Roi François I, etc., etc.

Correspondance intime du Roi avec Diane de Poitiers et plusieurs autres Dames de la Cour, edited by CHAMPOLLION-FIGEAC.

Preface to the above work: CHAMPOLLION-FIGEAC.

Récit d'un Bourgeois de Paris.

Etudes sur François I : PAULIN PARIS.

Conférences sur Marguerite d'Angoulême: LURO.

Marguerite de Valois: LA COMTESSE D'HAUSSONVILLE.

Lettres de Diane de Poitiers with critical introduction: GUIFFRY.

Margaret of Angoulême: MARY ROBINSON.

La Réforme: MICHELET.

Histoire de France: MARTIN.

CHAPTER VII

(1515—1525)

During the first ten years that followed the young King's accession, he divided his time between love and war. Italy, indeed, for which he fought so hard and so fantastically, was to him as a mistress ever pursued and never won. At home, amidst his circle of charmers, he was doing more than he knew: he was founding French society. This was one of the unexpected results of his gallantries. The presence of witty ladies at Court drew many other women thither— no mere maids of honour ruled by a Gouvernante and bound by etiquette—but women of mind and beauty, who mixed themselves up with affairs and quickly obtained an equal footing with men. Without this sort of equality, women cannot make themselves felt and there can be no real society. "Society without women" (says an old chronicler) "is like a parterre without flowers"—and he might have added without bees. Margaret of Angoulême and her mother contributed much to these new traditions of good company—they helped, if we may say so, to found them. But their society, had there been none other, would have been something of a côterie—a choice group of intellectual people; and it would have lacked the lavish luxury and gaiety which Francis brought with him.

The feminine element was richly represented at the Field of the Cloth of Gold (1520). The interview had long been talked of. It came off as the direct result of the Imperial Election (1519): before the three young monarchs, who divided the attention of Europe, had yet had the leisure to decide their relations to one another. Francis hoped that he might lure Henry into an alliance with France. The whole affair seemed like a Comedy of Diplomacy invented for the pleasure of ladies. Those of Francis' Court were present in full force, including Anne Boleyn, Margaret's maid of honour, whom Henry saw there for the first time. The gorgeous show was arranged with an eye to woman's taste and a wish for woman's approval. The French had golden trees with green silk leaves—the English a pavilion made of glass. There were combats of generosity, carefully planned to make an impression on Beauty. Francis and his Brother of England vied with each other in courtesy. The French King forced his way, ostentatiously unattended, at daybreak to Henry's tent, and offered to act as his valet and warm his royal chemise for him. Henry, deeply moved, hung a rich chain round his neck, and Francis retorted with a still richer bracelet. There were trials of skill: Francis shone as a rider and a swordsman; Henry was great at the bow, but heavy on horseback. He killed a man by mistake and, in a single tourney between the two Kings, was unfortunately overthrown in the presence of all the Graces. The good of the gifts and visits was undone, the conciliatory purpose of the meeting injured, and the two monarchs parted

amid a good deal of personal irritation. Margaret of
Angoulême, the wife that might have been, and Anne
Boleyn, the wife that was to be, retired with the rest into
private life.

If this had been the end, the consequences would not have
been of importance. But before King Francis reached home,
he had already had the news that Henry had met Charles V
at Wael, near Gravelines. There were no silken tents
and no ladies, but a great deal of business was done. The
results were not long in appearing. Charles, who did not
waste time, at once declared war against France on the
vexed questions of Milan and Navarre. It was not a fortunate campaign for Francis. He lost both possessions with
disastrous rapidity (1521—2), and the calamity was aggravated by his fears that Henry would descend upon Calais.

Amid all these doings Queen Claude was forgotten. She
counted for little, and nothing was asked of her except to
efface herself. She gave her fickle husband three sons and
two daughters, but the chief event in her blameless life was
her death, in 1524, during his absence in Italy. Her funeral
was as magnificent as if she had been the most courted and
dominant of sovereigns; and the neglected little Queen was
borne in state through Paris, its streets and squares hung
with crape and a wax taper before each house. Six bare-
headed "children of honour," dressed in black velvet, rode
the horses that drew her hearse. Margaret and Louise
followed her on mares with black trappings; twenty-four
"criers" in mourning cried her name; and before her, in
scarlet robes, went the whole Court and the Parlement,
heralded by the First Usher in his hat of gold. These

grandiose shows would have given her scant consolation.
Even now, while her body was being paraded through the
city, Francis was dreaming of a certain Clarissa of Milan
who had been described to him; contemporaries went so far
as to say that it was mainly to win her that he undertook
that year's Italian campaign.

Long before her death, Queen Claude had found herself
permanently supplanted by more important rivals. The
woman who ruled the first years of the King's reign was
Françoise de Foix, Duchesse de Châteaubriand—a true child
of the South, black-haired, olive-skinned, and passionately
in love with the light-hearted King. She must have been
a person of great charm. Her husband, Jean de Brosse,
who knew all about her royal attachment, was under her
spell to the end; and honoured her gifts and virtues by an
epitaph—ordered from Marot—which would be touching if
it were not absurd. She, meanwhile, wrote bitter complaints
to the King of her occasional visits to her home in the
country. "Everything seems difficult when I consider my
present circumstances, and reflect that all my life I shall
probably be nothing better than a woman bound to house-
keeping; a yoke which is the dreariest of all yokes." The
King's answers are light; he was not capable of love, but
he hid its absence by amorous conceits. "Ah! my friend,"
he exclaims, "let *me* bear the burden, since I alone am the
cause of it; it is not reasonable that innocence should suffer
the penalty of guilt.... I would far rather have the ruins
of love in my memory, than my memory without such
ruins.... The misery of parting lies in the longing to
return."

La Comtesse de Châteaubriand.
(Portraits des Personnages français les plus illustres du
XVIième siècle, avec Notices par P. G. J. Niel).

F. p. 112.

It is all very fine to talk about the bearing of penalties, but it is not easy to discover the burden that the King carried—for himself or anybody else; and his memory was strewn with so many ruins that they only served to make it picturesque. The Queen was not alone in her experience of him. Sooner or later he tired of wife and mistress alike. Even before Claude died, Madame de Châteaubriand began to see symptoms of a change in him and recognised the advent of a rival. She writes a letter in vehement dispraise of fair complexions, which shows the way the wind blew. "Blanche couleur," she says, "est bientôt effacée.... Blanche couleur n'est pas longtemps nette" (clear). She reproaches him in rhyme—but she is none the less bitter for that. She knew too well that her only chance was to amuse him ("Celle qui est noire" she calls herself); and when that fails, she breaks down and becomes pathetic. She writes her own epitaph and begs him, if he ever loved her, to look at it as he passes by. It must have been a deep sorrow which made a King's mistress natural, and there is the tragic force of sincerity in her cry:

> Une femme gisant en cette fosse obscure
> Mourut par trop aimer d'amour grande et naïve.

Francis ran no risk of such a death, and he found little difficulty in parting with his old love. The new one was ready—the golden-haired Mademoiselle d'Heilly de Pisseleu (afterwards Duchesse d'Etampes), deliberately chosen for him by his mother. The King relieved what feelings he had by writing a poem on the complication of caring for too many people at once. "I am constrained to love three

women," he sighs... "one of them is too much mine for
me not to love her." This rather dubious complaint refers
to his wife, and he proceeds to describe the other two. He
carried on this dual game till the Italian wars called him
away again. Madame de Châteaubriand, treated with every
indignity by the Regent Louise, retired with a broken heart
to a comfortable country-house. The rest of her life does
not belong to history.

Mademoiselle d'Heilly was quickly domesticated by Louise,
who refers to her as one of their "united trio." "La plus
belles des savantes et la plus savante des belles," Marot
called her. She was a young woman of sense and parts,
with a good deal of learning besides; and was afterwards
made governess to the King's little daughters, as if she were
a Maintenon or a Genlis. She was not altogether generous,
for she begged the King to get back the jewels he had
given to her predecessor, not because of their value (jewels
were then unfashionable), "but for love of the devices
engraved thereon and designed by his sister, who was a great
mistress of this craft." Madame de Châteaubriand responded
by returning the King's gifts turned into golden *lingots*.
"She has shown," said the King, "more courage and generosity
than I had thought possible in a woman."

Margaret's part in all this is difficult to realize. She
was a friend of Madame de Châteaubriand, but she was
intimate with Mademoiselle d'Heilly. Mademoiselle's Protestant leanings (which made her, as Duchesse d'Etampes,
the Patroness of the Reformers) must have been a bond of
union, but there was, besides, a real affection between them.
The truth was that Margaret always loved the people the

King loved. She saw him in everything and everybody. "I was yours before you were born," she wrote—"you are more to me than father, mother, and husband. Compared to you, husband and children count as nothing." This is the mysticism of love, and a mystic Margaret was, in heart as well as belief.

AUTHORITIES CONSULTED FOR CHAPTER VIII

Journal de Louise de Savoie.

Les Marguerites de la Princesse des Marguerites: MARGUERITE D'ANGOULÊME (with Biographical Preface by FRANCK).

Nouvelles Poésies: MARGUERITE D'ANGOULÊME.

Lettres de Marguerite d'Angoulême (Biographical Preface): GÉNIN.

Nouvelle Lettres (Biographical Preface): GÉNIN.

Life of Margaret of Angoulême: MARY ROBINSON.

Les Femmes des Valois: ST.-AMAND.

Conférences sur Marguerite d'Angoulême: LURO.

Marguerite de Valois: LA COMTESSE D'HAUSSONVILLE.

Vie de Rabelais: RENÉ MILLET.

Histoire de France (Vol. VIII): HENRI MARTIN.

La Renaissance: MICHELET.

La Réforme: MICHELET.

Dictionnaire Historique: BAYLE.

CHAPTER VIII

(1515—1525)

RELIGION at this moment was occupying Margaret's mind. It is said that people become Catholics for very different reasons; emotional, aesthetic, theological. In those unsettled times men and women were Protestants from motives quite as varied. These were the palmy days of Reform, before divergences of doctrine were defined. In France, the home of culture, alone of all countries, for the first twenty years or thereabouts, the Renaissance and the Reformation went hand in hand. Scholars, Reformers, Poets, Philosophers, Wits and Mystics, all made common cause against the rule of ignorance and convention, and the imprisonment of the imagination. Margaret of Angoulême adopted the new faith in great measure because she was a mystic, and rebelled against the gross shackles of dogma; because, too, her large-minded charity made tolerance a necessity in her eyes. Any thought that helped men to live more nobly she included within the pale of religion, and Socrates was no less a Saint to her than Augustine.

Of her actual dogmas we know little, except that she dwelled much on Redemption and little on the Fall. She thought a great deal about Immortality, but did not like many

words about it. Impatient at a preacher who constantly
harped upon death, she said that such talk was the last
refuge of clergymen when they were at an end of their
resources and did not know how to make any effect on
their audience. And when men of mind discussed Eternal
Life in her presence, she would shake her head sadly: "All
that may be true," she would say, "but we have to remain
a long time underground before we reach it." The love of
speculation was strong in her, but her love of good actions,
her reverent humility, were stronger. The creed that used
fewest forms and dwelled most upon practical Christianity
was the one that appealed to her. "The least word in the
Scriptures is too good for me," she said, "and the clearest
is full of obscurity. Alas, what choice can I make between
them, seeing that I cannot even understand why they differ?"
This is the saying of a modest and moderate person—one
who would not easily sever old ties. The heart is conservative, and the heart was Margaret's weakness as well as her
strength. She was born to purify an old order rather than
to found a new one.

She was bent on the conversion of her brother and her
mother—hitherto latitudinarians, but not pious as she was.
Louise seems, for a short while, to have inclined towards the
New Ideas, but her beliefs were beliefs of the brain; feelings
had nothing to do with them. Scorn of the Monks and a
taste for satire played a much larger part in her creed.
"My son and I," she wrote in her Journal, "begin by the
grace of God to know the hypocrites, black, white and
grey, and the hypocrites of all colours.... The Lord preserve us from them, for in all human nature there is no

more dangerous race." A religion such as this, founded on antipathy and common sense, was hardly of stuff that would endure. Policy was her real conscience; and when the new doctrines interfered with that, and endangered State as well as Church, then they became heresy and she persecuted more bitterly than anyone. Both she and Margaret were absorbed by the novel study of the Scriptures. To Margaret, who did not analyze the people she was fond of, her mother, whom she began by converting, afterwards figured as the perfect interpreter of the Bible. In the "Heptameron" Louise is probably portrayed as "Oisille"—the wise and calm lady who directs the conduct and devotions of her companions, and expounds the Bible to them daily with such charm and understanding that they are loth to leave her, even for Boccaccian pleasures.

The attitude of the King resembled both that of his sister and his mother. He was warm in intellect and eager to please all parties. But there was another side to his character. Selfish statecraft, pride of position, and relentless cruelty to opponents lay beneath the dazzling surface. When Reform seemed to threaten his prerogatives, he followed his mother's example and punished barbarously. In these early years of his manhood, however, all was serene, and Margaret had her way with him. Such love as hers was rather blind. She constantly gave thanks for his spiritual progress when he was really acting on the dictates of a shrewd mind. Happily it suited his views to play the Patron of the Reformers, whom he called "Mes fils" and "Hommes d'excellent savoir." Calvin dedicated his book to him. So did Zwinglius, Pastor of Einsiedeln and Vicar of Zurich, who promised him a place in heaven in the company of Hercules and Cato. The King graciously accepted their homage. " I have no wish," he said, " to persecute ; I should only be preventing clever men from coming into the country." This was to his credit, at a time when German princes were killing the monks of Antwerp—when even in England parents were burned for teaching their children the Pater and the Credo in English (1511). Like Margaret, Francis was fond of inviting the Reformers to his table, and discussing their subjects with them during dinner; and what he thoroughly enjoyed was getting a laugh at the Pope : the sly laugh of the schoolboy at the expense of a tyrant pedagogue.

Margaret was bent on the further conversion of both Francis and Louise. She introduced into the family circle a certain Michel d'Arande, a scholar of the new faith, whom she made her special " Reader." Unlike their brethren at Geneva, who read the whole of the Bible, the French Reformers devoted themselves to the New Testament. Michel d'Arande read portions of it daily to his three royal friends in their private apartment, and held debates as he went on. Louise and Francis became more heterodox, and Margaret rejoiced in her success. " The King and Madame," she wrote to a friend,[1] " are more than ever inclined to aid the Reform of the Church, and resolved to let the world know that God's truth is not heresy." Another of her converts was the sister of Louise, Philiberte de Savoie, widow of Leo X's brother. Philiberte returned from Italy to France and " fell

[1] Briçonnet. 1521.

in love" (so she tells us) with her niece, Margaret, who plied her with tracts and pious conversation. When the aunt was inconsolable at the thought of departing for Savoy, the niece begged Michel d'Arande to go and calm her with spiritual ministrations. She remained, like many others, under Margaret's spell, and a kind of Protestant mysticism became the fashion at Court.

It was greatly helped by the rise of a little group of men, eager for Reform, to whom Michel d'Arande belonged. These were the Mystics of Meaux, earnest thinkers and students, dwelling chiefly in that city and centering round its fashionable Archbishop, Briçonnet, Margaret's Director and correspondent. She was only second to him in importance amidst this band of Reformers, and all the best and least fanatical spirits gathered round them. Here was Lefèbre d'Étaples, translator of the New Testament and tutor to the King's son; Roussel, "the Red-haired," Margaret's preacher, who travelled in Germany, heard Luther, and shaped a creed of his own—neither that of Luther nor of Calvin; Berquin, a noble by birth, a soul of fire, doomed to perish for his faith; Farel, also an aristocrat, very small and fierce; Leclerc, a democrat and a weaver of Meaux, who supplied the popular image-breaking element and was born to be a martyr; Mazurier, who, with Lefèbre, defended Reuchlin against the Cologne Dominicans; and a few others no less fervent, if not as effectual as their fellows. They had, too, one or two outside associates: Duchatel, the King's Reader, and Guillaume Petit, his Confessor. But these men, now their admirers, afterwards took fright and turned against them.

In spite of occasional opposition, they continued to work
and strive. They got hold of the weavers of Meaux,
Leclerc's fellow-artisans, a handful of starving men, fit
subjects for religious revival. So matters went on till 1523.
That year the fanatic, Noël Béda, began a systematic
persecution and obliged them to scatter and to flee. Farel
went to the Dauphiné and sowed the seeds of Reform;
Roussel followed him there, but not for long. The indefatigable Margaret gave him the Abbey of Clérac. When things
were quieter she even got him a Bishopric, and the title
of Royal Almoner and Confessor to herself and the King.

It is remarkable that so many men of distinction, bound
to each other by kindred aims, should have left so little
mark behind them. The fact is that not one of them was
a real leader. They were all thinkers and theorists rather
than doers. Berquin, who was fervent, had no wisdom;
Farel, a man of action, lacked magnetism and did not
possess the requisite largeness of vision; and Roussel, with
his separate creed, left the high-road for a by-path. The
two most promising members were Briçonnet and his Grand
Vicar, Lefèbre d'Étaples; but they too failed, for reasons
peculiar to their characters.

Briçonnet's nature is summed up in Robert Browning's
Bishop Blougram—the man of good aspirations who com-
promised with the world. The son of a priest whom
Julius II excommunicated, he was first made Comte de
Montbrun, then took orders and obtained the confidence of
Louis XII, later of Francis I. Twice Extraordinary Ambas-
sador to Rome and Representative of France at Papal
Councils, he followed up his honours by gaining the rich

Abbey of St. Germain-des-Prés, reforming its abuses and increasing its library. He was a true lover and protector of Letters, and this was probably his first link with Margaret. "Madame," he writes to her, "if at the farthest end of the Kingdom there existed a Doctor, who by one single condensed verb could teach the whole of Grammar; and if he could also teach Rhetoric, Philosophy, and all the seven Liberal Arts, each by a like condensed verb, I vow that you would rush to him as a shivering man would to the fire." Later—and it is a matter for regret—their correspondence resolved itself into unintelligible mysticism. Its bulk is astounding, its contents more so. A stranger farrago of exalted dulness cannot be imagined, and its incoherence increases till it reads like a correspondence in a dream. Repentance and ecstasy are expressed in the extravagant language of love—a kind of spiritual euphuism, complicated by allegory. She dwells vaguely on a crushing sense of sin; Briçonnet absolves her in phrases that sound like gibberish. She was twenty-four years younger than he, but he signs himself "your useless son"; she varies between "your useless mother", and "your frozen, thirsty and ravenous daughter".... "Madame," he answers (unconsciously parodying himself), "what am I saying? I do not know what I *am* saying." No more perhaps did Margaret, for even she, on one occasion, asked him to "démétaphoriser" himself.

Sentimental though he was, this Court Bishop was no charlatan. He sincerely wished for Reform in the Church, and all through the Meaux period he was working for his cause. But when that cause became a dangerous affair, his opinions changed and he gradually cried off. To avoid persecution, he belied himself in the pulpit and made all the retractations required; yet, to his credit be it added, he never consented to persecute.

Lefèbre d'Étaples was of a nobler strain. He hated the abuses of Rome, and wished to revive the primitive Church. It was with this view that he translated the New Testament and made a Commentary on St. Paul. Professor of Letters and Philosophy in Paris, he had a good deal of interest in the world of cultivated people, and it was he who first communicated the new doctrines to Briçonnet. Appointed as his Grand Vicar, he went to live near him at Meaux and was among the first of his comrades to encounter the anger of the Sorbonne. His opinions do not sound very dangerous: they concerned nothing more vital than the lives of St. Anne and Mary Magdalene. Nevertheless, they were pronounced to be heretical, and he was forced to flee to Strasburg. Thanks to the efforts of Margaret, the Court intervened and rescued him. He was made Tutor to the King's youngest son and, later, when danger again threatened him, his Lady's Librarian at Blois. But the Sorbonne refused to leave him in peace, and Margaret, then Queen of Navarre, removed him thither, to her palace at Nérac.

Although we are forestalling the date, this seems the right place to complete the picture of the apostolic Lefèbre. In holy calm he lived on at Pau until he was a hundred and one, filling his days with charity and with wise conversation. He read to the Princess daily from the Gospels, or from pious books, and it was with him that she liked best to talk. He fulfilled, she said, her ideal of goodness and simplicity. He was at dinner with her a few hours before he died. "Madame," he said, "I have reached the age of a hundred and one, and I do not remember committing any fault with which to burden my conscience now that I am leaving this world—unless it be one only, which I feel it is impossible to expiate. How can I exist before the Tribunal of God—I who have taught the Gospel of His Son, in all its pristine purity, to so many who have suffered death for Him, whilst I have always managed to escape it? And this, too, in an age when, far from fearing it, I ought to have desired it." Margaret tried to comfort him, and she reasoned so well that at last he said, "There is nothing left for me to do but to go to my God Whom I hear calling me." Then, turning his eyes on her, he begged her to be his executrix; he left his books to Roussel, his clothes to the poor, and recommended the rest to the care of God. "And what of all your fortune comes to me?" she asked. "The trouble of distributing my possessions among the poor," he replied. "Gladly will I do it," said she; "and I swear that this gives me more pleasure than if my brother, the King, had made me his heiress." Thereupon he said farewell to those at table, and went straightway to his bed, where he died so gently that everyone thought he was asleep.

Perhaps Lefèbre d'Étaples was right about himself and he had, by his retirement, committed an unconscious crime against the French Reformation. But in England Protestantism established itself without the existence of great leaders. Had Francis I been a strong-willed and clear-sighted man of action, like Henry VIII—or had he even remained faithful to his trust as the Patron of Reason and

Reform—the Reformation might have taken root in France. But as it was, the typical Frenchman could not impose Protestant thought upon his nation—a sign, maybe, that such beliefs were not made for it and could not have flourished in its midst. It never took hold of the French people, but remained, from first to last, the concern of the cultivated aristocrats—an intellectual conception lacking democratic sinew. Excepting for a brave little band of weavers and cloth-workers at Meaux, and a few stray artisans of later days in Paris, the poor had nothing to do with this period of the French Reformation: the only period when it might have had big issues. Luther was the son of a miner and he needed the help of the German people to spread abroad his religion. It was a faith which depended on confident deed rather than on beauty-loving form. And thus it was that he succeeded where a thinker like Erasmus must have failed.

In 1525, there occurred an event which proved of significance to the Reformers—the fatal battle of Pavia. The war with the Emperor, which for the last ten years had been continued almost incessantly in Italy and the Netherlands, was now approaching a fresh crisis. Francis had, off and on, himself conducted his campaigns and had had his share of hard fighting. In 1524, he once again crossed the Alps and led his army in person against the forces of Charles V. He undertook the long siege of Pavia, which culminated in the great battle at which he was defeated and taken prisoner. It was a catastrophe for France, and, had they known it, for the Reformers: marking, as it did, the close of their best days—the days of tolerance and reason. [1] When the King returned from his captivity, persecution was already in the air. His mother, who looked upon Pavia as a judgment for heresy, had not been slow to fan the flames; and though he had occasional returns to his generous mood, 'he too joined the cry against Reform. Margaret alone remained staunch to her old friends.

The news of the disaster, which reached her at Lyons, overwhelmed her. She heard that a blunder on the part of her husband—the Commander of the Vanguard—had been a main cause of the defeat. It was difficult to get tidings. Rumours reached her that her brother was crushed by the blow; that he was leading the life of a monk. Adversity had, indeed, plunged him into a penitential mood, though it never shook his conviction that he was under exceptional protection from above. He received, as he thought, a special intimation of the fact. When, under a strong guard, he attended Mass in the Chartreuse at Pavia, with heavy heart and head bowed on his breast, his eyes fell on these words, engraved on the pavement at his feet: "It is good for me that I have been in trouble: that I may learn Thy statutes." Impressionable as usual, he took to fasting. Margaret heard of it and wrote off in agitation to say that it would ruin his health. He had much better read St. Paul's Epistles, which she sent him with her letter. She need 'not have been alarmed. Asceticism was not his strong point. He cheered his sackcloth and ashes by more mundane diver-

[1] There had already been some victims before this: Louise de Savoie was the chief instigator of their tortures. But their number was comparatively few and the real times of persecution came later.

sions: letters in rhyme to Mademoiselle d'Heilly, and her poetic replies, full of compliment and sympathy. Then there was his family correspondence. "Madame," he wrote to his mother, "pour vous faire savoir comment se porte le reste de mon infortune, de toutes choses ne m'est demeuré que l'honneur, et la vie qui est sauve." Tradition has the knack of epigram. This, it is interesting to find, is the real version of the famous, "Tout est perdu fors l'honneur."

Time wore on. There were incessant negotiations between him and Spain, whence Charles V watched his opportunity. He ended by outwitting his most Christian Brother, Francis, and persuaded him that the only means of settlement between them lay in a personal interview. Francis, believing him, was taken to Spain. He found the interview deferred, and his own person indefinitely consigned to a State imprisonment in a castle near Madrid.

This was a misfortune. But misfortune only spurred Margaret on to fresh efforts for her faith. She began a second mystic correspondence. This time it was with her cousin, Sigismund of Hohenlohe, a warrior-prelate, Luther's follower and Dean of the Chapter of Strasburg. He was ambitious, and dreamed of the conversion of France to Lutheranism. Having sounded Margaret, he found her a ready means to his end and he made the King's captivity a pretext for writing to her. The correspondence served as a congenial distraction to her grief. The idea of the Crusade appealed to her imagination. It was certainly a venture which her brother's presence would have prevented, and her action against his known views is difficult to understand. No doubt she thought she was helping his eternal salvation, and this conviction destroyed any scruples she may have had. "God is God," she wrote to Hohenlohe, "no less invisible than incomprehensible; and His victories are so spiritual that He is a conqueror when the world fancies He is conquered." The victories dreamed of by the Dean of Strasburg were not so abstract. He required three thousand foot-soldiers to achieve his purpose. Some two years later, on the King's return, Margaret went so far as to beg this force for her cousin, on the pretence that he needed it to repel Charles V. But the whole affair eventually fell through and ended by Hohenlohe's withdrawal; because, as he politely put it, he felt that the King would not make him welcome in France.

The defeat at Pavia and its consequences provided another Reformer with an occasion to write to Margaret. This was no less a person than Erasmus. She was made to suit his delicate mind—whether as a refined scholar, or a typical representative of that Reformation which best embodied his tastes. When she was at Lyons, he wrote to her from Bâle. They had never met or corresponded, but her admirers had urged him to address her now, amidst this tempest of troubles. He had been reluctant—scrupulous—but not for long.

"Fear and shame" (he wrote) "have yielded to the strange affection that I bear you. For I have admired and loved you this long while because of the many and goodly gifts that God has bestowed upon you: the prudence of a philosopher, purity, moderation, piety, an invincible force of soul and a marvellous contempt of all the vanities of the world. Who would not admire in a great King's sister the qualities

which are rare in priests and monks? And I would not
speak of them now, were I not sure of your knowing that
the merit lies in no way with you, but wholly with God,
the Dispenser of all good. So with the wish to congratu-
late rather than console you, I make this venture. The
calamity is great, I own it; but nothing in human affairs
is so terrible that it need cast down a courage truly founded
on the rock—the immovable rock—Jesus Christ. If you
ask me whence I know you, I who have never seen you,
there are many who know your Highness by your portraits
without ever having had the happiness of seeing you face to
face. As for me, many men of excellent parts have painted
your mind in their letters to me, more faithfully than any
painter could portray your person with his illusive colours.
You must not misdoubt my good faith. I praise you because
I know you, and I do not flatter your power, for I want
nothing from you except a return of affection. Long have
I loved the Most Christian King; or, to speak more truly, I
have returned his friendship—since he it was who first sought
for mine in divers ways. And a woman, a heroine such as
you are, I cannot keep from loving in the Lord. I owe to
the Emperor not only fair deeds, but piety—and that for
more than one reason. First, I am born his subject—then
I have long been his councillor and he has my oath of
allegiance. Would to God it were the Turks over whom
he had gained this victory!.... That would have been an
answer to our most fervent prayers.... Now, however
magnificent his triumph, I have not been able to congratu-
late him from the depths of my heart...." There follows
a noble exhortation to trust in God, "the great Workman

of secret counsel, Who brings good out of evil." The
Emperor's genius, the King's skill, will effect much. . . .
"Best of all," he continues, "I feel certain that they have
formed between them a bond of friendship, strong as a
chain of adamant. My hopes are grounded on the letter
which, just as the King was leaving for Spain, your Highness
wrote to the illustrious Polish Baron, Jean de Lascar. He
lives with me and love has made all things common between
us. In truth, your letter showed, not only a firm courage
to bear the heavy burden of destiny, but refreshed our
affectionate anxiety by words of good omen. If this hope
be fulfilled, we shall wish joy to the Emperor—and not
alone to him, but to all Christendom.

"I must before I end, ask a twofold pardon from you—
first, for having dared, at my own prompting, to write to
so powerful a lady; next for having done so impromptu: a
liberty which even a plebeian hardly permits himself towards
a friend. But my scruples were chased away by the confidence that I conceived when I heard the rumours of your
surpassing kindness. The Lord Jesus keep you in health
and safety—fresh in the full flower of prosperity in Him.
At Bâle; Saint Michael's Eve, 1525."

The letter from Erasmus and the plottings with Hohenlohe
came at a time when Margaret was preoccupied with domestic
tragedy. Her husband, the Duc d'Alençon, had died of a
broken heart. A keen soldier and the leader of the Vanguard,
a post of the greatest importance, he had commanded the
left wing of the army at Pavia; and his unaccountable
defection there was one of the dire calamities to which the
loss of the day was ascribed. The right wing, separated

from him by the Swiss, took fright. He caught the panic and retreated with his men, infecting the Swiss with his example and leaving the King unsupported. When his master was taken he returned, safe though desperate to France, to be hooted in each village he passed through. The country folk were all singing " Chansons de Pavie," and he must have been pursued, as he rode, by songs such as this one:

> Qui vit jamais au monde
> Ung roy si courageux
> De se mettre en bataille;
> Et delaissé de ceulx,
> En qui toute fiance
> Et qui tenait asseur,
> L'ont laissé en souffrance !
> Véez là le malheur ! [1]

To such music he probably entered Lyons. Here his wife and mother-in-law met him, and Louise lost no time in overwhelming him with reproaches. In this act of the drama, she appears in the part of the original mother-in-law of French farce. Crushed by shame, the poor creature took to his bed—whence he never rose again. His sense of guilt and humiliation was too much for him. Margaret tended him, body and soul, with conscientious devotion; it was the first time that he received much attention from her. When the last hour came, two months after his misfortune, she was kneeling by his bedside receiving the Sacrament with him.

Her feeling did not go deep; and it probably jarred little upon her when—the breath scarcely out of her husband's

[1] Life of Margaret of Angoulême by Mary Robinson.

body—Louise offered her in marriage to Charles V. It seemed the easiest means of delivering Francis from captivity. The Emperor did not even answer the proposal, and Louise, now appointed Regent, had recourse to other expedients. The crafty Francis sent his ring from prison to Soliman; he hoped to free himself by an alliance with the Turks. It sounds as if he were enacting one of his favourite Romances of Chivalry. No plan seemed too difficult to put into execution. He resorted to treachery, and agreed to a settlement which betrayed Italy and Burgundy into the hands of the Emperor. The time before his departure for Spain was full of ingenious machinations.

AUTHORITIES CONSULTED FOR CHAPTER IX

Histoire des Choses Mémorables: FLEURANGE.
Lettres de Diane de Poitiers (Introduction): GUIFFRY.
Histoire de France (Vol. VIII): MARTIN.
Histoire de France: DURUY.
Etudes sur François I: PAULIN PARIS.
La Renaissance: MICHELET.
Life of Margaret of Angoulême: MARY ROBINSON.

CHAPTER IX

(1504—1525)

CHARLES DE MONTPENSIER, THE CONSTABLE OF FRANCE

THE battle of Pavia was a turning-point in the personal
life of the King and of Margaret. It proved to be no less
so to Louise, the third person of the trio. Francis was,
we have said, the centre of his mother's existence; but
during one short act of the drama another figure played
the hero. This was Charles de Montpensier, Duke of Bourbon and Constable of France, whom she loved for a space
with all the passion of an exclusive nature. It was the
only love-story of her life; a tissue of hope and hatred,
which interwound itself strangely with the history of the
nation.

The Constable was one of those superb figures of the
sixteenth century who seem to have been invented by Shakspeare. He and his kind were a proof that the times the
poet lived in actually possessed the glorious peers and
princes, magnificent in their crimes as in their virtues, who
haunted his vast imagination. When Henry VIII saw the
Constable on the Field of the Cloth of Gold—"If that man
were lord of mine," he said, "his head should not remain
two days on his shoulders." He outdid the King in splendour, and the palace which he made for himself was the most

beautiful in France. By 1504, he was almost as rich as Francis. He had, in that year, married the sickly Suzanne —only child of Anne de Beaujeu and Pierre II, Duke of Bourbon—and his territory amounted to a kingdom.

It was probably about ten years later that he became the lover of Louise de Savoie. There is no doubt about *her* feeling; how far his was sincere and how far it was assumed, is a matter for speculation; but they seem to have gone as far as the exchange of rings, and actual promises of marriage when Suzanne should be no more. It was through the influence of Louise that Bourbon was made Constable; and ambition, rather than love, was probably the ruling power which guided the course of this Renaissance Lucifer. He had a right to his restless pride. His mother was a Gonzaga, and the blood of generations of Condottieri was in his veins. Somewhat later, soon after the King's first campaign in Italy, Bourbon was appointed Governor of the Milanese district and took up his abode there. Louise, desperate at his absence, resolved he should come back and intrigued for this end with Madame de Châteaubriand, who also desired his return because she wanted his post for her brother, Lautrec. They gained their point, but Bourbon, furious at his recall, swore he would never forgive Louise. In an outburst of rage, he told her that he had never loved her—that her daughter Margaret was the woman he really cared for and wished to marry. On the instant Madame's passion turned to hatred; she vowed revenge, and each bent an inhuman force on the task of destroying the other.

The King had always regarded the Constable with anxious jealousy. He was eager to propitiate him, but there was

Portrait du Connétable de Bourbon.
Cabinet des Estampes Bibliothèque Nationale ; d'après
un dessin du Musée d'Aix.

F. p. 136.

no love lost between them : little wonder, considering the
rumour that Bourbon had preceded him in the heart of
Madame de Châteaubriand. "Plus gris que vieux"—"grey
with experience not with age"—so the King wrote on the
portrait of the Constable in Madame de Boisy's Album. The
sympathy between these two Kings, the crowned and the
uncrowned, was not increased by the campaign of 1521 :
the campaign which culminated in the secret League of the
Emperor, the Pope, and Henry VIII against France; and
in the conduct of which Bourbon showed towards his sovereign a proud and impatient temper. Francis knew how
to retaliate. During his expedition to Hainault, he gave
to the Duke of Alençon the command of the Vanguard—
a post which by rights belonged to the Constable of France—
and contrived to dishonour him in minor ways, not one of
which was lost upon Bourbon.

In the same year of '21, Suzanne de Bourbon died. The
Constable wasted little time in beginning fruitless negotiations for the hand of Princess Renée, Queen Claude's sister,
a match which would have served his ambition. At this
moment, Louise de Savoie asked the King to give her the
Constable in marriage. Francis sent a Lord to apprise Bourbon of his will. An old Chronicler describes the scene.
"When the Duke heard these tidings, for a long time he
spake no word, but stood looking at the noble messenger,
his brother-in-arms, and at length he said to him : 'Is it
an act worthy of our friendship to bring me the offer of
such a woman . . . the dread of all nations? . . . I would not
do this thing—no, not for all the riches of Christendom.'"
When the King told Louise of his answer, "she, like a

woman bereft of her senses, began to tear her hair, saying that she had been a madwoman thus to abandon herself in order to receive such an answer. 'The matter shall not rest here,' quoth she in her rage; 'for by the Creator of souls, his words shall cost him dear. My son, I will not own you, I will condemn you as a coward King, if you do not avenge me.'"

The King, with his usual good sense, replied that the hour had not yet come—that the Emperor was going to Rome for Easter—that he meant to cut short Charles' imperial journey and, for this end, the Constable's help was necessary. "Bear with me, mother," he concluded. "When the time is ripe I shall know how to reckon with him."

Louise could not now have withdrawn, even had she wished it. The game between her and Bourbon became more acute and events helped their designs. The King and his unscrupulous Minister, Duprat—at the end of their resources—were busy concocting illegitimate schemes of taxation for getting enough money to carry on the war in Italy. At this moment (1522) Lautrec lost the Milanese possessions and returned to France. When the King reproached him, he coolly replied that Francis alone was at fault for not sending him—Lautrec—the sums he had demanded for paying the discontented army. The King, amazed, declared that he had instantly despatched a sum through the Treasurer, Jacques de Semblançay.

Semblançay was summoned; he remembered the incident, but said that Louise de Savoie had told him to give her the sum for her own use. Bourbon allied himself with

Lautrec in trying to expose her. Francis, infuriated, sent
for her and asked her to account for what had happened.
It was not so much from avarice that Louise had taken the
money as from a spiteful desire to injure Lautrec, who had
had the indiscretion to denounce her way of life; and now,
when she was accused, she lied brilliantly. She asserted that
Semblançay had slandered her and that the money he had
given her was not the King's, but a fund of her own
which she had entrusted to his care. Suspicion enveloped
Semblançay; he was ordered to bring his accounts and a
special Commission was appointed to look into the matter.
Duprat and Louise were active in their plots against him;
but the disasters of 1525 intervened and diverted their
attention from the affair. Louise, however, never forgot.

In 1527, after the King's return from captivity, the case
was reopened. Semblançay was again summoned; underwent
a mock trial; was condemned for corruption, and was executed
—one of the few honest men whom the King could boast
as his servants.

Meanwhile the first part of the episode was remembered
as a fresh score against the Constable. The Queen-Mother
now gave vent to her long-smouldering schemes of revenge.
When Suzanne de Bourbon died, she had bequeathed all
her lands—a large portion of the Kingdom—to her husband.
Louis XI had left them to her mother, Anne de Beaujeu,
under condition that if she died without a male heir they
should go to the Crown. But Louis XII had annulled
this edict by another which enabled Suzanne to dispose of
her property as she willed. Louise worked indefatigably till
this second Act was also annulled, and then she entered the

lists as heir to the Bourbon dominions. She based her claim on
the fact that she was Suzanne's first cousin, whereas the Constable's kinship was more distant. The lawsuit ended in a verdict which gave the lands to the Crown. The King presented
them to his mother—thus ruining Bourbon, who soon after lost
other territories left him by Anne de Bretagne. He appealed
against the decision of the Judges, and a Commission was
instituted to go down to the disputed province of the
Bourbonnais and enquire into the business. The Commissioners,
refusing to be responsible, referred the matter to the Parlement.

But the Constable was prudent as well as impetuous. He
knew how to make friends with the children of unrighteous-
ness. As early as 1521 he began his plottings with the
Emperor; in '22, they took more definite form; and in '23,
at Bourg-en-Bresse, he made a formal pact with Charles V.
Bourbon swore to serve him against all his enemies, in return
for a large sum of money, a leading position in the army,
and one of the Emperor's sisters, Eleonora or Catherine, in
marriage. Charles V was to invade France with his ally,
Henry VIII, and Bourbon was to have a free hand with
the English troops. At first he refused the condition imposed
by Henry,—that, when the war ended in the Allies' partition
of the French Kingdom, the Constable should acknowledge
the English monarch as King both of England and France;
but he acceded later, on the promise of the whole of Provence.
He was also to regain the Bourbonnais. With overweening
pride, he refused the Emperor's offer of the Order of the
Golden Fleece. It is difficult to detect the goal for which
his giant daring was making. It was probably nothing less
than the throne of France.

He made use of his present opportunities by going to England (where Henry VIII received him well) and afterwards to Spain—to arrange the marriage, which never came off, with Eleonora of Portugal. Sir Thomas Boleyn, Anne Boleyn's father, then Ambassador at Madrid, writes in praise of him to Wolsey. "The Constable" (he says) "has, according to his own showing, the noblest motives for his desertion of his country, which is purely owing to the badness of the King, the current abuses, and Bourbon's earnest desire to relieve and reform the people." From Spain he proceeded to Paris to look after the lawsuit, now in the hands of the Parlement. Whilst there he visited Queen Claude. The King came in and said, "It is true, I suppose, that you are going to be married?" "No, Sire," replied Bourbon. "But I know that you are—I am sure of it. I know all your traffic with the Emperor. You had best remember what I am saying." "Sire, you threaten me; I have not deserved to be treated in this manner." Whereupon he (the Duke) left the room, followed by all the nobles in attendance on the Queen. Perhaps nothing can give a truer measure of his power in the land than this behaviour, at a moment when his fortunes seemed sinking. Nothing, either, can convey a better notion of Francis' density when his vanity and his prestige were concerned. Once these were affected, he became both merciless and blind, however great the danger that stared him in the face.

The invasion was now fully organised—the position of each army defined. Francis, at last discomfited by the rumours abroad, tried at the eleventh hour to propitiate the Constable by offering him the Lieutenant-Generalship of the Kingdom, under the Regency of Louise, while he himself was with the troops in Italy. Growing uneasier, he resolved to interview him and try what he should have tried at first—generosity and forgiveness. He saw him at Moulins and told him that all should be forgotten, although he was fully aware of his deeds of disloyalty. Bourbon denied them; he said that Charles V had made him offers which he had refused; that he had only waited to inform the King until he should see him in person. He agreed to accompany Francis to Lyons, en route for Italy; but when the hour of departure came, he feigned illness and said that he would join him later. When at last he pretended to start, he branched off on the road and took refuge in his Castle of Chantelles, on the confines of the Bourbonnais. The King had, in the interim, learned all the details of the conspiracy and the names of the numerous nobles implicated in it. The discovery was made through a priest, to whom it had been confided under seal of confession by two of those who were involved. An order went out for the arrest of the Constable, who fled, disguised as a valet, to the mountains of Auvergne. The plans for the Allies' invasion were, for the moment, at an end.

We have now to glance at the events which led up to the battle of Pavia. Francis had no easy position, with England, Germany and Spain all arrayed against him. In 1523, Bonnivet conducted the war in Italy, where the fortunes of France were waning; and, early in the next year, the Constable appeared there with the Imperial forces. Not long after, the veteran Bayard first saved the French army at Gattinara, and then—mortally wounded—kissing the cross of his sword-hilt, he lay down under a tree to die. Bourbon came to look on him and offered his tribute of praise—sternly rejected by Bayard, whose last words were a rebuke to the traitor. There followed to the spot all the greatest nobles of the Imperial host, who stood with tears running down their cheeks and watched the death of their foe: the Chevalier "sans peur et sans reproche."

The conquest of Provence, in 1524, under Bourbon and his colleagues, had been the sequel of the Imperialists' successes in Italy; after which, against the Constable's advice, they proceeded to besiege Marseilles. The defence was gallant and much helped by "Le Rempart des Dames," made by the ladies of Marseilles. The King sent efficient reinforcements and the town was saved: to the great discomfiture of Bourbon and his troops. That autumn the King and his soldiers left France for Italy, and the four-months' siege of Pavia was begun. They were four months of degeneration; for Francis, as usual, mingled love with war and caprice with reality. The result was the battle of Pavia and his imprisonment, in 1525.

The news of the calamity spread dismay through France. In Paris, schoolmasters were ordered to forbid their school children to play at being King, or to sing "Vive la France ne son Alliance," in the streets. Disaffection was in the air. A band of men, on mules in green cloth hoods, rode through the city "and in their hands they held a scroll from which they recited divers joyous words," as if they were about to hold some sport; but it was merely a device to spread abroad a false report of the King's death. The Regent tried in vain to prosecute them—they escaped her vigilance. She, meanwhile, was laid low with pleurisy, "which (a contemporary notes) "came upon her from rage because of the war and all the troubles the King had suffered in his Kingdom." The battle was a terrible blow to the good fame of the nation and a rude shock to the King's fantastic dream of Italian conquest. From the days of Charles VIII, it had been a voluptuous vision—a ruinous mirage for France. But Francis' infatuation was not to end with his defeat. He had thrown away untold gold upon the Siren: he was fated to throw away still more. The lives that perished on the field of Pavia were not the last that were given to the aerial cause of Italy. And yet they should have sufficed. La Palisse, La Tremouille, Bonnivet, all lay dead there. It is said that when Bourbon found the corpse of Bonnivet —his rival in love for Margaret as well as in magnificence of state—he was filled with triumphant joy. Mercy was not his strong point.

There were songs enough to commemorate the dead heroes; they were sung on the roads and in the streets. They remain like the echo of a dirge.

Hélas, La Palice est mort,
Il est mort, devant Pavie;
Hélas, s'il n'etait pas mort
Il serait encore en vie.

Quand le roi partit de France
A la malheur il partit,
Il en partit le dimanche
Et le Lundi il fut pris. [1]

---

[1] Life of Margaret of Angoulême by Mary Robinson.

On the evening after the fight, the Constable went to pay the King his respects. Francis was sitting downcast in his tent when Bourbon entered. An eye-witness has told us that, when King and Duke stood face to face, both practised remarkable self-restraint. Francis showed no wounded pride, the Constable no galling commiseration. Bourbon's desire for revenge did not go the length of conniving at the King's removal to Spain. Neither he nor his fellow-general, Peschiera, knew anything about it. The journey was managed secretly, in the summer, by Lannoy, the Emperor's right-hand man. Louise, as we know, had all this time been busy with negotiations for his release, but manifold difficulties arose about an agreement. The main stumbling-blocks were the Emperor's desire for Burgundy and the final apportionment of Italy. So impeding was distance and so slippery the character of Charles V, that no arrangement seemed possible without the presence of a trusty delegate in Spain. Who so trusty, who so faithful and clear-headed as the King's sister? As usual she played a sacrificial part. Her mother decided she should go, and she went with a courageous spirit.

There were countless difficulties; protracted dallyings. The Emperor had no great wish for her. He promised her a safe-conduct, and waited for weeks before he sent it. Every hour was important to her. When the document arrived in September, she set out at once. Two Bishops accompanied her, so did the President of the Parlement. The hardships she endured in the burning heat would have been severe for a man, but her love for her brother carried her gaily through the ordeal. She wrote to him while her mules were resting—rather over-long verses, full of ornate encouragement—full of anything but herself. She hardly halted for food or sleep. Her long journey through Castile, in a litter, took her little more than a fortnight. When at last she reached her goal she was half dead with fatigue. But her hopes were high when she entered Madrid, and she lost no time in beginning her campaign of diplomacy.

THE SPANISH CAPTIVITY

AUTHORITIES CONSULTED FOR CHAPTER X

Lettres de Marguerite d'Angoulême.

Nouvelle Lettres de Marguerite d'Angoulême.

Dames Illustres: BRANTÔME.

Dames Illustres: HILARION DE LA COSTE.

Marguerite de Valois: LA COMTESSE D'HAUSSONVILLE.

Biographical Preface to Lettres de Marguerite d'Angoulême:
GÉNIN.

Conférences sur Marguerite d'Angoulême: LURO.

Margaret of Angoulême: MARY ROBINSON.

Biographical Preface to Les Marguerites de la Princesse des
Marguerites: FRANCK.

Les Femmes des Valois: ST. AMAND.

Histoire de France (Vol. VIII): HENRI MARTIN.

La Renaissance: MICHELET.

Histoire de France: DURUY.

CHAPTER X

(1525—1531)

THE SPANISH CAPTIVITY

FRANCIS I was lodged by the Emperor in the high tower of the Castle of Madrid. On his arrival in Spain, his good looks had created a sensation. When the Donna Ximena, one of the greatest Spanish ladies, saw him, she swore to marry none other; and when he left her country, she disconsolately retired to a convent. This kind of devotion was of no use to the captive. He tried more effective measures, and rumour went so far as to say that he offered his sister's hand as a bribe to the Constable. Rumour was probably untrue, but the Duke's attachment to Margaret seems to have been well known. When Charles V asked for her in marriage as a main article of his treaty with France, he casually remarked that Bourbon could find a wife elsewhere —and promised him Milan in compensation.[1] The King accomplished nothing by his manœuvres; he remained languishing in his tower, spending his time in reading his favourite romance, "Amadis of Gaul", in turn with St. Paul's Epistles. Charles V had resolved to reduce him to terms by a course of slow asphyxiation. The result was

[1] Wives and provinces were alike staple commodities of State traffic.

dangerous. The dulness, the want of air and exercise, told on his constitution, and he sank into a lethargy which soon became alarming. The doctors said he would die unless some hope were given him. So great was the impression he had produced on the people, that the churches were full to overflowing, and they prayed for his recovery as if he were an Infant or Infanta. The Emperor dared not take the responsibility of his death; he visited him in prison and tried the effect of a few cheering falsehoods about the future. But it was rather like the meeting of the fox and the crane, and the French King's condition remained the same.

This was the day before Margaret's arrival at Madrid. Charles V went to meet her at the Gate Alcazar. She was dressed in "black velvet without jewel or ornament, and a long white veil flowed over her shoulders." She curtseyed with dignity and grace; he kissed her on the brow. The accounts of her brother frightened her and she hastened to his bedside. He was unconscious—at the last extremity. The Bishop d'Embrun prepared to celebrate the Mass at his bedside. An altar was erected in his room, and all his French comrades, together with his sister and the servants, knelt side by side before it. At the Elevation, the Bishop exhorted the King to lift his eyes upon the Host. Francis awoke from his torpor and obeyed, raising his folded hands towards it. At his own request, the Sacrament was administered to him. "This is my God; He will cure me, body and soul," he exclaimed. Somebody objected that he would not be able to swallow the sacred bread. "Oh, but I shall," he said; and from that hour he began steadily to recover.

His sister's coming had given him fresh life, but it was to be expected that she and her orthodox suite should look upon his cure as a miracle wrought by the Host. Until his health was assured, she let business stand aside and devoted herself to his service, writing for hours at his dictation—state letters, business letters, love letters, probably, also. She "helped very much to make him well," says Brantôme, "for she knew his constitution and his temperament better than the doctors who were attending him." His convalescence was a gay one; all the grand ladies of Spain paid him visits: and, foremost amongst them, the Emperor's sister, Eleanor, widow of the King of Portugal. Her marriage with the French monarch had, from the first, been one of the main articles of the treaty with Charles, much to the disgust of the Constable, who had till then been sure of his bride. The business-like Emperor took his sister of Portugal —"the merriest lady ever seen"—to dance a Sarabande before Francis in his tower, by way of showing off her charms to the languid connoisseur. Margaret resolved to win her friendship—no very difficult task. We soon hear of them together, practising all the good old feminine fashions. "Elles se mirent à brasser"—and Margaret went to stay with her. She achieved more by her visit than by twelve months of public diplomacy.

As soon as the King was well enough she left him to set about her mission. She plied him with letters and details which time has by now made tedious. He was wise to leave all to her finesse. When he and the Emperor were left to each other, they could not get on. Margaret once told the Venetian Ambassador, Giustiniani, that her brother and

Charles "would never agree unless God re-created one of
them in the mould of the other." Perhaps it required a
woman to gauge the Reynard Emperor, and she certainly proved
a better match for him than Francis. How far she would
have been a stateswoman if she had not had personal
motives, is an interesting theme for speculation; her love
for her brother was always there to shape her policy. He
had leaned upon her judgment from the first. At home
she had taken part in all the Councils of the kingdom.
Ambassadors [1] lost themselves in admiration of her parts
and even enlarged upon them in their despatches.

There began between her and Charles a duel, which looked
like a Court game and was really a mortal combat. His
courtesy was impenetrable—his propriety immaculate. He
met her by appointment at Toledo, led her by the hand to
the palace prepared for her, and "me tint (so she writes)
fort bons et honnêtes propos." They talked for three hours
daily in their marble boudoirs, and the discussion always
ended with compliments and promises. She knew very well
that, if she trusted to his words, their conversations might
go on for ever: if she was to win, it must be by strategy.
With impetuous courage, she set about planning the King's
escape. There was a stage plot in which Francis was to
escape as a negro page. Like all stage plots it was discovered, and Charles, who had nearly been outwitted, loved
Margaret none the better for it. "She is," he sourly said,
"more of a prodigy than a woman." Her gentleness of
manner in their interviews had thoroughly deceived him.

[1] Dandolo and Giustiniani

He resolved, in revenge, to cheat her about her safe-conduct home, and to keep her as a hostage till he should have forced Burgundy from Louise. With this end, he added a clause to the passport: "She may pass (it ran) provided she has done nothing against the Emperor, or against the safety of the nation." At the end of her patience with his prevarications, she at last broke out on him with such eloquence that he for some time mended his policy. The next step she took—an unwonted one—was to appear before the great Council presided over by the Viceroy. She treated them with regal candour and informed them " that they had little honour and a great deal of bad will amongst them." The President says (she writes) " that he thinks I should go of my own accord to the Emperor, but I let him know that I had never yet stirred from my lodgings without being summoned; and when it pleases the Emperor to send for me again, he will find me." Soon after this she produced her scheme for a Treaty. She gave the Emperor the Duchies of Genoa and Milan; and offered him Burgundy for a stated time only. He rejected each clause in turn and continued his game of shilly-shally. Margaret posted to and fro between Toledo and Madrid, and went to Alcala and Guadalaxara, seeking to make many friends. She won love on all sides; the Spaniards were at her feet. They tried to keep her amongst them by constant parties in her honour. The ladies took to imitating her dress, her manners, even her way of speaking. She found her chief allies in the family of the Duke of Infantado, who was friendly to the King and the father of the exalted lady who became a nun for his sake. But the Duke was summarily informed that if he wished to keep the Emperor's favour, neither he nor his must speak another word with Margaret of Angoulême. "At all events," writes the Princess, "women are not forbidden me and I shall make up by talking double to them."

Convinced that she could effect nothing more by her presence, she resolved to leave her business still unsettled and to reach Bayonne by Christmas. But before she started, she and her brother made one more effort in their cause and tried a little further strategy. Francis resolved to abdicate the throne in favour of the Dauphin under the Regency of Louise. He would then be no royal captive, but an ordinary prisoner, bound by none of his former promises; and the French might make war upon Charles if they liked. The word of a prisoner, he said, tied him to nothing. So he laughed in his sleeve and pretended to accept the Emperor's conditions. He even went through a private marriage with Eleanor in his tower, although they were separated directly the ceremony was over. It was all-important that Charles should not see the Act of Abdication before Margaret had arrived in France. She was to have carried it with her, but there was some delay and she started without it. While she was on her journey, she received a sudden warning that a copy of the document had come into the hands of Charles V and that he intended to detain her. Legend says that the news reached her through the newly arrived Constable, as a last proof of his devotion; but however that may be, she lost no time in her use of the information. Her safe-conduct expired at the end of a given period, but she never dreamed the Emperor would cavil about times and seasons, and she had meant to travel at her leisure. This was no longer safe. If Charles V wanted to seize her, he had a right to do so were she found in his Empire a moment after the allotted date. She was still a fortnight's journey from the frontier, and her passport lasted for only half that time. If her strength held out, it was just possible for her to reach France before it was too late. Her spirit was up. She set off on the instant; accomplished in a single day the journey of four; and reached the frontier in one week instead of two, an hour before the expiration of her term. The Emperor was successfully checkmated; he had not taken his Queen, and the Queen did not easily forgive his behaviour. Years afterwards, when he was passing through Paris to the Low Countries and making a stay with Francis, Margaret, finding herself one evening seated at table between them, maliciously reminded Charles of his famous safe-conduct and was able to enjoy his embarrassment.

His cunning, and his bad faith to his prisoner made him so universally unpopular that, after Margaret's return, he found it advisable to change his course. All the Powers of Europe took up the question; the great Scholars agitated for the King's release; and Erasmus was not the only man of letters who wrote to the Emperor demanding it. The abdication had come to nothing, but at last Francis' cousin, Montmorency, was able to conclude negotiations. Francis was set free, on condition that he ratified the inglorious Treaty at the first French town he reached. It gave up Burgundy besides the King's Italian territories, and promised the two little princes as hostages to Spain—not to speak of numerous minor concessions. Lannoy conducted the King to the frontier, and there he put him into the returning boat which had just brought his hostage sons, with Lautrec as their guardian. The exchange of himself for his boys does not seem to have affected his easy-going heart. As he leaped from the boat and his foot again touched French soil—"In one moment I have become a King," he shouted, and mounting the horse that was ready for him, he galloped to Bayonne. Here he was expected by Louise and her Court, with Mademoiselle d'Heilly in attendance; and he gave himself up to festivity. Lannoy, his Spanish escort, dared to remind him of the Treaty, but Francis put him off by feasting him, and said that he was only waiting for a deputation from Burgundy. When the deputation arrived, it would not allow the Duchy to be given up to Spain. Francis did not stick at trifles. He altered the Imperial Treaty and sent Lannoy back with a refusal to yield Burgundy. The Emperor, angry at being cheated, accused the most Christian Monarch of cowardice; but the French King was backed by a new alliance with the English, made through the influence of Wolsey. The Cardinal had had a difference with the Emperor and was at that moment well disposed to the French.

It was not long after this that Henry VIII began thinking of the divorce from Catherine of Aragon—a project which made him hostile to her nephew, Charles V, and anxious for alliance with France. Serious plans were set on foot for his marriage with Margaret of Angoulême. The Bishop of Tarbes went to England about it, and Wolsey desired its completion. "There is a woman in France who is above all other women," he said to Henry, "none other is so worthy of your hand"—and he added her portrait to his persuasions. Margaret was a long time unconscious of the scheme, but when she heard of it she rejected it with pride. "Never speak to me again of a marriage which would take away the life and happiness of Catherine of Aragon," she said, and, for the second time, the match with the English King was dropped.

Charles V was taking his own course and, if we are to follow the fortunes of Francis and his sister, some slight outline of the war becomes necessary. The Emperor had lost no time in asserting himself in Italy, and had sent his generals and his army to crush Milan with their cruelty. The groaning people under their weak leader, the Duke of Urbino, had not the heart for an organised resistance till Bourbon appeared upon the scene. He had been chafing at his enforced inactivity, and now (1526) he arrived on his own account with his private troops: nominally on behalf of Charles. Secretly, however, he had vowed to desert him as soon as he had wrested to himself the promised Duchy of Milan. The Milanese saw in him a welcome deliverer and prayed him to save them from their oppressors. He swore he would do it, or die; obtained a large sum of money; attempted to fulfil his promise—and failed signally. The impoverished Milanese were obliged to give in, while the Constable pursued his usual policy of avoiding Nemesis. He left them for Germany, where he saw fresh chances for himself.

State-craft—embodied in the First Diet of Worms—had at this moment obliged Charles to pursue the line of religious tolerance; and the Lutheran Princes had, in con-

sequence, grown friendly to him. Bourbon had not much
trouble in persuading some of them to join him, as Charles'
representative, in a raid upon Italy and Catholicism; though
the Emperor afterwards declared that he knew nothing of
the plan. Bourbon promised the Germans untold wealth if
they came with him. He himself, he said, "was but a
penniless horseman, no richer than they were, not by one
farthing." He created enthusiasm by distributing all his
plate and jewels amongst them, and only kept for himself
his clothes and a coat of cloth of silver.

In 1527, he started for Rome. He was soon the leader
of a motley army, consisting indifferently of French lords,
polyglot outlaws, Italian bandits, and German soldiers. His
principal colleague was the Lutheran Baron, Freundsberg,
who carried a gold chain in his pocket with which he meant
himself to hang the Pope. Clement VII, when he heard
of their approach, fled into his fortified castle of St. Angelo,
and they reached the Roman ramparts in safety. It was
Bourbon who planted the first ladder against the walls and
scaled it in front of all the rest. "Silence à vous, César,
Annibal et Scipion—vive la gloire de Bourbon!" cried his
soldiers, as he mounted. But even as he did so, a bullet
hit him and he fell back into the trench, mortally wounded.
Benvenuto Cellini, the great braggart of autobiography, tells
us that it was he who took aim and fired the fatal shot;
but considering the multitude of his lies, there is no reason
to believe him. Whoever dealt the blow, it killed the
Constable and put an end to the vital force which gave
impetus to his army. He might have been able to restrain
his men from the hideous cruelty which disfigured the famous

sack of Rome; and might, perhaps, have opposed the policy which kept the Pope for six months a captive in his castle. Francis I and Henry VIII declared themselves Clement's allies and condemned his imprisonment; Francis even went so far as to challenge Charles to a single-handed duel on account of it. But the Pope's freedom was finally gained by his own ignoble bargain with the Emperor, who laid all the blame of the affair on Bourbon. He himself, he declared, had had nothing to do with it.

After the sack of Rome, and all through 1528, Lautrec and his army performed wonders and regained the lost territories of France. They crowned their victories in the North by taking Naples. Francis might have established his dominion in Italy, had it not been for his density. He had no faculty for the measurement of issues and never knew where to yield. This defect was emphasized by the puerile impetuosity which often made him begin an enterprise with fire and throw it over when he tired of it. It was these faults which detracted from his political importance and prevented him from being a real force in history. They found a strong foil in the Emperor's dogged persistence which lent weight to his despotism and left its stamp upon his age.

With petty tyranny, Francis refused the passionate entreaty of the Genoese for self-government and took measures to ruin the commerce of Genoa. Stung by these affronts, the great Admiral, Andrea Doria—who, with his fleet, had hitherto fought for the French—avenged himself by going over to the Emperor, and thus turned the scale of naval power in his favour. Disaster for France ensued and, little

by little, she once more lost all her Italian territories.
The last blow came when Francis' pseudo-ally, the Pope,
made a solemn "Pact of peace and eternal alliance" with
the Emperor—a move which decided the game.

Francis' one wish was now for peace, but Charles was
not ready. It was the Turks who finally forced him into
it. They had invaded Hungary and deposed its monarch,
who was his brother-in-law. The Archduke Ferdinand
lost no time in urging his claim to the throne. But
they set up an opposition King, a Hungarian, and marched
to the walls of Vienna to support their claimant against
Austria

Not the Emperor, but the women on either side, saw
that a truce between France and Spain was the only
safeguard for Europe. Margaret of Austria and Louise de
Savoie met, in 1529, in full splendour at Cambrai, where
Wolsey also arrived to hold counsel with them. The result
was the Ladies' Peace, the famous Treaty of Cambrai. It
was to be ratified by a public marriage between the French
King and Eleanor of Portugal. Charles gained all his
desires save Burgundy; Francis ceded every right, present
and future, in Italy. The rapacious Charles also got a good
many prizes in the Netherlands, and a huge sum for the
ransom of the royal hostages.

The only excuse for Francis' baseness to his country was
his anxiety for his sons. It had been slow to wake, but
now he was really alarmed. Charles had separated them
from their French attendants and was cruelly neglecting
them. The children were sent back with Eleanor of Portugal and welcomed in state at Bayonne. There was any

amount of speech-making. Marot, Margaret, and Louise
wrote stilted verses on the event; princes, poets, and states-
men thronged to greet them. Francis celebrated his marriage
with Eleanor, and national disgrace was eclipsed by family
rejoicing. But, for all that, Francis kept an abiding sense
of his humiliation and could never bear to look at anything
that recalled his captivity. "He hates the sight of a Spanish
dress as if it were the Devil. . . . I entreat you to remove
every single Imperialist from the Court"—so wrote his
Ambassador six years later to Montmorency. Perhaps his
merry wife reminded him too strongly of Madrid. They
had, it seems, pleasant relations, but she was not of much
importance to him, and he spent his time with Mademoiselle
d'Heilly. He had married her, for appearance' sake, to a
respectable French noble. She was soon to become the
Duchesse d'Etampes, the real Queen of France..

The reception of the hostages was the last festival at
which Louise was present. She had carried through her
task as Regent, if not nobly, at least with a strong hand
and an astute eye. She felt that she had re-purchased the
Deity's interest in her son by lighting the fires of persecution.
Her plots and counterplots had, in minor ways, established
his prosperity, and she never saw its decline. She lived,
too, to see her widowed daughter married to the King of
Navarre and to feel that she was suitably provided for.
That was in 1527. The end came in 1531. A comet had
appeared, much to the excitement of the Court, who looked
upon celestial phenomena as connected with royal destinies.
Louise de Savoie had always been a lover of astrology.
She lingered late one evening to watch the meteor, and

caught a chill which proved fatal. She died on September 2nd, with her son's name on her lips; and left behind in her coffers the astonishing sum of 1,500,000 gold coins— enough to account for all the Semblançay affair. Her children were probably the only mourners who really sorrowed for her loss.

LA·ROYNE·HELYONNEVR

Eléanore d'Autriche, Reine de François I.
(Portraits des Personnages français les plus illustres du
XVIième siècle, avec Notices par P. G. J. Niel).

F. p. 162.

THE QUEEN OF NAVARRE

AUTHORITIES CONSULTED FOR CHAPTER XI

Lettres de Marguerite d'Angoulême.

Nouvelle Lettres de Marguerite d'Angoulême.

L'Heptaméron: MARGUERITE D'ANGOULÊME.

Les Marguerites de la Princesse des Marguerites: MARGUERITE D'ANGOULÊME.

Oraison Funèbre sur Marguerite d'Angoulême: CHARLES DE SAINTE-MARTHE.

Récit d'un Bourgeois de Paris: edited by LALANNE.

Histoire de Béarn et de Foix: OLHAGARAY.

Œuvres de Brantôme, Vol. VII.

Dames Illustres: BRANTÔME.

Dames Illustres: HILARION DE LA COSTE.

Livre d'Etat de Marguerite d'Angoulême: LE COMTE DE LA FERRIÈRE.

Marguerite de Valois: LA COMTESSE D'HAUSSONVILLE.

Conférences sur Marguerite d'Angoulême: LURO.

Les Femmes des Valois: SAINT-AMAND.

Biographical Preface to Lettres de Marguerite d'Angoulême: GÉNIN.

Biographical Preface to Les Marguerites de la Princesse, etc.: FRANCK.

Life of Margaret of Angoulême: MARY ROBINSON.

Jeanne d'Albret: Miss FREER.

Le Château de Pau: LAGIÈZE.

Dictionnaire Historique: BAYLE.

Caractères et Portraits: FEUGÈRE.

Histoire de France (Vol. VIII): MARTIN.

La Renaissance: ⎱ MICHELET.
La Réforme: ⎰

CHAPTER XI

(1527—1540)

I

MARGARET of Angoulême and Alençon now changed her title and became the Queen of Navarre. It was a position of finer sound than substance, for Navarre had become a tributary kingdom dependent on Spain. In the preceding generation it had stood by itself, but Henri's father, Jean, or Juan, d'Albret, had lost the freedom of his realm. "Don Juan," said his strong-minded wife, Cathérine de Foix, "if we had been born, you Catherine, I Don Juan, we should never have lost the kingdom of Navarre." Margaret brought her husband the Duchy of Alençon and the province of Berri, which the King had given her on her first marriage; and, soon after her second, he bestowed upon Henri the governorship of Guienne. But the dowry she most valued was her brother's sacred promise to win back Navarre and restore its independence—a promise he never meant to fulfil, and which proved the cause of Margaret's first disenchantment about him. Happily she never knew the worst: his secret despatch to the Emperor, begging him *not* to help Henri to re-conquer his kingdom, "even though he hath taken to wife my dearly beloved and only sister." It did not suit his interests to have another King for a neighbour.

She first met her second husband at Queen Claude's funeral and straightway fell in love with him. It was perhaps a superficial love and her passion for her brother was still paramount in her heart, but she was dazzled by Henri d'Albret. "I have only seen one man in France, and that man is the King of Navarre," said Charles V, who was not easily impressed. Such a hero was bound to be taken prisoner at Pavia, and he only escaped a worse fate by pretending to be ill and getting away in his servant's clothes. Margaret easily succumbed to this young Olympian. It was, to all appearances, a risky match. She was his elder by eleven years, he being twenty-four and she thirty-five at their marriage, in 1527. She had more than the philosophy of her age, he more than the impressionableness of his. His veins were full of Southern blood, and yet, with all the fire of a Spaniard, he possessed the airy lightness of a Frenchman. He was born to make a woman unhappy; for his mind was finer than his character: fine enough to encourage hopes of his reformation. He shared Margaret's love of learning, even to the extent of demanding it in women; but the strongest bond between them was his sympathy for the Reformers,. though he was more of a Trimmer than she was.

Secular reforms were more to his taste. While Francis I was still growing richer by the labour-tax, Henri was the first ruler to remit it; and his kingdom—a model of legislation—had its own system of agriculture, its national Library and Printing-press; its special industries and code of Laws, all invented or re-organised by him. He chose the right wife to help him. His attitude towards her was one of perfect confidence; and "he always reverenced her mind," for (as an old historian quaintly observes) he was not one of those "who keep their wives in such a state of slavery that they do not dare to cough in their lord's presence." But he regarded her more as a mother than a wife, and often behaved roughly as well as faithlessly towards her. Even Francis was roused by his rudeness and summoned him to receive a royal scolding, at least so says the princely gossip, Brantôme. "Henri d'Albret," he writes, "treated the Queen, his wife, very badly and would have treated her worse, had it not been for her brother Francis who rated him soundly, and ended by threatening him, because he had been disrespectful to his sister, in spite of her high rank." Margaret showed a queenly reserve about her troubles, and only alluded to them with the lightest of pens. "You are better as a relation than the King of Navarre is as a husband," she wrote to a cousin; but she liked best to disguise herself in fiction; and in one of her plays she figures pathetically as "Mal-Mariée." She was always subtle even in her confidences.

These facts belong to her later history. The earlier days were happier—among the happiest of her life. They were full of work and pleasure. Her husband took her to visit his kingdom, but they lived a great deal in France. Alençon was a good field for her benevolence; it owed its large Hospital to her. The King, too, in a tender mood, gave her a grant for a Foundlings' School in Paris: la Maison des Enfants Rouges, it was called, because of the scarlet dresses of the children. "Our very dear, deeply-beloved and only sister, the Queen of Navarre," runs the Deed of Gift, "has heretofore instructed us in the great poverty and misery . . . endured by little children deserted by their Fathers and Mothers . . . in the Hôtel Dieu of Paris; because the aforesaid little children after the death of their parents stay on in the Hôtel Dieu, where the air is so foul that straightway they fall ill and die. Therefore our sister, from the compassion she bears to little children, entreated us to succour them, and help towards their maintenance" . . . .

The picture we have of her at this time is a radiant one. She generally wore a bodice of blue velvet, and a jewelled girdle which fell to the hem of her white satin gown. The slashes of her puffed sleeves, fastened by diamond clasps, showed her white arms, and bands of chesnut hair lay beneath a hood of pearls encircled by a golden crown. Her smile, we may believe, apart from courtiers' euphuisms, was the finest adornment of all. Experience had matured her sweetness and made her an adept in the arts of graciousness. "We are very different from each other"—she writes of a friend—"she is from Normandy and she smells of the sea; I from Angoulême and I smell of the gentle waters of the Charente."

And the portrait of herself comes home to all who have seen the bright tranquil stream, sheltered by alders and elder boughs, flowing like a silver ribbon below the town that is hung on the hill—the sweet green city of Angoulême. She was full of charming acts of kindness. She would send the tit-bits from her table to the old friends she wished to honour, "to eat for the love of her: because," said she, "these little graces are better than ceremony, they touch the hearts of the receivers." Obvious emotions she disliked and she had fantastic ways of showing it. Brantôme's brother, Captain Bourdeille, had fallen in love with Mademoiselle de la Roche, against the wishes of his father; and he brought her, at her own entreaty, to live at Margaret's Court while he was at the wars. The Princess espoused her cause and gave her a trousseau. On this the Captain departed with an easy conscience. Three months later he returned, but the girl had died in his absence. It was Margaret who had to break the news to him, but she waited till they were in the open. When they came into the churchyard of Pau,

"Cousin," she said, "do not you feel something stirring beneath your feet?"

"No, Madame," he replied.

"But ponder well, my cousin."

"Madame, I have pondered well, but I feel nothing stir, for I walk on a hard stone."

"Nay, but I warn you," she resumed, "that you are upon the tomb and the body of poor Mademoiselle de la Roche, who lies buried here beneath you; the tomb and the body of her whom you loved so dearly. And since our souls still feel after death, we must not doubt that this constant woman, who died of care, was moved as soon as she felt your step above her. Though you did not feel it, because of the thickness of the tomb, you must not doubt that she thrilled at your presence; and because it is a pious office to remember the dead whom one has loved, I pray you give her a Pater Noster, an Ave Maria, and a De Profundis, and sprinkle her with Holy Water. You will win the name of a faithful lover and of a good Christian."

Does Margaret believe in him or no? or does she think

that, soldier-like, he has forgotten? It is hard to say. There is a smile behind the tears—a hint of elusive irony—but it vanishes as we question it, and the scene remains painted in half-tints, Margaret's favourite colours.

She liked society as long as society was intimate; but she hated crowds and public places and only frequented them, says Brantôme, so that, she might know all things and, above all, the secrets of the King. Her best happiness was at home, for these early days had brought her the fulfilment of her wishes. She had become a mother. In 1528, a daughter was born to her, and the birth of a son at Alençon, two years afterwards, seemed all that was wanting. But he did not stay with her long. Having known a mother's joy, she was to know a mother's agony, and when he was a few months old, he died. "She went into her room and without the aid of any womanish action, she kneeled down and very humbly thanked the Lord for all the good it had pleased Him to do her." Then she gave orders that the Te Deum, the popular hymn of rejoicing, should be sung, instead of the funeral hymn, throughout the city of Alençon; and that on its walls should be posted placards, bearing the words: "The Lord hath given, the Lord hath taken away. Blessed be the Name of the Lord." The only sign of mourning that she showed was in her dress; and from the day of her baby's death, she wore nothing but black. Later it became her taste and her ladies were not allowed to wear anything else.

Francis showed his best side in sorrow, and his letter of sympathy about her sorrow has an elaborate sweetness which reminds us of his early years. He had himself lost two children and, however capricious he might be, he was a tender father and knew the nature of grief. " My darling," he wrote, " if Fortune had not tried our resolute patience through all these years, I should say she was right to make fresh proof of her power. But having learned by sure experience that what is mine is yours, she should also have considered that what is yours is mine. And so, since you bore the pains of Death when my—your—first children died.... it is for me now to bear your pains as if they were my own. You must not, in troth, like a rebel, forsake the fight with the Common Foe, but remember that this makes the third of yours, and the last of mine, whom God has called unto His blessed company. They have gained with little labour what we desire with infinite travail. Forget your sad tears in obedience to God .... and accept from yourself the clear and pure counsel which, in like case, you once gave to me." She was destined to perform that office again for him six years later, when the young Dauphin died of a sudden and mysterious illness: poisoned, it was credulously said, by the orders of the Emperor. Amboise, the scene of their own childhood, had been the Dauphin's birth-place. "I can no longer believe that Amboise is Amboise"—writes the sister to the brother—"It is now only the source of infinite memory and pain."

Soon after her loss, the King and Queen left France and went to live in the province of Béarn, in their kingdom of Navarre. They took up their abode in the Châteaux of Nérac and of Pau, where the most important part of Margaret's life was spent. Here passed the first two years of little Jeanne's childhood. All was going smoothly and happiness seemed certain, when the King came down on the peaceful little group and carried off Jeanne to Tours. He had suspicions, not unfounded, that her parents wanted to betroth her to the Heir of Spain. This did not suit his purposes at all. He put her in his Castle of Plessis-le-Tours, Louis XI's grim, iron-barred fortress, and here he had her educated. He had determined to bring her up in orthodox Catholicism, and this may have confirmed him in his course : however that may be, he succeeded in breaking his Mignonne's heart by the separation, and though she treated him as a deity, her spirit was sore within her.

It is easy to imagine her terror when, Jeanne being eight years old, she suddenly heard that the child was mortally ill at Tours. The distance from that town to Paris, where Margaret was staying, was no slight matter in those days; and, when the news came, her servants were not at hand and none of her vehicles were obtainable. She borrowed her niece's litter and reached Bourg that evening, going straight to the Church to escape the crowd of Courtiers that awaited her at the door. She would take no one with her but her favourite duenna, the Sénéchale de Poitou ; and as she entered, she said that all hope had left her. Weeping and praying, she prostrated herself before the Crucifix and accused her own sins as the cause of her child's illness. When she rose again, she was calm : "The Holy Spirit has promised me my daughter's recovery," she said. Once in her lodging, she sat down with her suite to supper, and all through the meal she talked of God's pity and mercy and "the miseries and tribulations of men, with a great gravity of language." After this, she sent her company away,

returned to her devotions and opened the Bible on the song
of Hezekiah, which she took as a good omen. At this very
moment a postilion's horn sounded in the street with a
note that seemed to mean haste. "What news?" she cried,
rushing to the window—but no answer came: the postilion,
whom none dared question, had gone to the Bishop's Palace,
and she resumed her prayers. It was thus, kneeling almost
prone against a stone bench, that the Bishop of Séez found
her when, a few minutes later, he entered the room. There
was a pause before she rose; at last—"Ah, Monsieur de
Séez," she said, "have you come to tell a suffering mother
the death of her only child? I know full well she is now
with God." Such was her state that he had to break his
good news to her and make her gradually understand that
the danger was past. She showed no exuberant joy, but
lifted her hands to heaven, thanking and glorifying God.

Sad though she was in her solitude, she never seems to
have blamed her brother, either for separating her from her
child, or for his behaviour about Navarre. A letter to her
cousin, Montmorency, begging him to try and persuade the
King to keep faith about her kingdom, is her only mention
of her wrongs; but she must have been thinking of Francis
when she wrote in after years that "she had learned to live
on paper more than on anything else." Her letters to him
are loving and effusive as ever; as for his to her, she never
tires of saying that they are a cure for all her wretchedness,
even for her colds and indigestions; and she kisses them
"at least once a day" and wears them as relics. She went
so far as to make her poor husband do the same. There
is no length she will not run. In order to be with Francis

she will gladly renounce her royal blood to be "the serving-maid of his washerwoman." "And I give you my word, Sire," (she ends) "that without regretting my cloth of gold, I much desire to put on a disguise and to try being your servant." There was one occasion when he sent her a New Year's present of a Crucifix, accompanied by some rather trite verses he had composed. "When" (she writes) "I behold an object so divine, so well made, so rich and excellent. . . . I can do nothing but embrace the finely-carven figure, for the honour and the reverence that I bear my two Christs."

She wrote these rhapsodies in all sorts of uncomfortable places—often while travelling about on one of the rather un-christian missions of the most Christian King. Now she is posting hither and thither as escort to one of his lady-loves; now awaiting her arrival and catching a chill in a draughty inn by the roadside. And when the war breaks out in Provence and in Picardy, she becomes, as she says herself, "Penthilisea, Queen of the Amazons"; reviews his armies, first in one province then in another; and examines the fortifications in the North. "Would to God," she writes, after watching a battle in Provence, "that the Emperor would try to cross the Rhône whilst I am here! I would wager on my life that, woman though I be, I could prevent him from doing so."

II

The other personage who at this time played a part in the life of Margaret was Anne de Montmorency, the

successor of Bourbon as Constable of France. Their relations
were complicated. He was her cousin, the playmate of
Francis at Amboise, the friend of her early days, and the
correspondent to whom all her first letters were addressed.
They were on the most intimate terms; she confides in him,
scolds him, rallies him about his flirtations, as the mood
takes her. It is charming to catch her in her lighter moods.

"I showed your letter (she writes) to Mistress Margaret
of Lorraine, who, in spite of her grey nun's habit, has never
ceased to remember old days; she assures you that she
acquits herself so well in praying for you, that if all the
ladies who have sported with you did as much, you would
have no cause to regret the past; for their prayers would
carry you to Paradise, where (after a long and a pleasant
life) wishes to see you,

"Your kindly cousin and friend,
"MARGARET."

There are graver and more political letters written to
him after Pavia and during the Spanish journey. Her trust
in his judgment seems unbounded. He was clever, but
reckless in his arrogance. He was like the Constable Bourbon in his superbness. His Palace of Écouen, built by
Philibert de l'Orme, outrivalled the Château de Madrid.
Chantilly was also his, besides a third estate; and his hunting
array of Arab horses, Turkish hounds, and falcons from
Tunis—sent him by Soliman—were the talk of France.
He filled eleven different offices, and his income was nearly
double Margaret's own. A keen soldier and a potent ally

of the King's, insolent, rough, splendid, and uncultivated, he was universally disliked. Literature and refinement he despised, and he could not bear the fact that Greek and Latin Scholars took precedence of gentlemen at Court. He boasted that, in spite of his great fortune, he had never given a crown-piece to a man of letters; and the Reformers he hated even more than the learned.

It was this aversion for the New Ideas which caused his gradual separation from Margaret. From being her comrade he became her worst enemy, and, after he was made a Constable, he was constantly seeking to injure her in the King's opinion. He may have been actuated by ambition, but he was an incorrigible mischief-maker. According to Brantôme, he fanned quarrels between her and her husband: but, however that may be, he was sincere in his wish to suppress her Protestant tendencies. He tried to persuade the King of her heresy, but Francis remained loyal. "Oh," he answered Montmorency's accusations, "as for her, don't let us mention her—she loves me too much. She will never believe anything except what I want her to believe, and will never accept a religion which does the slightest injury to my State."

The King's mind still leaned towards Reform, though his policy often pulled him the other way. Margaret tried her best to soften his spirit towards Protestantism, and now and then succeeded. "Oftentimes," says an old historian, "she talked to him about it, and tried by light blows to hammer some pity of Luther into his heart." Public events had hitherto helped her. In the course of Henri VIII's proceedings with regard to his divorce, he had applied to Francis to get the opinion of the Sorbonne. On its expressing disapproval of the divorce, the King of France, nothing daunted, called an irregular Council, which justified Henry's course and then registered its decree as that of the Sorbonne. [1] This did not make that Faculty more friendly to either monarch; and when Henry married Anne in the same year (1531), it was equivalent to an anti-papal proclamation. The destinies of Europe at that moment depended on the attitude towards the Pope of the three great sovereigns— Henry, Charles and Francis. Charles V had no choice in the matter. For the sake of his aunt, Catherine of Aragon, he was forced to represent the Catholic cause. His enemy, Francis, was swayed by other influences; as the ally of England he found himself personally obliged to assume a certain amount of tolerance. But he could not keep it up. The Sorbonne, the Parlement and his mother—until her death—proved too strong for him; while the Reformers themselves became their own worst enemies and harmed their cause by their rashness.

The history of persecution makes ugly reading, and a mere list of tortures is futile; but some slight account of the progress of the New Ideas since the battle of Pavia is necessary, if we are to follow the dealings of Margaret with their advocates.

When the Pope wrote to ask Louise de Savoie what cure she prescribed for heresy, she answered, "The Inquisition," and lit its fires throughout France. The "Citizen of Paris" who kept a diary, notes one hideous spectacle after another. A hermit is burned in the pig-market, because he said

---

[1] Martin: Histoire de France, Vol. VIII.

Christ was born like other men, "et néanmoins il n'était point clerc et ne savait A ni B;" or Pierre Piéfort is killed for stealing Ste. Geneviève's cup, though the King took, without demur, "three or four golden statues of Apostles" from the great Church at Laon to help him in his wars. There were martyrs of six and seven years old; there were decrees of the utmost rigour against printers who published Luther's books, and writers who translated St. Paul's Epistles into French.

In spite of all this, Margaret had been able to protect her friends. The Faculty condemned Erasmus; she took up his cause. It persecuted Calvin; she received him at her Court. She was not so successful with Berquin—Berquin, famous at Meaux and the chief martyr of Protestantism; Berquin, "le plus savant de la noblesse," whose spirit knew no turning. Twice was he imprisoned and in danger of his life, and twice she saved him by her influence over Francis. In vain his friend Erasmus tried to modify him. "The time has come," replied Berquin, "to humiliate the School-men." Erasmus retorted that he was wrong—that the time had come to temporize with everyone. "Do not trust to the King's protection; do not commit yourself with the Faculty of Theology!" he exclaimed. But the gospel of compromise was not for Berquin. "Do you know what I have gained?" asked Erasmus in despair—"I have only given him fresh courage."

It was not so much his own daring as the King's puerile superstition that finally brought about Berquin's fate. In 1528, occurred the famous affair of the broken statue. A figure of the Virgin with the Child in her arms stood "against

the wall of the house of Maître Loys de Harlay," near the
Church of Little Saint Antoine.   One day it was found
mutilated; the heads of both figures had been knocked off,
and no trace of the destroyer was discoverable. " Whereupon the King, who was in Paris, being told thereof, was
so much angered and so far undone that, saith report, he
wept bitterly."   The deed was trumpeted for two days
through Paris, and a reward offered to the finder of the
desecrator; but in vain.   Then came a season of processions
to the Parish where the sacrilege took place. First the
University and the Schools of Paris, then the King and the
prelates, marched to the scene of the crime, " with instruments
of music and hautboys, and many bugles and trumpets, beautiful to see and sweet to hear."   Next the King, and a Bishop
in full dress, bore to the spot a new figure in silver beneath
a red silk canopy, with a statue of the King to stand below
it; they set it up to the sound of music, with " three deep
curtseyings before it," and carried off the broken Virgin as
a relic.   Unfortunately, at this moment, Berquin was for
the third time in prison on charge of heresy.   He sent a
letter to his servant, bidding him burn his books in a
certain place which he indicated.   The servant, in carrying
them there, had to pass the new silver statue and, as ill
luck would have it, just as he reached it he turned faint
and fell down.   Some bystanders, running to his help, found
inculpating letters upon him.   They took them to a priest
hard by, who conveyed them to Béda, the persecuting
leader of the Sorbonne.   Berquin underwent a mock trial,
the scholar Budé in vain urging him to make some form of
submission.   He refused, and was condemned to death.

Margaret was away from Paris, so was the King; and the Sorbonne took advantage of their absence to have him burned at once (1529). "You would have said," wrote Erasmus, "when he was led forth to be tortured, that he was at home in his library, pursuing his studies, or in a temple, thinking of holy things." The diary of the Paris Citizen also commemorates him. "Le dit Berquin," he says, "était moult grand clerc, expert en science et subtil;" and he wore, he adds, "a velvet gown.... and golden stockings.... for he was of noble birth."

There is no record of Margaret's feelings when she got the news, but Berquin was only the chief of a long array of martyrs. The King was panic-struck and encouraged every ingenuity of cruelty. Margaret must have needed an uncommon strength of mind to hold as she did to her opinions. In 1533, she produced "Le miroir de l'âme Pécheresse," a long high-souled poem—mystical, almost Evangelical. The Sorbonne, headed by Béda, seized their long-desired opportunity and fell upon it. It made, they said, no mention of the Saints or of Purgatory, and they summoned her to appear before them for heresy. They had a second string to their bow: a Book of Hours, which Briçonnet had arranged for her, leaving out certain prayers to the Saints. Nothing perhaps so clearly shows the influence either of Margaret or the Sorbonne as the power of the latter to command a Queen to attend its court, or her power to pay no attention to its orders. Guillaume Petit, Bishop of Sens, managed her affairs for her and silenced the Sorbonne. The matter might have blown over, had it not been for the priests and students. A monk chose to make her the subject of a sermon, and told his congregation that she deserved to be put into a sack and thrown into the Seine. The audacious students at the University went farther and got up a farce all about her. It began with her desertion of the distaff for the company of a Fury—who presented her with a Bible; and, when the play ended, she was left upon the stage transformed into a Fury herself.

This was more than Francis could endure. He sent his Archers to seize the guilty students and would have had them executed, had it not been for Margaret's entreaties. His royal affections were ruffled; his royal prerogative was outraged. He had to rest content with milder punishment and a retractation of his censure of the Sorbonne. But he soon found occasion to arrest the bigot, Béda, and afterwards to imprison him in Mont St. Michel, where he died. As for the compromising book, it gained a great reputation : which only proves that what one century admires makes the tedium of another. The poem was translated by Queen Elizabeth when she was eleven years old, and presented by her to her step-mother, Catherine Parr. Evidently the French volume had come into her hands through her mother, Margaret's former maid-of-honour; and the English Princess' manuscript, "The Mirrour of a guilty Sowle," lies in the Bodleian Library, bound in faded blue and gold—the half-forgotten memorial of two literary queens.

There seemed again a chance that Reform might flourish unmolested, but Clement VII's arrival at Marseilles with his niece, Cathérine de Médicis, as a bride for the Dauphin, gave fresh impetus to persecutions. This time the Reformers themselves helped them on by their folly. In the autumn

of 1534, the King, then at Blois, rose one morning to find
a placard against the Mass fastened on his palace wall;
similar posters were found throughout Paris and the provincial towns, and no one could discover their authors.
The King, equally outraged in his dignity and his faith,
decided on extreme measures.   In January 1535, bare-headed,
with a taper in his hands, he led an expiatory procession.
It started from St. Germain l'Auxerrois, and carried with it
the relics of all the shrines in Paris.   On the night following,
after dining with the Bishop of Paris, Francis got up into
the pulpit before Court, Parlement and Ambassadors, and
pledged himself to stamp out heresy: he would slaughter
his own children, he said, if they showed any signs of Protestantism.   Margaret in alarm chose an orthodox Confessor
and took the Communion in public.

Auto-da-fés raged, and such were the excesses of the
King's "execrable justice," as the "Citizen of Paris" calls it,
that Paul III himself was obliged to interfere.   He wrote
a letter to Francis in June, begging him to stay his hand.
"No doubt," said the Pope, "'le Roi très Chrétien' was
only doing his best to justify his title.   And yet God, the
Creator, when He was in this world dealt more in mercy
than in justice, nor is it the duty of man to use severity.
It is double cruelty to burn a man alive, for otherwise he
might return to faith and law.   And therefore"—ends the
mandate—"the Pope requires the King to appease his fury...
and to pardon."

When Popes begin to plead for tolerance, kings have no
choice but to obey.   For three years there was a truce, of
which Margaret took advantage.   She persuaded Francis to

invite Melancthon to Paris to dispute with the Sorbonne, and the King went so far as to ask for the permission of Melancthon's master, the Elector Palatine, to let him come. The Elector refused, and the plan came to nothing. But Francis' unstable conduct continued to bewilder his friends and his foes, and to vary exactly as his interests required. When he was irritated by Clement VII, the Emperor's ally, he behaved like a schoolboy and vowed to the Nuncio that he would turn Lutheran. "Frankly, Sire, you will be the first man to be ruined by it," said the diplomat; "you will lose more than the Pope, for a new religion spread amongst the people soon demands a change of Prince."

This was unfortunately the view to which Francis returned. He ultimately became too much frightened about his temporal safety and his eternal salvation to run any risk of endangering either, and Margaret's little court in Béarn became the only haven for the Reformers.

To that court it is pleasant to turn. Under the Pyrenees stood the feudal castle of Pau, the southern capital of her kingdom. She had also the Castle of Nérac, her capital in the north. These were to be her principal homes for the remainder of her days. She at once saw their possibilities. Bands of Italian workmen came with her and helped her to realise all her dreams of beauty. Surrounded on all sides by the bleak Landes, or overshadowed by grim mountains, there arose these palaces of delight, embosomed in groves and gardens, with terraces and fountains like those of Touraine. They abounded in books and sculptures and their rooms were marvels of art.

Into this Epicurean setting stepped Calvin in all his

sternness.   Stepped is, perhaps, too leisurely a word.
Margaret had been keeping him for some time in hiding
at Nantes and at Angoulême, and now he fled to her,
disguised as a vineyard-labourer.   He found a troop of
penniless Protestant Scholars—as incongruous as himself—in
her palace.   Chief among the new names were two of whom
there will be more to learn hereafter : the restless, revolution-
ary poet, Bonaventure des Périers; and the free-thinking
philosopher and pamphleteer, Etienne Dolet, both of them
constantly in mischief.   And there was the sweet old Maître
des Requêtes, Margaret's future biographer, Charles de Sainte-
Marthe—broad of mind, but too gentle of spirit to be dangerous—and the peaceful librarian, Lefèbre, whom Calvin set to
work to censure for his "cowardly" want of initiative.

A court was certainly not Calvin's element; he was a born
controversialist, urged alike by an unflinching courage and an
unresting brain.   Although he was little over twenty, his
character and creed were already set.   He was a born despot,
and countenanced no method of belief but his own.   Of
Margaret's tolerance, which he praised when directed towards
the Calvinists, he severely disapproved when it was given to
others.   Her readiness to help all the persecuted, whether
Romans or Genevans, seemed a weakness to him; eclecticism
offended him like a crime, and all the race of broad-thinkers
—"libertins" he called them—were outcasts in his eyes.
After he had left Béarn, [1] he shot forth a terrible pamphlet,
"Ex Libertinis", in which he bitterly reproached the Queen
of Navarre for harbouring two fugitives belonging to no

[1] 1545.

Church and both tending to free-thought. "It is impossible,"
he wrote to her soon after, " not to wish that your house should
prove worthier of being the true family of Jesus Christ;
instead of which certain of its members deserve to be called
the slaves of the devil : his slaves, I repeat, and his colleagues...
I was told that a servant such as I am, was neither useful
nor agreeable to you. And, indeed, when I do myself justice,
I recognize that I cannot be of much use. It seems as if,
among your servants, you had no need of a man of my sort."

Margaret, who did not care a jot for the condemnation of
the Sorbonne, was deeply hurt by Calvin and reproached
him with maltreating her friends with his pen.

"And yet (he replied) it is not affection fory ou which I
lack. Even if you regretted and scorned my devotion, I
should none the less keep for you the same faithful attachment.
Those who know me, know how far I am from seeking the
favour of princes. It is quite enough for me to have been
admitted to the service of a greater Master. . . . Thy most
devoted, thy ready servant, even to obsequiousness,

"JOHN CALVIN."

He probably said the same things in the sermons which,
while at Nérac, he constantly preached in her presence.
Roussel, her other special Preacher, had a temperament the
opposite of Calvin's and, pious though he was, he took
pleasure in the Court Society. It must be owned that her
life in Navarre was not such as to please a rigid Puritan.
It was a strange jumble of brilliance and gravity, and even
its religious practices showed the same contrast. It is a

mistake to think that the New Ideas meant universal austerity,
or that Margaret, Saint of Charity as she was, was only
given up to good works. Gaiety was almost as needful to
her as self-discipline, and her high spirits often led her into
a kind of intellectual exuberance which bordered on irreverence. Devotions alternated with sacred farces and pastorals,
many of them written by herself. Clerks who joked about
the Virgin and Saints, churchgoers who spent their fortunes
on dogs and mistresses, were encouraged to act the Scriptures
on her stage She herself made "a tragi-comic translation"
of nearly all the New Testament, and got a troupe of the
best comedians "qui fussent lors en Italie" to act it before
her husband. The actors interspersed their drama with
"rondeaux" about the Clergy, and directly it was over the
King and Queen went on to "Prèches", a kind of sermon-
service held in the King's room by Roussel and another
fugitive priest. One of Roussel's duties as Chaplain was to
contrive plays for edification; but edification was a wide
term including satire against Rome, and was indifferent
to the means by which it arrived at its moral.

Another strange rite of the Reformation was in vogue at
the Château of Nérac. This was the heterodox "Messe à
sept points," or "Messe à deux espèces," held in the cellars
of the palace. No elevation of the Host, or adoration of
Species was allowed, no commemoration of the Virgin and
Saints; the officiating priest was not obliged to be celibate.
He wore lay dress, took a common loaf, ate of it and gave
it to the congregation, who all together communicated in
both Species at once. There was psalm-singing, too, in the
midst of which any priest inclined to be a wag would burst

into jokes and songs against the " Gent Papiste "—Margaret laughing with the best of them. Her husband's attitude towards these ceremonies was changeable. At first he took part in them. But as he grew older, he became more timid and more orthodox. He made all sorts of petty restrictions, and scolded if the Reformers at his Court did not appear in the monk's dress that caution had inspired him to prescribe. His wife's freedom began to disturb him. The story runs that on one occasion he went to her room, making sure he would find her with a certain Lutheran who was trying to convert her. He meant to thrash him for his pains, but when he reached her apartment the bird had flown and he found Margaret in solitude. He was not a man of words. " You want to know too many things, Madame," he said, and boxed her soundly on the ears.

In this matter he could count on the sympathy of his brother-in-law. Alarmed at the reports of Margaret's heretical festivities, Francis summoned her to come to him and administered a lecture. He told her that women who followed new doctrines were hateful and that she must alter her ways. Roussel he also cautioned and hinted, with rather ominous wit, that his " Messe à sept points smelled of faggots." Margaret exonerated him and herself. " The King will find that Roussel is worth something better than the flames," she wrote... " Believe me, had I ever seen the faintest shade of unfaith in him I could never have borne the contaminating poison for so long, or have allowed my friends to pollute themselves." Both she and Roussel evidently took the royal hint, for Francis eventually made him Bishop of Oléron. The appointment was a bold one. One day, when he was preaching, a fanatic against Reform cut the supports of the pulpit and he fell. He was badly hurt, and died some time after from the effects of the accident.

Calvin, no doubt, considered it a judgment. In his eyes prosperity was worse than tolerance, and to be a Bishop meant to be a villain. The letter that he wrote to Roussel on his getting the Bishopric can hardly have flattered the new prelate's feelings. "Everybody," it ran, "goes about saying that you are very happy—the darling of Fortune, so to speak. I pity your disaster from my soul.... As long as you remain of the troop whom Christ called the robbers... and murderers of His Church, *you* may think of yourself as you like. *I* shall never consider you a Christian, or a good man. Adieu."

Calvin was an awful correspondent. His pen was a rod and his eye a search-light. His bad digestion may have had something to do with his acrid conscience. It must have been a relief when he ended his long stay in Navarre and betook himself to Bâle. Here he published his "Institutions." It is interesting that he was still allowed to dedicate his work to Francis and that he continued to look upon the King as his Patron. "You can afford to tolerate us in all conscience—we are not heretics," he had once ventured to write to him. The times had changed. Now he sent him his book with "Non pacem sed gladium" for its motto—hardly the device for Church and State.

He did not return to Margaret's Court. She had, however, other and more insidious opponents. Her heterodoxy brought her more than once into danger, and there was a strong party against her who did not stop at words. There were actual plots against her life. At one time she was obliged to celebrate Mass in her room, because she heard that the incense burned before her in the church had been poisoned for her destruction. Apart from such disturbances, she pursued her way in peace. She enjoyed the classics with Paul Paradis, history and poetry with other friends. They read out to her and, while she listened, she embroidered classical fables, or the rites of the Church, in tapestry-stitch. Her work was said to be like painting, but she never worked for work's sake. If she were not being read to as she sewed, she dictated her meditations to her Secretary. "She was used," says Sainte-Marthe, "to hold a book with greater ease than a distaff, a pen rather than a spindle, and her ivory tablets in place of a needle." She had one Secretary to write her letters and another to copy her verses. Sometimes she made them for her dearly loved lute: songs, thin and sweet, still precious to the collector. What she liked best was to ride about the country on her mule and make the peasants sing her their country-songs, which she jotted down at their dictation. It was her way of getting to know her people and their language, which she picked up quickly—and they soon grew to love her with devotion. In the evening she and her ladies made music, or told realistic romances ("Nouvelles" they called them) in the drawing-room: stories that ranged from coarse fables about drunken monks to idyls of purest love.

Or they made conversation. Even if we allow the usual deductions for flattery, Margaret's talk must have been remarkable. There remains a record of an impressionable Spanish gentleman who came to visit her. He found her

in the midst of a discussion with Gérard Roussel. "Except
ye be as little children" was their theme, and Maître Gérard
was quoting St. Augustine; another Scholar, St. Jerome; while
Sainte-Marthe broke in with St. Chrysostom and St. Hilary.
Then the princess took up the tale and the appreciative
Spaniard "was as one who saw a vision and remained in
speechless ecstasy at her eloquence." Another of her guests,
not so sweet of temper, went away mightily offended because
she had not spoken a word to him, but continued her abstract
dialectics with "Je ne sais quels bonnets ronds." She came
in for a fair share of ridicule from people outside her circle.
The world accused her of affectation, because she preferred
the conversation of "gens de robbe" (the learned professions)
to that of noblemen and courtiers; but the world did not
affect her. At dinner she chose her talkers, and her topic
for the day. Strangers were sometimes admitted to hear
her. She conversed about all her usual subjects, bookish
and ethical; or discussed medicine and hygiene with her
Doctors. They took their meals with her and carefully
watched her diet. Her eloquence converted her financier
to Woman's Rights. "It is blindness—a very ditch of
error," he exclaims, "to object to the study of philosophy
for women. Why on earth should we forbid them to read
the same books as men?" But he hastens to remind us
that, with all her brilliance, "she remembered the advice
of Plutarch and of St. Paul to women... She could easily
have chattered with the best of them before her husband—
she could easily have interrupted him when he talked."
But she never did so, or allowed any debating in his
presence; far from the case of those women (says her

chronicler) "the cackle of whose inanities you would take
for the clattering of saucepans, tambourines and bells."

Margaret's Court was perhaps the most literary on record
—le Parnasse Béarnais it was called. Her society drew to
Pau and Nérac a large company of poets and artists, besides
those who lived on her bounty. She was, says another
emotional contemporary, "the precious carnation in the
flower-garden of the palace; her fragrance had drawn to
Béarn, as thyme draws the honey-bees, the noblest minds
in Europe." Of her old friends at Paris and Blois many
came to her; Postel and Mélin St.-Gelais were amongst
them. The second Clouet painted for her, [1] and a charming
illuminator, Adam Martel, took up his abode at Court to
illustrate her "Heptameron." Frugal though she was, she ate
her sparse meals off gorgeous plate, ordered from Benvenuto
Cellini and his rivals. There is an order in her account-book
for a salt-cellar in the shape of Susannah rising from her
bath—no trifle as far as expense went. She had enamels
from Léonard Limousin, first of enamellers; she had finely-
wrought jewels from struggling artificers. The sums spent
in ornaments for art's sake—even for the maintenance of
tailors and embroiderers—are surprising.

She allowed the men and women of her suite twenty-five
crowns a year for their dress; but she gave more to the
slovenly and ungainly, because they needed more clothes to
make them look nice, and "she liked to see comely people
about her person." She kept up the princely tradition of
providing her "Demoiselles" with trousseaux. Eight ells of

---

[1] The fourth Clouet was at one time also employed by her.

black velvet at seven francs an ell; eight of black satin at four francs ten sols an ell; a cloak lined with lamb's fur and trimmed with Spanish cat; with a supplement of thirty francs for a mule—such is the entry in her ledger of the bridal provision that she made for one of her ladies. Her own dress was of plain black velvet: from the skirt, half hidden by the long cloak—cut away under the arms—to the cornette, or square hood, coming down low on the forehead. She wore no jewels or trimming; but her high collar was lined with marten's fur and fastened by pins in the front; and it left room for a little white chemisette, which was drawn up in folds to her throat.

Her whole personality, at this mid-day of her life, seems to have been stamped with royal dignity. "If she turned her eyes upon you," says Sainte-Marthe, "there was in her countenance I know not what of divinity, which would so have amazed you that you would have been powerless, not only to advance a step, but even to move your foot to get nearer to her." Like all true sovereignty, hers had an element of severity and she inspired awe when she wished to do so. She made a code of rules for her Court, condemning all things that made against a Christian life. She included cowards and "criminals by the tongue" in her list of immoral persons. Disobedience to these laws meant exile, even, as it afterwards fell out, when the offender was her favourite poet, Bonaventure des Périers. For a first offence she was content to admonish, and her words were not easily forgotten. Towards any real delinquent "she used great gravity, but with such a manly majesty that he who had erred wished himself at once a hundred feet below the

earth. ... She never uttered an insult, but she lashed him
hard with her tongue.... and when she thought she had
gone far enough, she was careful to mix honey with the
aloes." To the poor, the humble and the timid, she was
gentle as ever, and her charities were as constant in Navarre
as in Alençon. She liked walking almost alone in the streets
of Pau, that they might approach the more easily and talk
frankly to her. "To see her you would never have thought
she was a Queen, for she went about like a simple *demoiselle*."
"No one," she said, "ought to go away sad or disappointed
from the presence of a prince; for Kings were the ministers
of the poor, not their masters: and the poor were the
members of God." She would like (and she said it with
tears in her eyes) to be the servant of all who served the
lowly; and the Prime Minister of the Poor was the title
that she gave to herself. She visited them in their homes
and sent them her own Doctors. All her officers of relief
(Mademoiselle St. Pather was her "Chief Almoner") had
orders to act without delay. Her capricious husband, as
we know, was not capricious in works of public spirit. He
had begun them without her and they continued them
together. They imported labour from the Berri and Sologne,
and planted vineyards all over the kingdom. Margaret went
a step farther and urged civic reform. She devoted her energies
to her town of Pau, giving it a Parliament and an Exchequer,
and maintaining order by means of her private purse.

Her purse might have belonged to Fortunatus; it subsisted
on miracle—the miracle of the heart. For Margaret and her
husband presented the anomaly of a really poor King and
Queen, and their circumstances were not improved by having

a poet for Minister of Finance.   Their poverty alone would
make them interesting.   At one time Margaret had to
borrow from one of her ladies-in-waiting to pay up her
charities.   The King allowed her a pension of £1000 a year,
but their whole income was only about £1630, on which
they had to provide for all their liabilities as Royalties and
art-patrons, philanthropists and entertainers.   Her treasury
never kept its contents for long.   Fines which might have
gone to swell it were remitted by her quixotic generosity.
As sister of the King of France she was obliged to keep
up a certain state.   The number of retainers considered
indispensable was out of all proportion to the size of Navarre.
She had ten Maîtres d'Hôtel, twenty Valets de Chambre,
seventeen Secretaries, four Doctors, two Chamberlains, a
Chancellor, and twenty-eight Ladies—besides Lawyers, Coun-
cillors and Financiers.   It was etiquette to allow a fund of
£800 a year for lawsuits; and dowries and pensions must
be added to this.   Besides the endowment of convents, there
was the education of destitute students—a legion of them.
The most distinguished was the Greek Scholar, Amyot,
whom her ready hand saved from penury.   Nor did she
only give to the poor.   In spite of Francis' treacherous
conduct, he had the audacity to borrow largely from her and
she lent him a fortune in plate.   She was doomed to be
exploited : and always by the people she loved best.   Later
it was her daughter who remorselessly ruined her; and her
needy sister-in-law, Isabeau d'Albret, lived upon her gifts. [1]

[1] Amyot came to Paris as a boy, determined to get into
College; starved in a garret on one loaf a week, sent him from

Wherever she turned there was someone ready to spend her
money for her.

"Plus vous que moi," was one of her devices. It could
not be more apt. Who more amply fulfilled her own saying
that "To love God one must first love a human creature
perfectly"? She might perhaps have added that to love
human creatures perfectly you must consent to be disappointed in them. That was certainly her case. It had
happened with her brother, it was to happen again with
her child.

the country by his mother; succeeded in entering the College
of Cardinal Lemoine, and afterwards taught for a living. He
became teacher in the family of one of the King's Secretaries
and came under Margaret's notice. She sent him to Bourges
as Professor of Latin and Greek, after which his fortune was
made.

AUTHORITIES CONSULTED FOR CHAPTER XII

Papiers d'Etat du Cardinal de Granvelle: quoted in the Appendix to Lettres de Marguerite d'Angoulême.

Nouvelles Poésies de Marguerite d'Angoulême.

Epitres de Jeanne d'Albret à sa Mère.

Oraison Funèbre sur Marguerite d'Angoulême: SAINTE-MARTHE.

Jeanne d'Albret: MISS FREER.

Livre d'Etat de Marguerite d'Angoulême:

LE COMTE DE LA FERRIÈRE.

Château de Pau: LAGIÈZE.

Marguerite d'Angoulême: LURO.

Marguerite de Valois: LA COMTESSE D'HAUSSONVILLE.

Marguerite of Angoulême: MARY ROBINSON.

CHAPTER XII

(1537—1545)

ALL Margaret's affection centered upon Jeanne, who remained an only child. There is a record of twins who were born about 1540, but they died directly after birth. Jeanne, like many daughters, had a character the opposite of her mother's. A person of convictions rather than of sympathies, she saw one thing at a time and did not want to see more. Cold and strong, she despised those who gave themselves away for anything but ambition; and stoicism was a virtue she understood better than charity. There is a characteristic story that just before the birth of her son, her father had had a gold chain made for one of his mistresses. It went thirty times round the neck, and the mistress would have duly received it had it not been for Jeanne, who sang so merrily while she gave birth to Henry IV that her father was moved to present her with the jewel. The incident shows her as she was. Hard and gay she remained, with a Gaulois gift for satire—great, if pedantic, intellectual powers—and a faculty for absorbing knowledge: the faults and the virtues of an *esprit-fort*.

As she grew older her mother was often with her at Tours, but she still lived there under the eye of her royal

uncle. The King and Queen of Navarre took great pains
to find her a tutor and chose a man of parts, Nicholas
Bourbon, who had taught an English nobleman's family in
England. She had a duenna also, to instil the social graces
—Margaret's great friend, Madame de Silly, born Aimée
Lafayette, who held the purse and kept Jeanne's accounts.
A good deal of money went in theatricals. Jeanne's
taste for them was even stronger than her mother's and she
had her own private performances. An entry in Madame's
ledger for the scaffolding of a Passion play, to be acted
before the little girl, then eleven, still bears witness to the
cost. She lived to see the development of a real drama—
classic tragedies and social comedies—but in early years the
plays of Béarn contented her.

She had, too, a natural bent for elegant pedantry, and
the fashionable knack of rhyming. She and her mother
kept up a learned correspondence in verse. Anything colder
than Jeanne's letters—than their stilted compliment and
hyperbole—cannot be imagined. It is a comfort to find that
she had a child's sense of fun, even though it was not a
delicate one. She delighted in jokes against the monks.
One day she found her mother's embroidery—the Celebration of the Mass was its subject—and she took the trouble
to work in foxes' heads to cover the heads of the priests.
Freaks such as these were premonitory of her views. In
after years, when she definitely espoused Protestantism, it
was from hatred of the Catholics and a sense of the absurdity of asceticism, rather than from any enthusiasm for
the Cause.

Childhood in those days, especially royal childhood, was

early overshadowed by matrimonial complications. There is something half droll, half tragic, in the thought of these infants playing the part of the heroines of drama. Once in the hands of royal matchmakers, even Jeanne becomes pathetic. The history of her first marriage with the Duc de Clèves is one of the strangest upon record in a strange period: a period when, we must remember, Kings still had divine rights; when authority meant tyranny; and coercion must not be regarded with the humane eyes of nine-teenth-century parents.

Her father and mother had plans for marrying her to Philip, the son of Charles V; but this did not suit the interests of Francis I. To prevent any schemes but his own, he continued to keep her in confinement at his Castle of Plessis-le-Tours. She was not an agreeable little prisoner. "Her sojourn," says a quaint old Chronicler, "was very griev-ous and very wearisome to her. She filled her chamber with wails and the air with sighs.... The dark red of her cheeks grew discoloured by the abundance of her tears; her hair remained dishevelled and undressed, her lips without the ghost of a smile." When she was eleven, Francis sug-gested her union with an ally of his own, the Duc de Clèves, who had a remote claim on the Spanish throne. He had reckoned without his host. Jeanne flatly refused. The Duke was a heavy German; she could not understand his language. She did not love him, she said, and she would not have him. A mere Duke, she protested, was no fit match for a Princess. In vain did her uncle pay her a state visit. He coaxed, he threatened, he declared he would never speak to her again. "I would rather throw myself into a well," she replied. A Marshal and a Cardinal (the famous Cardinal of Tournon) were sent to lecture her; but they left her unmoved, and Francis, in despair, sent her home to her parents.

It is disastrous to find Margaret supporting her brother. Disobedience to the King was treason in her eyes—a sin endangering salvation; rebellion against parental fiats was a vice without precedent; she herself had made no complaint when she married the Duc d'Alençon. All the same, the mother who felt so tenderly for her child's illness might have had some compunction at causing that child so much misery. Her servile love for the King seems sometimes to have acted as a poison, perverting her nature and deadening her affections. She wrote him almost abject letters, and ordered the State-Governess to thrash Jeanne daily till she consented to the match.

We do not know how many beatings were administered. Finding her plaints of no avail, the brave little girl took more practical steps. She assembled the chief officers of her household and read them a solemn Protestation—though how she contrived to get them together, or even to escape from her governess, History does not relate.

"I, Jeanne de Navarre," ran her speech, "continuing the Protestations I have heretofore made (in the which I persist) say and declare ... that the marriage my family wishes for me with the Duc de Clèves, is against my will; that I have never consented and never will consent to it, and that all that I do or say hereafter which they can construe into my consent, will be wrung from me by force, in spite of me and my desires, through fear of the King of France, and of the King my father, and the Queen my mother. I further declare that they have threatened me and had me beaten by the Baillive de Caen, my governess. It was by my mother's orders, and she has many times pressed me to yield, saying that if I did not do all that the King wanted with regard to this marriage.... I should be so severely thrashed and ill-treated that it would bring about my death; and that I should be the cause of the ruin of my afore-mentioned parents and their House, the fear of which fills me with terror. I know not to whom to turn, unless it be to God, now that I see that my father and mother have forsaken me—they who know well what I told them: that I shall never love the Duc de Clèves and that I will not have anything to do with him. And therefore I declare at once that if it falls out that I am married, or still considered as the betrothed of the Duke, in whatever way it happens, it will be... against my heart and inclination: that he will never be my husband, that I shall never consider him as such, that the said marriage shall be null, and that I call God and you to witness thereof—so that you may sign my Protestation with me, and remember the violence and com-pulsion used towards me in the matter of this marriage.

" Thus signed

> Jehanne de Navarre.
> J. d'Arras.
> Francis Navarro.
> Arnauld Duquesse."

This was pretty strong for a girl of barely twelve.   She
made a last desperate effort and, the very day before her
wedding, read another Protestation, as vehement as the first.
But it did not help her to escape the ceremony of marriage.
It took place at Chatellerault.   The fatal hour arrived.   Her
mother led forth the miserable little bride to the room—a
ball-room—where the Altar was set up.   On her childish
head was a royal crown, and she was crushed by the weight
of her gold and silver dress, thick with jewels, and by the
long violet satin cloak, bordered with ermine, which fell
round her shoulders.   The King stepped forward to take her
to the church where the public service was to be celebrated ;
but the rebel Jeanne, determined to hold out to the last,
fell back in her chair and said she felt too ill to walk.
Her uncle, more than her match, gave orders that she should
be carried.   The Constable Montmorency had irritated him
by his pride : this seemed the moment to humiliate him,
and Francis commanded him to lift the bride in his arms.
This was looked on as a menial office and equivalent to
disgrace.   " C'est fait désormais de ma faveur.   Adieu lui
dis !" he exclaimed, but he had to obey and bear the
reluctant Jeanne to the church-door.   Margaret was not
displeased at the discomfiture of her new enemy and old
friend, " Voilà," she said, " celui qui me voulait ruiner autour
du roi mon frère, qui maintenant sert à porter ma fille à
l'église."   The Constable could not bear the ignominy and,
after the " dîner des noces," he took his departure.   He
retired to Ecouen, nor did he re-appear at Court till the·
reign of Henri II.

In the end Jeanne got her way ; for after the wedding

festivities she instantly parted from her bridegroom and returned home to live with her parents. About three years later the Emperor descended on the Duchy of Clèves (the war had been resumed in 1541) and took one place after another. The dismayed Duke thought discretion was the better part of valour, met Charles at Venloo, capitulated to him, and went over to his side. It had been decreed that Jeanne should join him, but when his treachery was known, Francis annulled the marriage. Even then there was some delay in getting the Pope's dispensation. But the indefatigable Jeanne was not to be done out of her freedom. She resumed her policy of Protestation. This time she assembled the Chapter of Tours, the Cardinal, and a crowd of ecclesiastics, in the Chapel of the Castle at Plessis. After receiving the Sacrament, she read them a solemn Remonstrance. It is a surprising picture—that of the slender figure standing in the centre of the long shadowy aisle, surrounded by the tall forms and gorgeous copes of the prelates. The Princess was equal to the moment.

"My Lords—Cardinal, Archbishop and Bishop here assembled"—she said, "I declare to you again that I desire and intend to persevere in my aforesaid protestations. I persist in them and shall never do anything else. And since . . . . I cannot express my meaning as well as I understand it, I have had it here drawn up in writing and have signed it with my hand. I will read it to you, and I swear by the Godhead I have just received that what is here written contains the truth."

The resolute little lady got her deserts : she was freed. She continued her life at Pau, where her extravagance soon

became a serious incubus.   It devoured her mother's pension
from the King, besides a large allowance for "menus plaisirs"
and almsgiving—£3250 in ten months, as Margaret's account-
book shows us.   The girl's retinue was enormous, and separate
from that of her parents.   "The King of Navarre and myself
find it insupportable," wrote her mother, "and we have not
the means to maintain it."   None the less, she gave without
ceasing.

Jeanne's need for money from her was perhaps their
closest tie. The girl seems, if anything, to have disliked
her mother. She was probably scornful of Margaret's outgoing
nature. They found, we may hope, common ground in their
taste for learning and Reform, and they liked the same sort
of people. The audacious Jeanne developed with surprising
quickness, even for those days of early development; and
when she entered her teens she was already an accomplished
woman—a brilliant new element in the literary Court. She
was lucky enough to live at a moment when books were
the fashion—when those who wrote them occupied an honourable position.

There had been many changes in the world of literature:
new forms were becoming visible; new ideas were coming to
the front. They were the result of a gradual Movement
that had begun long before: a Movement to the growth of
which it is now time to turn.

BOOK III

RABELAIS AND HIS CONTEMPORARIES

AUTHORITIES CONSULTED FOR CHAPTER XIII

Œuvres de Clément Marot.

Œuvres Choisies de Clément Marot (Biographical Preface):
HÉRICAULT.

Cymbalum Mundi: BONAVENTURE DES PÉRIERS.

Récit d'un Bourgeois de Paris (edited by LALANNE).

Dictionnaire Historique: BAYLE.

Tableau du Seizième Siècle: SAINTE-BEUVE.

La Littérature française: RENÉ DOUMIC.

Trente Ans de Jeunesse: DE MAULDE LA CLAVIÈRE.

Marguerite d'Angoulême: (Biographical Preface to "Lettres"):
GÉNIN.

Le Livre d'Etat de Marguerite d'Angoulême: LE COMTE DE LA
FERRIÈRE.

Marguerite de Valois: LA COMTESSE D'HAUSSONVILLE.

Conférences sur Marguerite d'Angoulême: LURO.

Les Marguerites de la Marguerite des Princesse (Biographical
Preface): FRANCK.

CHAPTER XIII

(1495—1544)

I

CLÉMENT MAROT

FOR the last fifteen years and more, from the battle of
Pavia onwards, there had been a marked progress in the
literature of France. The National movement was beginning
to assert itself, though here its development was slower than
in the sister arts. Since the days of its first great progenitor,
François Villon, and of Charles d'Orléans, the ballade-singer,
it had been chiefly represented by the Drama. The "Fraternities" were the first actors, and "Mysteries," as in other
countries, the first plays. These dramatized versions of the
Scriptures were acted in the Hôpital de la Trinité and the
Hôtel de Flandre, of which the "Fraternities" obtained the
monopoly; and the people flocked to them without interfer-
ence until the time of King Francis. The rise of the
Reformers was the death-blow of the Mysteries. In 1542,
the Provost of Paris objected to the performance of the Acts
of the Apostles and protested against Mysteries in general.
They kept their audience from Mass, he said, lasting as they
did, from ten o'clock until five; and they made the Priests
hurry over the service, or even abandon it in their eagerness
to reach the play in time. And then there was the political

danger. The Mysteries and their jokes were an important
tool in the hands of the Reformers : just as in England
they were supposed to promote Catholicism and were forbidden by Henry VIII. In 1543, Francis I ordered the
Hôtel de Flandre to be demolished, but the actors, unabashed,
got possession of part of the Hôtel de Bourgogne and built
a theatre there. They could not procure a license till the
next reign ; and even then they found themselves hedged
in with restrictions and only allowed such plays as were
"profanes et honnêtes" in their subjects. Mysteries went on
sub rosâ, under the name of Pastorals and Eclogues, till the
growth of the classical Drama gradually extinguished them.

Meanwhile Comedy was developing apace. It is characteristic of France that the mirror of society—the art which
is synonymous with social development—should have already
been so much more polished than it was in contemporary
England. While we had nothing less primitive than "Ralph
Royster Doyster" and "Gammer Gurton's Needle," the French
were playing satires which have something to amuse us even now.
The two great companies were the *Enfants sans souci*—
consisting of young noblemen who performed "Sotties," the
most extravagant form of skit imaginable—and the Company
of the Lawyers, or *Basochiens*, who acted simple farces.
There was, however, no stickling for property, and the two
troupes interchanged their plays and acted them all over
Paris—strolling players at best, yet of no small importance.
If the Mysteries were of use to the Reformers, the Sotties
were still more so. Their subjects show us why. In one of
them Louis XII, as the "Vieux Monde," is discovered asleep,
surrounded by trees in which the "Sots" are imprisoned.

There they vegetate. Enter "Abus," the spirit of corruption. He releases them—gives them fresh life; they emerge and run riot: the "Sot dissolu" in the garb of a cleric, the "Sot trompeur" as a lawyer. "Abus" looks at the drowsy Vieux Monde and thinks that his appearance needs altering. He shaves him, but the change is for the worse and he only seems uglier than before. Then he resolves to make a New World. He begins to build it, but his blunders bring down the scaffolding. The noise awakens the Vieux Monde. He sits up in his chair and moralizes on events. And when he has said his say to the younger generation, he resumes his "train de Gros-Jean."

Les Halles preferred "La Mère-Sotte," which was given on Shrove Tuesday, 1511. The Church, disguised as the Pope, was unmasked by her prelates and discovered to be the Mother of all Fools. The authorities got wind of the Mère-Sotte and the actors found themselves in prison. No Lord Chamberlain would have passed the plays of that time, and their audacity is astounding. At the "Sacre" of Francis I, his last flirtation was enacted under his nose. He appeared on the stage as a Salamander: the reigning beauty as a barn-door fowl. This entertainment came under the category of "Sottye, Sermon, Moralité et Farce, avec autres choses morales et bonnes remonstrations." The author was a priest and his tonsure alone saved him, after this, from being thrown into the Seine.

When we turn from the Drama and look for the national movement in literature, the progress was slower. Many parties were still in the field: the Boccaccian and the French, the learned and the colloquial, or, as Sainte-Beuve puts it, the Court and the Country. The Country seemed in abeyance. For a hundred years or so after Villon and Charles of Orleans, there was hardly a poet of the National School. "The call to create was not yet distinct from the desire for knowledge.... Men professed verse-making, as they professed medicine or law, theology or history; and any literate man of that day could, at a pinch, rank among the Poets." [1]

The name of such mediocrities was legion. Jean Marot (the greater poet's father), Budé, Héroet, Bouchet, Dorat, and de Bézé were recognized lights amongst them: the rest can safely remain in the oblivion which they have deserved. These Savants, whose aim was to write rhymed chronicles and metrical eulogies, looked down on the more natural verse-writers as the frivolous creatures of a drawing-room. Had they not been blind, they might have read the signs of the times. French was becoming the official language: the Law Courts were ordered to use it. There was growing up a new group of writers—men of the town, not of the study—who appealed to a larger audience than the bookmen had done: who spoke in a tongue which was stronger than that of their elders. They needed a voice to proclaim their ideas; and the voice was there—it was that of Clément Marot.

His are the only poems that have come down to us of the hundreds composed by his contemporaries. [2] They were amply rewarded by the fame they had in their own age.

---

[1] Sainte-Beuve: "Tableau du XVIième Siècle."

[2] The best among these contemporaries were Melin Saint-Gelais, Brodeau (whom Marot called his son), Charles Fontaine, Bonaventure des Périers and Maurice Scève.

Melin Saint-Gelais, [1] the nephew of the Bishop Octavien, was, in his lifetime, almost as famous as Marot. Now he is covered by kindly dust.

The *"gentil Maître Clément"*, as Marot was called, made a great deal of noise in his time, some echo of which has sounded down through posterity. His career was that of a typical French poet in the sixteenth century. "It combined all that was piquant in his generation—the valour of a soldier, the manners of a courtier, brilliant gallantries, literary feuds, quarrels with the Sorbonne, and visits to the Prison of the Châtelet." Born about 1495, his life began in the purlieus of the Court. He was the son of Jean, or Jehannot Marot, poetaster in the retinue of Anne de Bretagne: first her Secretary, then her Valet de Garde-Robe, together with Jean Clouet (also the father of a famous son) and Jean Perréal, the Painter. A grander friend than these was the attendant of the Princess Renée, Madame de Soubise, who faithfully protected Jean's interests at Court. No wonder that his son said that he wished for no better fate than to step into his father's shoes. But Jean Marot's favourite crony was his fellow-poet, Jean Lemaire, who had—so says tradition—a good deal of influence on the boy, Clément. We can imagine the two men discussing metre in the Marots' parlour. Or we see him "rather late at evening" —as he himself describes—the lamp on the table, *le bon veillard*, his father, "working beside him, watching over him as carefully as shepherdesses, crouching near their

---

[1] He had a still grander connection. He was supposed to be descended from "La Fée Mélusine," a strange lineage for one who was originally brought up for the Church.

cottage fires, watch over their starlings or their magpies."
Clément's education was not elaborate; probably Nature
and that same "*bon veillard*" were responsible for his accom-
plishments.   He himself has recorded them:

> J'appris les noms des quatre parts du monde,
> J'appris les noms des vents qui de là sortent,
> Leur qualités, et quel temps ils apportent,
> Dont les oiseaux, sages devins des shamps,
> M'avertissaient par leurs vols et leurs chants. [1]

While still very young, he was sent to the University in
the Rue Fouarre at Paris—a strange, jolly villainous Paris,
hardly the safest place for a boy not yet in his teens.   He
saw more of it when he had done with College and become
a Basochien, a student of the Law, able to wander at his
will.   It was a paradoxical city: an inconceivable mixture of
polish and barbarism, integrity and felony, free-thought and
superstition.   A Countess indites Latin love-letters to her
Lord.   The public executioner is burned to death in his
house for refusing to behead some unpopular victim of the
pillory.   A procession carries the "Châsse" of Madame Sainte
Geneviève through the town, in the hope of arresting a
drought, "*dont depuis ne cessa de pleuvoir par l'espace de
trois mois.*"   Three rich Bakers, who have been for months

---

[1] "I learned the four quarters of the globe, I learned the
names of the winds which issue thence, their qualities and
what weather they bring, of which the birds, sage soothsayers
of the fields, were wont to warn me by their flight and their
song."

in prison for selling bread of insufficient weight, have to march disgraced through the streets. And yet money thefts are winked at in high places and Cardinals may sell what they like.

The Basochiens were among the wildest spirits in Paris, and Clément Marot was the wildest of the Basochiens. They had convivial relations with other companies who vied with them in adventure: the Enfants Sans Souci, the Clerks of the Châtelet, and the Clerks of the Empire of Galilee. Together with these boon-companions, Clément hobnobbed with all the ragamuffins of the city, lived with the watermen on the river-bank, fought the Watch, and scandalized the Law-court and University by the strange friends he brought there. The public Squares—the Halles, the Grève, the Place Maubert, the Pierre-au-lait—were his favourite haunts. He would loiter too by the Cloître des Innocents, near St. Thomas du Louvre, "where singers and players of instruments made music;" he would stop, as he strolled, at the church-doors, before which bands of alchemists in rags, crucible in hand, sought the philosopher's stone, or pursued the more profitable business of writing love-letters for chambermaids. The favourite taverns, crowded with roystering students, each with his bumper of red wine, were the Pomme de Pin au Castel, the Magdaleine à la Mule, or the famous Trois Poissons in the Faubourg St. Marcel. By the time he was fifteen, Marot was the Prince of Swashbucklers. At about that age he became, like all young gentlemen, the page of a Parisian nobleman—Monsieur de Villeroi. The life of a page in the provinces was a discipline of pious courtesy and soldierly exercise; but the same service in Paris

meant nothing better than an elaborate training for Ras-
caldom. The next year, mercurial and precocious, Marot
left his place, indulged in a love-affair and was made, like
his father before him, a royal valet-de-chambre.

His master was the Heir-Apparent, Francis, to whom, on
his accession in 1515, Mercury presented his first poem,
"*le Temple de Cupidon.*" The King took a fancy to him
and, after this, was constantly seeking his company—" *mon
bien aimé varlet-de-chambre,*" as he called him. Clément
had a reckless tongue and a lively store of anecdote, and
his sovereign, who dreaded dulness more than death, always
took him as his travelling companion. He was a person-
able man : his eyes were brown and vivid, his skin bronzed,
his forehead broad and round, his look flashing yet shifty.
The Prince of Swashbucklers was bound also to be the
Prince of Quarrellers, and the rest of his Court life was a
tangle of loves and quarrels. His friends and enemies among
the Court beauties were innumerable. At one time he has
a quarrel with "all the ladies of Paris" and pursues it in
embittered verse; at another he conceives a passion for one
of them, an unknown Diane, who fixes him for rather longer
than her rivals; and all the time he is flirting with a score
of charmers and writing sonnets to their eyes, their girdles
and their spaniels. He fought with the King at Pavia and
—it is said—saved his life by covering him on the battle-
field. Made a prisoner with his master, he was, like many
others, speedily liberated in consideration of all the booty
that was taken. On his return to France, finding that Diane
had grown cold, he abjured his love and turned his active
imagination into new fields. It was about this time that

he joined the Reformers, more from a love of adventure and of skirmishing with the police than from any real conviction. He was, if the truth be told, incapable of deep feeling, either in love or religion; but he needed to use his energies and, it must in justice be added, that his keen mind took naturally to enlightened ideas.

This phase of his life brings us to an interesting episode —one which, perhaps, drew out the best that was in him. He was made valet-de-chambre to Margaret of Angoulême. Poets, as we know, became Secretaries and Valets, even Bishops and Canons, at the shortest notice in reward for their works. Servant both of brother and sister, Marot gossiped with the one and was inspired in his art by the other. Some of his most appealing verses are due to Margaret. He wrote to his patroness in the language of love, and spoke of her charms in terms that were vivid, if sometimes rather coarse. On this fact has been based the story of his love for her, and (which is far more incredible) of hers for him. It has even been asserted that she was his mistress. But Lavaux, another of her dependants, Jean Lemaire and many others, wrote with the same extravagance to the ladies who protected them. It is only Marot's superior fame which gave him singularity and thus stigmatized his addresses to his princess. Besides, it is impossible to accept as true an incident so wholly out of keeping with Margaret's life and character. She was a bountiful provider of all his needs and his constant refuge in times of persecution. For henceforward Marot's scrapes are nearly always religious.

There is a vein of pathos in this gay creature—with his

slight dilettante taste for Reformed doctrines, yet fated for
many years to lead the life of the victim of belief. One is
inclined to think that so much privation for a Cause must
have gradually turned him into an enthusiast. His taste
for guerilla warfare was at all events convenient, and the
Reformers often used him as a ready tool. Close upon his
return from the war and during the absence of Margaret,
he was cast into the Prison of the Châtelet for bragging
with some impudence about the New Ideas; and was severely
summoned before the Bishop of Chartres. He must have
had something childish and disarming about him, for the
prelate only condemned him to confinement in a comfortable
house close to the Episcopal Palace. There is a story that
the townsfolk of Chartres used to stand below his window
and sing his own songs to cheer him, but his durance was
very short. It was well for this quarreller—this harlequin
of the Reformation—that he had powerful friends at Court
besides Margaret and her brother. The Constable Montmorency; Chancellor Duprat; Treasurer Robertet; the Cardinal de
Tournon; Guillaume du Bellay; the King's Mistress, Madame
de Châteaubriand; Madame d'Albret, and the Lorraine
family, were allies not to be despised. And, strange to say,
he had quite as many in his own profession. Brodeau and
Melin Saint-Gelais were his best-loved comrades, and men like
Rabelais, Dolet, Bonaventure—men of scholarship and science
—were also of his circle.

No effort of friendship, however, could keep Marot out
of prison. He was there again in 1527, this time for
fighting the police and helping their prisoners to escape.
He was set free again by a special order from the King.

In 1530, Francis took him with him to Bayonne, when he went there to receive his second wife, Eleanor of Portugal—"*la plus joyeuse dame qu'oncques* [1] *on vit*," as Marot wrote of her. In this year he married; but though he had a family, this was a fact that hardly counted in the life of a man who could not bear the slightest tie, and proclaimed his dislike of staying in a place for more than two weeks together.

The following years were filled by vicissitudes. He was robbed; he was ill; he was again imprisoned—for eating bacon in Lent; he petitioned the King in prose and verse, and finally landed himself in comparative prosperity at Lyons. This town, the Academe of France, grew into a favourite haunt of his; and he soon became a member of its choice literary circle—the friend of all its scholars, of its poets and poetesses. To one of these blue-stocking Muses, "Jeanne Gaillard de Lyon, Femme de bon scavoir," he dedicated some of his airiest verses; another, and the most famous of them, Louise Labé, can have been no more than an infant prodigy at the time of his visits; but he evidently knew her, for a local rhymer, anxious to please her, sends some inflated lines to promise her the praises of Marot. He accompanied Margaret and her retinue to his native town of Cahors, that he might do the honours to his lady; but on the top of this, in 1533, came the terrible persecution of the Protestants. Marot was denounced as the "Leader of a party," and a domiciliary visit to his house in Paris resulted in the discovery of various books of magic and of

---

[1] Ever.

scandal, besides suspicious papers. He had been staying
with one of his grand friends at Blois, and had just returned,
when a hasty messenger warned him of his danger and he
fled to Margaret's court in Béarn. Even that was not safe,
and, leaving her his son as a page, he escaped to Italy and
made for Ferrara.

Here he was not without allies, for the Princess Renée,
Louis XII's second daughter, who had married Hercules
d'Este, Duke of Ferrara, had taken with her to her new
Court Madame de Soubise, Marot's first patroness in the
days of Anne de Bretagne. Renée herself was a centre of
the Renaissance, with strong Protestant leanings. She was
plain and lame, like her sister Claude, but learned, subtle
and a great talker, given to astrology and speculation. The
Italians she disliked and she surrounded herself with French
courtiers, though she tolerated a few Ferrarese poets who
wrote verses in her honour. She was fondest of the women-
scholars of France, to whom she and her friend, Mademoiselle de Pons, gave the tone; and she loved to gather round
her the French Reformers—impelled at once by her friendship
for Calvin and her distaste for Papal cavillings. This was
in spite of her husband, a fervent Italian and a strong ally
of the Pope and the Emperor. She received Marot like
Ovid: so he tells us in his "Coq à l'âne," which was
written at Ferrara. But the Duke, hampered by her pedants
and in nervous dread of the Reformers, sent them all
packing, Marot amongst them, and hedged in his wife with
Italians.

Marot went to Venice, whence he implored the Dauphin
to help his return. At last, greatly owing to Paul III's

plea for tolerance, the Protestant fugitives were pardoned on condition that they abjured their heresy. In 1536, Marot travelled with a crowd of them to Lyons, and though his retractation has never been proved, it is probable that he made it. At any rate, three years later, the King again received him. He found an unexpected enemy at Court in the poet Sagon, the Voice of the Sorbonne, who looked upon Marot as a pernicious innovator, and organized against him a formidable party of busybodies—versifiers and ladies— Madame de Châteaubriand, Marot's former friend, with the rest. His rhymes, his invention of words, his person, his character, his religious views, were sharply attacked. He met the assault well supported by his allies, Bonaventure and Fontaine, and, in the end, seems more or less to have triumphed. The faithful King gave him a house and garden, but, even so, he could not settle down. He mixed himself up in Court intrigues and then proceeded to Paris, where he plotted for the Reformers once more. He endangered his luck by a friendship with Vatable, the heretical commentator on the Psalms and Proverbs.

It may have been this friendship which inspired Marot with his idea of writing a rhymed version of the Psalms— a task which he accomplished so successfully that Calvin had them set to music. They became the rage, both at Court and in the market-place. Francis presented thirty of them to the Emperor Charles V when he passed through Paris, and Charles paid for them handsomely with imperial gold. Every royal personage, King, Dauphin, Dauphine and Margaret, had a special favourite which they knew by heart, and sang even while out hunting. They were an excellent

refuge too for temper. When the Dauphine, Cathérine de
Médicis, was too much aggrieved with her faithless husband,
she took refuge in chanting:

> Vers l'Eternel, des opprimés le Père,
> Je m'en irai lui montrant l'impropère
> Que l'on me fait.

It is difficult to recognize the Psalm, but easy to imagine
the relief the words must have given. Humming Marot's
Psalms quickly grew into a fashion; it was a sign of good
tone—which largely increased their circulation. They were
set to other airs beside those which Calvin had circulated:
to Vaudeville and to dance-tunes: le Bransle de Poitou and
the like. They did much for the Reformation—more than
many weightier works. The gay diffusion of propaganda
seemed a fitting mission for this butterfly of the Protestant
Cause and this, at least, he achieved without disaster.

His prosperity, as usual, did not last long. The Sorbonne
grew venomous about the Psalms; the King at last turned
against him and he was once more forced to flee, this time
to Genèva. He was now surrounded by displeasure, neither
party approving of him. The Conservatives thought him a
heretic; the Reformers, aggravated by his mundane popularity, condemned him as lukewarm, They would not let him
stay in Geneva and he went to Piedmont, his last place
of exile. Here he wrote his poem to celebrate the King's
victory at Cérisole, and he may have enjoyed its success,
for soon after its despatch he was allowed to return to
Court. His triumph was a short one, lasting only for a
few months. He went to Turin and died there, in 1544.

He was not yet fifty, but he was worn by his motley fortunes; and he left few legacies behind him—unless it were an illegitimate daughter whom he bequeathed to the care of Margaret. "Tel fut l'existence passablement agitée du gentil Maître Clément." So we may end with the old Chronicler and find there is little more to say.

> Sur le printemps de ma jeunesse folle
> Je ressemblais à l'hirondelle qui vole
> Puis ça, puis là; l'âge me conduisait
> Sans peur ni soin où le cœur me disait. [1]

Thus he wrote in one of his serene moods. Poets can believe anything of themselves, and at such times he also imagined that he loved a quiet literary life—at least he said so to a friend.

> Tous deux aimons la musique chanter,
> Tous deux aimons les livres fréquenter,
> Tous deux aimons à d'aucun ne médire,
> Tous deux aimons un meilleur propos dire,
> Tous deux aimons gens pleins d'honnêteté. [2]

It is a sunny good-natured picture of himself—true enough as far as his character went, and a good specimen of his

---

[1] In the spring-time of my wild youth, I was like a swallow flying now here, now there. Age led me, fearless and careless there where my heart bade me wander.

[2] Both of us love to sing music; both of us love to seek the company of books; both of us love to speak evil of no man; both of us love to tell a good story; both of us love the folk that are full of goodness.

easy-going poetry. It is hard at this distance of time to estimate him rightly. His verses were the bedside book of Turenne. La Fontaine reminds the great soldier, in a letter, how once when he was journeying to take command of the Army and La Fontaine was his travelling companion, Turenne beguiled the way by quoting one after another of Marot's poems. But Turenne belonged to an age more artificial than Marot's, one to which he might well seem the embodiment of candour. There are delightful bits of autobiography in his "Adolescence Clémentine," which he wrote in the midst of his troubles; there are lines which have the charm which arrests. But if at his best he is charming—"le poëte du sourire," as he has been called— at his worst he is very dull, and whoever has the courage to search for his smiles must make up his mind to wade through pages of tedium. His true vocation was being natural. He described the flight of a bird, or a peasant's cottage, with a simple pen dipped in colours so fresh that they seem of yesterday. But much of his time went in a laureate's duties. Compliments, hyperboles, conceits, flowed with mechanical plenty from his hand. His native grace does not desert him even here, and some of these state lyrics are fascinating. There is a delicious little Ballade, pretending to come from the Baby Jeanne de Navarre, and inspired by joy at re-union with her mother. It is all about nothing: her journey home down the Loire, with her squirrel and her parrot, "vêtu de vert comme un bouquet de marjolaine"—her resolution to learn the "Danse du Compaignon"; but it is tossed off so airily that the verse itself seems a sylph-like dance—something that charms us by its movement.

As to his intellectual claims, he was quite aware of his purpose. He tried to revive Villon and re-edited him himself. He was, it has been said, an amateur—belonging to the New Ideas by his taste more than by force of mind. But belong to them he did, and very consciously. "You will find," he wrote to the still unborn child of the Duchess Renée, "a century in which you can quickly learn all that a child can understand. Come then boldly, and when you grow older, you will find something better still : you will find a war already begun—the war against ignorance and its insensate troops."[1]

To know how to snap your fingers gracefully in the face of "the insensate troops" is an art in itself: to be on the right side, a yet greater one. Perhaps these are not the least among Marot's titles to fame.

II

BONAVENTURE DES PÉRIERS

The life of Clément Marot was practically over before Jeanne d'Albret became prominent at her mother's Court. Other names were attracting attention, and by the time she had grown up, two men had become conspicuous there, too important in their own time and in their relations to the Queen of Navarre to be passed over slightly, though they are little known to posterity. These were the free-thinking Scholar-poets, Bonaventure des Périers and Etienne Dolet. The first really belongs to the days before Jeanne's return

[1] "Avant-Naissance."

to her parents, but his short story is so tragic that it finds
no place in a general picture of the Court. Bonaventure
was one of the group of men who had, in 1532, translated
the whole Bible into French. Calvin and Lefèbre were his
colleagues. He soon proclaimed himself a champion of the
New Ideas. An adventurer in thought, he belonged to no
sect. He had a daring tongue which often brought him
into danger. His constant refuge and the object of his
chief affection was Margaret. She made him her valet and
her secretary early in his career, but she could not ensure
his safety. After the affair of the Placards he had to
flee to Lyons, the metropolis of tolerance, and here he saw
the best literary company to be had in France. When
matters had smoothed down again he returned to Margaret,
who kept him on in spite of his frequent turbulence and
the censure she received for supporting a heretic.

He was safest when he was in harness—editing Marot's
works or writing his own. His versatile pen followed his
changeful moods. It varied between careless mirth and reckless
sarcasm: between his "Nouvelles récréations et joyeux devis,"
and his great book, "Cymbalum Mundi"—a Pantagruelian
satire, which was burnt soon after it appeared, by the common
hangman. It was the publication of this volume which put
an end to his sojourn at the Court of Nérac. It drew
down condemnation from Calvin and Robert Estienne, besides
the wrath of the Sorbonne. It was also an offence against
Margaret's code of Rules for a Christian life, and Bonaventure had to take the consequences. He was exiled from
Béarn and his name was erased from the list of her Staff.
But her heart was tender towards him; the court discipline

forced her to severity, but none the less she understood his
wild and bitter sincerity.   She kept sight of him at Lyons,
whither he returned, and put him under a friend's care;
she helped him with money from afar, through her gracious
almoner, Mademoiselle St. Pather.

He presently repented with as much force as he had
sinned, and Margaret, moved by his distress and the prayers
of his friend, Diane de Poitiers, consented to take him back
into her service.   The experiment could hardly have been a
success, for, a short time after, he was once more in Lyons
where deep despair overtook him.   His courage deserted
him; his brain was full of gloomy imaginings.   In a fit of
black melancholy he threw himself on his sword and died,
leaving his writings to Margaret—"the prop and safeguard
of all goodness", as he called her in his last testament. [1]
His death was a great shock to her—he was one of the
people she loved.

He was also one of her many links with the city of
Lyons.   Etienne Dolet, whose record was longer and no
less tragic, is another.   A third, and a greater, was the
immortal Rabelais who lived there for so long.   To understand these men it is necessary to understand the intellectual
atmosphere of their favourite town, and the people that
they found in it.   Both spent their best days there and
were for some time fellow-citizens: but Rabelais was the first
to arrive and had published his "Gargantua" in 1533—a
year before Dolet became his neighbour.   If we look at
Dolet first, it is only to clear space for the Titan Rabelais:
for the figure that made an epoch in the history of the world.

[1] 1548.

AUTHORITIES CONSULTED FOR CHAPTER XIV

Histoire de Lyon: PARADIN.

Histoire de Notre Temps: PARADIN.

Œuvres poétiques de Louise Labé.

Le Débat de l'Amour: LOUISE LABÉ.

Les Soupirs: OLIVIER DE MAGNY.

Œuvres de Clément Marot.

Poëtes français depuis le 12ième siècle jusquà Malesherbe.

Vie de Louise Labé: BLANCHEMAIN (preface to her works).

Collection Littéraire: KERALIO.

Dictionnaire Historique: BAYLE.

Dictionnaire de Colletet.

Dictionnaire de la Croix du Maine.

Causeries de Lundi: SAINTE-BEUVE.

Vie de Clément Marot: HÉRICAULT (Biographical Preface to
Œuvres).

Vie de Rabelais: MILLET.

CHAPTER XIV

J'ai trouvé plus d'honnêteté
Et de noblesse en ce Lyon,
Que n'ai, pour avoir fréquenté
D'autres bêtes un Million:

CLÉMENT MAROT.

THE town of Lyons had a fateful association with Margaret's fortunes. Here she heard the news of the disaster at Pavia; here her first husband died and all her friends, one after another, took up their abode; here, in 1541, she lingered with her brother, and here she arrived seven years later to learn the suicide of Bonaventure des Périers. She was lodging in the Convent of the Célestins, and she wrote a song to the rose-tree in its garden to commemorate her sorrow and associate it with her favourite city.

Lyons was at that time the Athens of France. It was on the frontier of Italy, a position which made it a centre alike of wealth and of beauty. Italian merchants kept up a ceaseless traffic of stuffs and jewels; Florentine architects settled there and, before the reign of Charles VIII, had already enriched it with exquisite buildings and given it a reputation for taste. Its pageants on state occasions were the prettiest in France, and the booth of the Florentine Confectioners at one of these functions was a nine days' wonder in the kingdom. All the artists and scholars, travelling to and from Italy, stopped there, often for months, on their way. Others were attracted by the famous Lyonese printing-presses to which they brought their works for publication, and nearly every writer of repute came there at some time in his career. Besides this, the incessant Italian wars made it a frequent pied-à-terre for King and Court—a fact as good for society as for trade.

All these intellectual influences created an atmosphere of free-thought and tolerance which soon turned it into a refuge for every sort of spiritual outlaw, though more of these were thinkers than active Reformers; created, too, an atmosphere of poetry and letters which added charm to solid scholarship. At first these philosophers and students of Lyons, in their zest for enlightenment, practically made one party with the Mystics of Meaux. But later, when sects grew more defined, they divided; and Reform and Renaissance were the watchwords of separate, if friendly circles. It is the distinction of Margaret that she always belonged to both, and the writers of Lyons owed much to her.

Athens of old was practical as well as literary, and Lyons followed its example. Its civic and philanthropic arrangements could teach more than one sound lesson to us of 1901. Its Corporation had apparently discovered the art of combining Christianity with economics. Their excellent organization began in the days of famine, early in the fifteenth century, when they did wonders with their public kitchens and their impromptu shelters for the outlying poor and for foreigners. When the dearth was over, the eight

famine-officers who had superintended the affair remained,
and became permanent "Recteurs de l'Aumône" and voluntary servants of their town. A Marchand des Blés was
added, and under them worked eleven paid officers, including four Beadles, "pour tenir les pauvres en crainte," and
two "Pédagogues" of Homes for the destitute. There was
one for orphan boys, who were tenderly educated, "selon la
capacité des petits enfants"; and a Priory disgraced for its
abuses was given by the city for this purpose. And there
was a corresponding Home for girls under a woman, where
they learned to sew and to spin and even to read. Every
year there was a procession of the schools and their "Pédagogues"—men and women—followed by the monks and Corporation and the poor of the town : the little boys singing
"Fili Dei, miserere nobis"; the little girls, ignorant of
Latin, "Mère de Jésus, priez pour nous." Sunday was the
day which these wise people of Lyons devoted to their
Committees and visits of inspection. Every Sabbath the
Rectors visited the schools, and chose the children best
suited to the "gens de bien" who required them for service
and trade, or sometimes for adoption. They were always
taken on two weeks' trial and then, if all was well, the City
gave them their clothes. On Sundays, too, out-door relief
was administered, and the Rectors met in the Cloister of
St. Bonaventure's Convent to hear the complaints of the
poor and give or refuse assistance. "Since the needy take
advantage of Truth," says the chronicler of Lyons, the
Corporation gave one of the city-towers for the confinement
of such as disobeyed the Rectors; but then, as he adds,
"les gens d'honneur" have no wish to be severe, and the

punishment was not very rigorous. Lyons seems, indeed, to have been the home of organized indulgence. The citizens did not wait for *noblesse* to oblige them; they found *richesse* enough incentive and gave with open-handed generosity. There was a Moulin de l'Aumône on the Rhône, which ground grain for the destitute and for all the charitable institutions; a public granary that stored it for them; and a free bakery that baked their bread. There was a great hospital, a model of its kind, managed by women; and another one for the pest—a disease which consequently disappeared from the place. Vice, says the old historian, became almost as scarce; and if we cannot quite accept this statement, we need not wholly reject it. Philanthropy is seldom picturesque because it is seldom personal; but the order and kindness of the Lyonese citizens affect us like a fine Flemish picture, full of light and warmth, and their civic arrangements read like the ideal community of a Thomas More or a Rabelais. Their town might well have been the capital of Utopia—independent of nationality, untrammelled by prejudices, open to all the friends of Truth.

In spite of their lavish gifts to the poor, the beauty-loving people of Lyons showed no economy in personal adornment. "Les accoutrements étranges dont les Seigneurs et Dames de Lyon usaient en ce temps," is the title of a contemporary's description of their fashions. "Changefulness and caprice in dress," he says, "have always been natural to the French more than to any other nation"; and Lyons seems to have been distinguished for taste in its caprices.

Yet its people were not frivolous in daily life. Its society was as different as its charity from that of other places. It was a city of poets—particularly poetesses—and men and women compared their poems with each other. They and their fellows in the world of letters formed a charming little circle, " la Société Angélique", which met at la Montagne Fourvière, the house of a certain Sieur de Langes. Marot belonged to it when he came to Lyons, and so did most of the visitors of distinction. Of the resident " Angelics" most are only known in the historical heaven to which they have long since departed, but they were prophets in their own day. There was the interesting family of the Scevés, all poets: two sisters, Claudine and Sybille, and a brother Maurice—the most gifted of the three—architect, painter and musician, as well as sonneteer. And there were, besides, the usual Scholar-rhymers, a charming Pleïade of women whose names have survived their songs. A list of women's names—women of a past century—is like a list of flowers, which does not burden the memory, but conjures up certain sweet scents by the mere virtue of sound. There was Jacquelin Stuart, the most beautiful amongst them; and Clémence de Bourges, an academic siren who played upon sweet instruments; and Jeanne Gaillard of the golden pen, to whom Marot wrote verses; and Louise Labé, the leader of them all, with Pernette de Guillet, second to her in reputation.

Louise Labé cannot be dismissed with the rest. Both as woman and as poet she was a personage, and created romance wherever she moved. Pernette also deserves more than a word. Contemporary Lyons was almost equally proud of both ladies. Criticism was not the strong point of the sixteenth century; it could hardly have existed together with its generous, undiscriminating enthusiasm for all talent and learning. Genius was a word unused; or, if used, it applied alike to scholar and to creator. "De deux dames Lyonnaises, en ce temps excellentes en scavoir et poésies," is the heading given by the old chronicler of Lyons to his chapter on these two Muses. " In this reign and in this century," he begins, " there flourished at Lyons two ladies, like two radiant stars; and two noble virtuous spirits—or, rather, we should say two Sirens. Both overflowed with a great plenty and mixture of all happy influences and precious understandings—more than any other persons of their sex in our time. The one was called Louise Labé, the which had a countenance more angelic than human, but it was nothing in comparison with her mind . . . . created by God to be marvelled at as a prodigy by mankind. . . . . The other lady was called Pernette de Guillet, very witty, very gentle and most chaste, the which has lived in great renown, because of her widespread knowledge." [1]

It is quite refreshing to find this chapter of heated hyperbole followed by another, " Concerning a wondrous Drought in the Lyonnais," and to escape from such overpowering intellect and beauty. But the chronicler might have found more to say about his goddesses. Pernette, who died in 1545, was an expert in tongues, dead and living, and also a graceful musician—" so well-skilled in all instruments of music, whether lute, spinet, or others, that she astounded the most experienced." In spite of her gifts she was modest, and could sometimes be natural in her verse.

[1] Paradin: Histoire de Lyon.

Sans connaissance aucune en mon printemps j'étais;
Libre sans liberté, car rien ne regrettais
En ma vague pensée,
De mots et vains désirs follement dispensés. [1]

So she wrote and her song is not without melody. She
published a volume of her poems: "Rimes de gentille et
vertueuse Dame Pernette de Guillet"—about love and friendship—which ends by her giving the palm to "honnête amour":
a very proper conclusion for an accomplished spinster who
had the good and bad fortune to live in the days of the
Renaissance.

Louise Labé had a different sort of fame and was a good
deal more than an illustrious blue-stocking. In her intense
feeling she is a modern. Though her lyre has but one or
two strings, they are such as continue to vibrate and make
us respond to them. She could touch the chord of suffering—the suffering of a woman's heart—with an impulsive
force that astonished in those heartless days of stilted grief.
Her lyric eloquence and her story have no parallel, unless we
turn to Georges Sand; and although the term is relative, she
may not unjustly be called the Georges Sand of the Renaissance. Her father was a rope-maker and she was born at Lyons
in 1525 or '26. At sixteen, "la belle Cordière," as she was
called, was already a prodigy of learning and a very pretty
poetess, as well as a notable rider and unerring shot. In
spite of the old chronicler, her "angelic countenance" was

[1] I lived without any sort of knowledge in my spring-time;
free, yet innocent; for among all the words and vain desires
that I squandered so gaily, my vague thoughts never found one
to regret.

really a very plain one, if the only existing portrait of her is to be trusted; and her motto, "Belle à soi" (the anagram of her name), may be a piece of subtle irony on her part. But she must have had the gift of fascination which sets beauty at nought. It was at this time—about 1542—that the French army rode through Lyons on their way to besiege Perpignan, then occupied by the Imperial troops. Louise, tired of her sedentary life and excited by the tramp and stir of the troops, resolved to turn soldier and share their fortunes. So she joined them in full armour on her horse, and rode away from Lyons to the wars. A rumour obtained afterwards that the Dauphin, who was with his regiment, had seen her and admired her in the town and that this was the occasion of her departure. Or perhaps it was she who fell in love with him. At all events the "Capitaine Loyse," as she was called, for all her soldierly shooting and endurance of hardships, lost her girl's heart before the walls of Perpignan and it was said at the time that the Dauphin was the cause.

When the French won the day and the siege came to an end, Louise returned to Lyons. She found suitors there in plenty. The well-known Italian poet, Luigi Almanni, proposed to her; but she rejected him and married a certain Ennemond Perrin, a rope-maker like her father. He worked hard at his trade and allowed his young wife as much latitude for her heart as for her head. They lived in a house at the corner of the Rue Nôtre Dame de Comfort, close by the meeting of the Rhône and the Saône, and she made herself a large library, the shelves of which were gradually filled by choice books and manuscripts. In this

room she collected round her all the artists and persons of
interest within reach, to discuss fact and fancy, or to hold
fencing-bouts of wit with her. The talk was varied by
music, for she, like Pernette and Clémence, was a charming
musician. Sometimes the company assembled in the garden—
a delicious place watered by fountains and divided into
"copse, flower-garden and greensward; sometimes she re-
galed them with a "collation d'exquises confitures." The
meetings became an institution. Poets from distant places
attended them—old friends like St.-Gelais and Charles
Fontaine amongst them. It grew into a regular salon:
the first of its kind in France, the land of salons. Louise
was fitted to found the dynasty of hostesses; she understood
the social art of uniting an interest in subjects with an
interest in their votaries.

But she was a woman and a poetess and, apart from her
salon, the personal was bound to prevail. She had lovers—
in succession. While she held her brilliant parties down-
stairs, her husband, who did not care for intellect, sat upstairs coiling his ropes. He seems to have behaved like a
second father to her, and Louise gave him nothing more
than a rather supercilious affection. At first she was satisfied by the friendship of her admirers. Maurice Scève was
for long her favourite crony, her help and her teacher in
poetry. Like our English Drayton, and so many of his
contemporaries in all nations, he was a Platonist with a
belief in the Idea, and tried to work out his theory in his
verse. Often he worked in Louise's company—in the cool
library most likely, where they could put out their hands
and take their "Phaedo" from the shelves. But as far as report

went, there was no thought of love between them. Friendship with women meant quite as much to her as friendship with men. She had the most romantic relations with Clémence de Bourges and at one time she was inseparable from her.

This lady, half poet, half pedant, whose gift for the spinet made the Dauphin and Cathérine de Médicis wish to know her, was one of the many "pearls of Lyons," and almost on a level with her friend. She repaid the love of Louise and dedicated her verses to her; and Louise, for her part, wrote her the already-quoted letter exhorting women to assert their minds and become the companions of men. But Clémence lost her heart to a lover who returned her feeling. Louise was her confidante and Clémence, in despair at her own rhymes, implored her comrade to make some love-poems for her. Louise complied and determined that her poetry should take the young man by storm. She succeeded so well that he fell in love, first with the verses and after-wards with herself. Clémence was deserted, and it is small wonder that she broke with her friend and never spoke to her again. She ended by dying of a broken heart, on the death of the man she was engaged to. He was killed in the war of 1562; de Peyrat was his name, but whether he was the same as the hero of the quarrel has not been ascertained.

The Capitaine Loyse had affairs with other men, generally poets, but nothing had hitherto gone deep and the real drama of her life was to come. In 1550, there passed through the town of Lyons a certain grand gentleman, the Seigneur de Saint-Marcel, who was on his way to Rome on an embassy to the Pope. In his train he had a young

secretary, anxious for travel and adventure, Olivier de
Magny, himself a poet and a friend of the great Ronsard,
the new star just rising over France. During his stay he
was, as a matter of course, presented to Louise. He was
"vif, ardent, bien pris de sa petite taille," and four or five
years younger than she was. Louise, then twenty-five, was
tall, with full lips, golden hair, and black eyebrows. In her
eyes he seemed illumined by all the glory of Parnassus.
The name of Ronsard had a powerful attraction for her
and lent a glamour to the man who was his friend. His
own gifts did more. They fell in love at first sight—driven,
as he tells her, by destiny—and he lost no time in pouring
out sonnets to her.

> "Car dès lors que fatalement
> J'en approchai premièrement"—

so he begins one of them.

> "Le voyant aimer fatalement
> Pitié je pris de sa triste aventure"—

Such was her answer, hardly truthful, for she seems to
have loved as instinctively as he. In spite of Maurice
Scève and Plato, she had hitherto achieved nothing better
than songs for the lute; but now, under Magny's inspiration, her lyrics acquired a deeper significance and rose from
verse to poetry. Her sonnets to him still vibrate with
emotion and are as simple as his to her—and his "Soupirs"
express the quick experience of his heart. They met in
"the little gardens" of the city, and wrote their poems in
the brief hours of their separation. The husband behaved
as conveniently as ever. He came into the room, says

Magny, dressed in a greasy apron; and when he found him
with his wife, out he went again with the greatest com-
plaisance. This went on for a while; but ambassadors have
to depart and their secretaries must follow them. The lovers
tore themselves asunder. Olivier de Magny started for Rome
and, while he was crossing the Alps, Louise spent her time
in writing Elegies. Though inconsolable, she allowed her
friends to read them. Like others of the poetic race, in
time she let them persuade her to publish, and one of the
great printers of Lyons brought out two volumes in one year.

Gratified vanity and constant ennui helped to cool her
passion; she could not live without immediate excitement and
Olivier's absence began to pall upon her. Louise was nothing
if not literary, and this time her choice fell on a young
lawyer—of course desperately in love with her—who was writing a history of Lyons. But all the while she was conscious
that she was merely using him as a distraction and that her
heart belonged to Olivier. She felt she was degrading herself and resolved to give up the lawyer. She was in process of separating from him when Magny suddenly returned.
He had been consoling himself in much the same way in
Italy, but his real feeling was for her and, impelled
by it, he broke away from Rome to catch one sight of
her face. He was greeted in Lyons by the story of her
faithlessness and found the rumours but too true. Her
renunciation of his rival was of no use. Magny, infuriated,
had but one wish: to avenge his love. His means of fulfilling his aim were not very creditable. He wrote her a
sonnet so insulting that it broke her capricious heart. She
was in sorry plight. The lawyer was as bitter against her

as Magny, and she had not only lost two lovers, but made two enemies. The sonnet did a great deal of mischief. The ladies of Lyons had long been feeling jealous of her social success and always talked of her with scorn as a Plebeian. Now they shunned her, and her salon (for she bravely maintained her literary traditions) was only attended by men. Her easy-going husband was faithful to her, but he did not live long after her parting with Magny. When he died he left her his fortune, and she retired to her country-house at Parcieu, a little way out of the town. Here she remained, and only appeared on rare occasions at Lyons. On one of these, when staying with an old friend, a Florentine merchant, Tommaso Fortini, she was seized with a violent illness. It broke her health and she died at Parcieu, that year or the next—1565 or '66—leaving large sums to the poor. Her death was a test of the love that her town bore her. "Her funeral was a sort of triumph," says a chronicler; "she was carried through the city with her face uncovered, and her head crowned with flowers.... Death could do nothing to disfigure her, and the people of Lyons covered her grave with tears and with blossoms."

"Enfin elle savait tout et même beaucoup plus qu'elle n'eut dû savoir.... Courtisane commode, mais courtisane commode pour les gens d'esprit." Such is the summary of an old critic who lived long enough after her to give an impartial judgment. We cannot be surprised that Calvin condemned her; so did many others who were less rigorous than he. To recognize her powers we have only to turn to her book of poems and listen to its music—to the cries that came from the depths of a heart truly human, however it was misgoverned. Here is one of them :

> "Je vis, je meurs: je me brûle et me noye;
> J'ai chaud extrême en endurant froidure;
> La vie m'est et trop molle et trop dure,
> J'ai grands ennuis entremêlés de joie,
>
> . . . .
>
> Mon bien s'en va et à jamais il dure:
> Tout en un coup je sèche et je verdoye.
> Ainsi Amour inconstammement me mène.
> Et quand je pense avoir plus de douleur
> Sans y penser je me trouve hors de peine."

She says that "le temps met fin aux hautes Pyramides," but that her love, far from waning, grows stronger as it grows older. Sometimes her verse becomes more impassioned :

> "Si de mes bras te tenant acollé,
> Comme du lierre est l'arbre encercelé,
> La Mort venait—de mon aise envieuse—
> Bien je mourrais, plus que vivante heureuse."

Or there is this sonnet :

> "Tout aussitôt que je commence à prendre
> Dans le mol lit le repos désiré,
> Mon triste esprit, hors de moi retiré,
> S'en va vers toi incontinent se rendre.
> Lors m'est avis que dedans mon sein tendre
> Je tiens le bien où j'ai tant aspiré,
> Et pour lequel j'ai si haut soupiré
> Que de sanglots j'ai souvent cuidé fendre. [1]

[1] I have often thought I should burst.

Oh doux sommeil, oh nuit à moi heureuse !
Plaisant repos plein de tranquillité
Continuez toutes les nuits mon songe !
Et si jamais ma pauvre [1] âme
Ne doit avoir de bien en vérité,
Faites au moins qu'elle en ait en mensonge."

She had her playful as well as her intense moods. Her longest work is a poem interpersed by prose, "Le débat de la Folie et de l'Amour," dedicated to Clémence before their quarrel. Folly and Love contend for mastery, in language that is full of delicious affectation and dainty conceits. It gives us much the same pleasure as some trim grove of clipped trees, where artifice is charming for its own sake and makes no pretence to seem natural. The characters of the piece discuss, amongst other themes, the metaphysics of elegance.

"He," says one, "who makes no effort to please anybody, whatever perfections he possesses, gets no more pleasure from them than he who wears a flower inside his sleeve.... But he who wishes to please broods on his aim without ceasing; mirrors and remirrors the creature he loves; pursues the virtues he knows will please her, and dedicates himself to such tastes as are the contraries of himself.... even as he who carries a nosegay in his hand can tell for certain from which flower cometh the perfume which is most pleasant to his senses.... And what shall we say of women whose dress and ornaments are made, if anything is made, to please? Is it possible to adorn a head more excellently

---

[1] "Poure" in the original text.

than women do—and will go on doing to eternity? Is it possible to have the hair better gilded, waved, or curled? Head-gear more becoming than when they are dressed à l'Espagnole.... à la Française... à la Grecque? And with all this splendour, their garments are clean—as clean as the leaves round summer fruit."

The words of Louise Labé leave us with a portrait of herself—the sumptuous woman of the Renaissance, ready for all sides of life—the poet dreaming over her lyre—the scholar intent on her Greek, and yet not too proud or too busy to look in her mirror.

ETIENNE DOLET

AUTHORITIES CONSULTED FOR CHAPTER XV

Life of Etienne Dolet: CHRISTIE

Dictionnaire Historique: BAYLE.

Le Second Enfer etc.: ETIENNE DOLET.

Deux Dialogues de Platon, Philosophe divin et surnaturel, nouvellement traduites en langue française par Etienne Dolet:

LYON, 1544.

CHAPTER XV

(1520—1546)

IF Lyons was a town of poets, it was also a town of printers. Bâle and Geneva had hitherto been the centres of printing and it was not far from either. There were two hundred presses in Lyons and all the most famous printers lived there: Jean de la Tourne, Juste, Gryphius, Nourry, and eventually Dolet. The Rue la Mercière, near the river, was given up to them; it gleamed with the great gilt signs hung out before each house: a griffin for Gryphius, an axe for Dolet, and so on for the rest. Inside, Correctors stooped over their desks and authors came in and out to superintend the publication of their books. Gryphius was the publisher of learned works—he brought out Rabelais' pamphlets, and Rabelais and Dolet were his Readers; Nourry was the man for popular writers, and he printed "Pantagruel." Erasmus, Budé, everyone of note, sent their manuscripts to Lyons, and even the Estiennes' firm in Paris was eclipsed by its younger rivals. This was the world to which Etienne Dolet was to belong. His figure stands out in his generation as boldly as that of Louise Labé. "C'est assez vécu en ténèbres!" he once cried, and that cry was the epitome of his history. He did not flee from the shadows; he fought them, sword in hand, to the end.

Fierce and fastidious, half cynic, half enthusiast, his path in life was bound to be a chequered one. His pugnacious instinct was even stronger than his love of study, and his bitter tongue cost him many friends. Perhaps this loss meant the less to him because his friendships were rather of the mind than the heart; but his turbulence marred his fortunes. The one thing that soothed his troubled spirit was music. "I care nothing," he wrote, "for the pleasures of food and gaming and love .... music, alone of all pleasures, takes me prisoner, holds me fast and dissolves me in ecstasy. To music, in truth, I owe my life itself." Such was Etienne Dolet. Every man of importance has his particular painter. Dolet is a born Rembrandt: pale, struggling, driven by wild energies—full of deep shadows and intense light—a creature who knew nothing of prosperity.

He was born at Orleans in the early years of the sixteenth century, but his real life—his intellectual life—began in his boyhood at Paris. When he was at school there (he was about sixteen) he came across a volume of Cicero and found in him the master of his choice. For the rest of his days Cicero was his Bible and he read him morning and evening. After five years at Paris, he went to the University of Padua. Padua was at that time the centre of classical criticism: the home of a group that might be described as the group of classical aesthetes. Chief of these was Cardinal Bembo, the sumptuous scholar, who had retired to collect books and coins at his famous villa. Under the shadow of Bembo's trees there gathered an Italian Academe, where

Cicero and Plato, life and death—according to the philosophers—were discussed with untiring eloquence. Eminent
among the disputers, when Dolet came to Padua, was the
Latin professor, Simon Villovanus, a broad and beautiful
spirit, enamoured of Cicero. With him Dolet formed a
friendship so romantic that it satisfied even his stormy and
questioning soul, and the early death of Villovanus, in these
opening days of Dolet's manhood, was an enduring grief
overshadowing the rest of his life. It confirmed his natural
inclination and made him retire more and more into the
pleasures of the mind.

As an undergraduate he quickly distinguished himself
and plunged, with an almost savage courage, into the
scholarly disputes that disturbed the town. These corresponded more or less to the differences which had already
appeared in the literature of France—the feud between
Ancients and Moderns—the Classical and the Natural. Later
in the century it re-appeared in England and stirred up
the English stage, where Ben Jonson as a Classic and Shakespeare as a Modern fought out the issue between them.

In Italy the Ciceronians were the counterpart of the
Ancients. Cardinal Bembo and Villovanus, who had a
large and metaphysical mind and a grasp of Cicero's ideas,
represented the best side of them, and Dolet became their
partisan. "Let others choose other masters," he said, "I
approve only of Christ and Tully; Christ and Tully are
enough for me." He and his friends confined themselves
to admiration of Cicero's thought and to fervent imitation
of his style. Unfortunately they were not typical of their
party. The Ciceronians, as a rule, were narrow and pedan-

tically conservative, like the Aristotelian Schoolmen. They
declared that no word should be used, no idea broached
that was not to be found in Cicero. They performed feats
of ingenuity. The Virgin was known as "Virgo Lauretana";
the Trinity as "Dii Majores." Erasmus launched his irony
against them in a Socratic Dialogue which appeared in
1531, and was answered by an indignant treatise from the
pen of the braggart Ciceronian, Julius Cæsar Scaliger.
Dolet also took up the cudgels and gave the public another
imaginary dialogue—between Sir Thomas More and Villovanus.[1] His only reward was the enmity of Scaliger, who
accused him of plagiarising from his pamphlet and heaped
unclassical invective on his head.

Dolet's language to Erasmus was cleverer, but it was
almost as scurrilous. His attitude towards him is unintelligible. There was something in Erasmus' wit that offended
Dolet's grim mind; he called him irreverent and, later, had
no words contemptuous enough for the "Praise of Folly."
No doubt the quarrel about Cicero had something to do
with his dislike. The constant difficulty with Dolet is to
disentangle the personal from the impersonal, and the complications this caused in his lifetime seriously impaired the
value of his judgments. His fortunes were founded by the
Bishop of Limoges. He was a literary Bishop with a hobby
for architecture, for which he found an outlet in his episcopal city. Just then he was bound on a special embassy
to Venice. On his way there he saw Dolet at Padua, discovered his talents, and took him as his secretary for three

[1] This was written when he had left Padua—the quarrel
prolonging itself until after his arrival at Lyons.

years. The young man had ample opportunities for studying men besides books, and he found a staunch friend in his patron. It was by his advice that Dolet, his secretaryship at an end, went to Toulouse and took up the study of the law at the University of the town. The choice was not a wise one and he soon dropped it. Toulouse, the place where St. Dominic founded his Order and still the stronghold of bigotry, was the worst place for him. It forced him into rebellion, and into the brilliant but violent paradox already too natural to him. "There is the same hatred of letters and the same love of stupidity that there always has been," he writes. "Not to be tedious, the fools are as numerous and of the same species as ever." He became reckless, and his gift for epigram gave permanence to his recklessness. His epigrams seem to have had so much reputation that one of his numerous friends begged him to make one on him, that so his name might go down to posterity.

Dolet created a great stir in Toulouse by acting as representative of the Students and making a free-thinking Oration on their behalf. The town authorities looked upon him with suspicion—and with reason. Most of his friends were heretical and so was he, but not in the sense which they usually gave to the word. Latitudinarian though he was, he detested the Lutherans: "that foolish sect," he calls them, "led away by a pernicious passion for notoriety— putting their lives in danger by their ridiculous self-will and unbearable obstinacy." The attitude that he took up was not one to ingratiate him either with Papists or with Protestants, and he quickly found himself out of favour with both parties. His antipathy for the Lutherans sprang

more from a fastidious taste and a scholar's dislike for too
much zeal than from any religious conviction. He admired
Lefèbre and Sainte-Marthe without sharing their doctrines.
A free-lance in all directions, an inveterate foe of superstition, he still considered himself within the pale of the Church;
a religious-minded Pagan he was—he would have called himself a Christian.

Yet he seems to have shown scant signs of holding any
Christian beliefs. "I saw nothing of Christ in his hands
or in his books," wrote a German scholar who had met
him in Lyons, "God knows whether he had anything in
his heart. This, however, I know from his own mouth,
that when he fled into France he brought with him, as a
consolation in the wretchedness of his journey, neither the
Old nor the New Testament, but only the Familiar Epistles
of Cicero." He was a Theist in theory, but it was an intellectual theory—a formula of intellectual pride asserting
the supremacy of mind over matter. His conception of
soul is much the same: "a certain celestial force," as he
calls it, "by which we live and move and are partakers of
reason." Perhaps the strongest article of his creed was his
faith in immortality; but the nature of his faith varied
with his mood. Sometimes he believed in the endurance
of personal consciousness; more often he did not, but
dreamed that the individual would be absorbed in universal
spirit. After the death of his friend Villovanus, he uttered
a cry of despair at the thought that he would not meet
him again; yet when his own time came, he seemed to have
a more supporting hope.

However this may be, he was hardly the man to suit

the authorities of Toulouse. When he had been there more than two years, they lost patience with him and banished him for contempt of their Parlement. Lyons was evidently the home for him, and there he settled in 1534. We have a picture of him at this period, drawn by the pen of Erasmus' Secretary. He was tall and stooping, with fierce eyes and leaden complexion; his hair was dark, his expression harrowed, and his general appearance gave an impression of poverty. He found Bonaventure des Périers at Lyons and began life there by working with him at a Latin Commentary : no mere verbal dictionary, but a classification of words according to ideas—a whole encyclopedia of biography and philosophy. It was printed in the town, Paris having refused to publish it; and was followed by other and more creative works, poetic and scholarly, from his hand. He wrote both in French and Latin, and his name began to be more widely known. But the scholar's peaceful existence did not keep him quiet for long. A short while after the appearance of his Commentary, the law-students of Lyons stirred up a riot which ended in the closing of the Law Schools. The King and the Court happened at that moment to be passing through the city : and Dolet, angry with the civic authorities, appealed to Francis in the matter. This was the occasion of his introduction to Margaret who was with her brother; but as she departed with the Court, Dolet did not then have any prolonged intercourse with her. They most likely corresponded, and it must have been between 1535 and '38 that he stayed with her in Navarre.

It was a breathing time in his history. Margaret was calculated to draw out his better and more ideal side, to modify the exaggerations of his character; and while he was with her, he got into no trouble. She helped him, doubtless, with her purse, as she helped all her struggling guests; and as, soon after his visit to her, he married, she probably went on aiding him. His marriage does not seem to have had much effect on his career; but his love for his little son played a strange part in his fortunes. This is, however, to anticipate events.

Soon after the Court left Lyons, Dolet had the ill luck to kill a painter who had attacked him in a brawl, and he was forced to flee to Paris to get a pardon from Francis. Through the influence of Margaret and the help of his friends, he obtained it; but it is a blot upon his fame that in the childish vainglory which belonged to his nature he afterwards denied the fact of their assistance.

He had by this time attained to a recognised position in literature. While he was in Paris he strayed into the shop of the Estiennes, and taking up the book of a fashionable poetaster, he chanced upon an ode in which he figured as one of the fifty-one great poets of France. Parisian society, and especially the literary circles, hailed him. They gave a dinner in his honour, and he found himself at table with Rabelais, Marot and Budé, discussing Bembo and Erasmus. Dolet seems to have had a special gift for inspiring warm friendships in the first men of his day and for quarrelling with them afterwards.

Rousseau alone could have rivalled him in the number of the ruptures that he had with his acquaintance. It seems as if there must have been a vein of madness in him to account for all his misadventures. With Budé, the hero of scholars, still unknown to him, he began in youth a hero-worshipper's correspondence which ended in an intellectual intimacy— and that was a relation abstract enough to remain tranquil. Nicholas Bourbon, the scholar and the tutor of Jeanne d'Albret, was also one of the adoring friends from whom he separated. Clément Marot was another. In 1538, Dolet became a printer and, not long after, he published the poet's works; but the two great quarrellers of the day had an irreparable breach and Marot wrote verses against him. It was much the same with Rabelais. He and Dolet began with a charming comradeship. Rabelais probably attended him as a doctor when he fell sick of fever, just after arriving at Lyons. Dolet wrote a poem to Rabelais, after his famous dissection of a body before the students of Lyons; and Rabelais sent Dolet from Rome what *he* would certainly have esteemed more highly than any production of his pen— a recipe for " Garum," a celebrated sauce, long lost to the world. In spite of this suave exchange, a feud ensued. In 1542, Rabelais published an edition of " Pantagruel," an expurgated edition to escape the censure of the Sorbonne. From Dolet's press, in the same year, came forth an unauthenticated edition of the work in its original form, according to the unexpurgated editions of '37 and '38, and pretending to appear with the author's permission and corrections. Rabelais was indignant, and well he might be, in an age when the Sorbonne's disapproval might mean death. Even with a Dolet in the case the affair needs some explanation, and it is just possible that Dolet never saw the title-page; for when the book actually appeared, he himself was in prison.

He became a printer, as we said, in 1538 and for the first four years was fairly prudent. But in 1542, his invincible impetuosity broke down his caution and he published no less than thirty heretical books—among them the Treatises of Erasmus, the works of Berquin, and Lefèbre's Commentary on the Bible—not to speak of selling Melancthon's Commentaries and Calvin's "Institutions." This list alone proves that his contempt for the Lutherans did not extend to other Reformers. Erasmus' death, too, had softened him, and he had composed elaborate compliments in his honour. His last publications were his ruin. He was arrested and brought to trial in the Ecclesiastical Court. It was the custom for the Inquisition to act as the Bishop's Assessor, and the Inquisitor-General presided on this occasion. Dolet was condemned, and appealed to the Parlement of Paris. The King's Reader, Duchatel, got the ear of Francis, who was willing to send a pardon, but in vain: the Parlement refused to register it. However, after fifteen months of trials and imprisonments and the burning of the books he had printed, Dolet was liberated and returned to his family at Lyons. His enemies were not contented, and resolved to re-capture him at all costs. They collected some contraband copies of the condemned books, put them in a parcel and wrote his name, as the sender, on the cover. Their stratagem succeeded. He was again condemned and imprisoned, but he was not daunted. He met ruse with ruse. His eloquent tongue—so fortunate and so fatal—won the gaoler to allow him to visit his wife and child in his house by the river. He bribed him by a vivid description of the Muscat wine in his cellar, and one morning, before dawn, they walked to Dolet's home. The inmates contrived to admit him alone, and quickly shut the door upon the other. He lost no time in escaping by a passage to the Saône, took boat and got away in safety. But the longing to see his boy again was too strong for him. After some time he returned to visit him, and was seen, taken and tried, this time in Paris.

His persecutors had a fresh charge against him. Just before his re-capture, he had brought out a new volume and dedicated it to the King of France. "Being at Lyons," he wrote in the dedication, "in the contentment of my spirit, I did not forget to examine my ' treasures ... I chanced to light upon two Dialogues of Plato which I had sometime since translated ... One is not unsuited to my condition, being upon the miseries of human life; and the other is to show you that I have made good progress in the translation of the whole of the works of Plato. So that either in your Kingdom or elsewhere (since without cause I have been driven from France), I promise you that with the help of God, I will give you within a year the whole of Plato, translated into your own language." His "Second Enfer"—an account of his second imprisonment—and a "Defence" of his opinions, appeared with these two Dialogues. They were called "Axiochus," and "Hipparchus," and were supposed to be Plato's until after the days of Dolet. It is the more pathetic that, apocryphal as they were, they should have been the practical cause of his death. In "Axiochus" there occurs the following passage :

"Pour ce qu'il est certain que la mort n'est point aux vivants; et quant aux défunts ils ne sentent plus; donc la

mort les attaque encore moins. Parquoi elle ne peut rien
sur toi, car tu n'es pas encore prêt à décéder; et .quand
tu seras décédé, elle n'y pourra rien aussi, attendu que tu
ne seras plus *rien du tout*." [1]

Dolet had added the words, "rien du tout," to elucidate
the meaning of the original. The literal translation of the
Greek phrase is "For thou wilt not be": a sentence which
"taken by itself seems ... even to be opposed to the doctrine of the immortality of the soul, though this is by no
means the case when taken in opposition with the context." [2]
But Dolet's judges chose to declare that he had changed
the sense of the passage and deliberately turned it into a
proclamation of materialism. The case was left undecided,
and the verdict was not given till two years later, during
which he was kept in close imprisonment.

In his "Commentaries" he had written a prayer which
almost proved a presentiment. "Ye Gods," it ran, "the omnipotent rulers of all things, grant me this one, only this one,
piece of good fortune. The material goods of fortune are
fleeting and vain things which I deem unworthy of your
care; nor do I for the sake of them seek to weary you
by my prayers. But grant this to me: that my reputation,
my safety, my life, may never depend on a judge. Grant
this, I implore you ... with the same ardour with which I
reverence your divine will and contemplate ... your power."
The gods had not answered his petition, but he did not lose
courage. He knew well what his sentence would be. Yet,

---

[1] The italics are not in the original translation.
[2] Life of Etienne Dolet: CHRISTIE.

while he lay in the Conciergerie, he found consolation in
his high and intellectual philosophy.

Si sur la chair les mondains ont pouvoir,
Sur vous, esprit, rien ne peuvent avoir;
L'œil, l'œil au ciel, faites votre devoir
De là entendre.

So he wrote in his prison. He was never tired of in-
voking Margaret with deep affection and admiration; and
though hope had deserted him, he remained unshaken in
his faith that "she protected men of learning as much as
in her lay." But in his case, she was powerless. In 1546,
the First President of the Court of Justice "pronounced
him guilty of blasphemy and sedition," and condemned him
to be hanged and burned.

He was fearless in death as in life. He had long been
tired of the "tenèbres" which obscure the truth; tired of
stupidity and ignorance; tired of peril and pursuit. "I
now come to the subject of death, the extreme boundary
of life, terrible to those who are about to die"—so he had
written under the word "Mors", in his "Commentaries."
The end brought him serenity. He had a proud claim upon
eternity and, when he died, he was able to realize his own
saying: "The power of death is nought against men who are
fenced about with such strong barriers of immortality."

AUTHORITIES CONSULTED FOR CHAPTERS XVI AND XVII

Gargantua et Pantagruel: RABELAIS (édition de Rathéry et Desmarets).

Epîtres de François Rabelais à Monseigneur l'Evêque de Maillezais. Ecrites pendant son voyage en Italie.

Lettres du Cardinal Jean du Bellay contained in l'Entrevue, de François I et Henri VIII, papiers inédits: LE PÈRE HAMY.

Œuvres de Marot, Ronsard, Joachim du Bellay.

Œuvres Choisies de Ronsard: SAINTE-BEUVE.

Œuvres Choisies de Joachim du Bellay: BECQ DE FOUQUIÈRES.

Vie de Rabelais: FLEURY.

Vie de Rabelais: RENÉ MILLET.

Dictionnaire Historique de Bayle.

Dictionnaire de Chauffpié.

Tableau du Seizième Siècle: SAINTE-BEUVE.

Causeries de Lundi: SAINTE-BEUVE.

Histoire de la Littérature Française: RENÉ DOUMIC.

Portrait de Rabelais.
Cabinet des Estampes de la Bibliothèque Nationale ;
d'après un dessin de Gaignères.

F. p. 258.

CHAPTER XVI

(1445—1553)

I

RABELAIS

S'on nous laissait nos jours en paix user,
Du temps présent à plaisir disposer,
Et librement vivre comme il faut vivre,
Palais et cours ne nous faudrait plus suivre. . .

. . . .

Las ! maintenant à nous point ne vivons
Et le bon temps périr pour nous savons,
Et s'envoler sans remède quelconque :
Puisqu' on le sait, que ne vit on bien onques ?

MAROT (A F. RABELAIS).

THE name of Rabelais is the greatest in the roll of
Lyons. He did not come there till the middle of his life,
or publish the first part of his book till he was near forty.
The exact date of his birth is uncertain, but it was probably about 1495. [1] He was thus the exact contemporary
of Francis I and Margaret of Angoulême. He was not

---

[1] The date of Rabelais' birth is much disputed. An old
tradition relegates it to 1483. But there are many reasons that
make this improbable, and the later authorities are agreed in
thinking he was born in the last decade of the century, probably
in 1495.

among her dependants, nor does he appear to have had
intercourse with her. But their intellectual relations were
close ones, and she seems to have been the one woman
whose mind he respected, whose personality he admired.
He dedicated to her the third book of his great work.
There was none of the courtier's hyperbole about him, and
he meant what he said when, by way of dedication, he wrote:

> Esprit abstrait, ravi et extatique,
> Qui fréquentant les cieux, ton origine,
> As délaissé ton hôte et domestique:
> Voudrais tu point faire quelque sortie
> De ton manoir devin, perpetuel,
> Et ci-bas voir une tierce partie
> Des faits joyeux du bon Pantagruel?
> . . . .

It is impossible to approach the figure of Rabelais without
a thrill of awe and excitement: the sense that we are in
the presence of a primeval force: a Titan whose mirth
shook the old world and gave birth to the new. He is
the Michael Angelo of laughter—sinewy, purposeful, Olympian; huge always, chaotic often; one in whom dignity of
outline served instead of grace. His laugh has a nobleness,
even a solemnity of its own; for laughter partakes of the
nature of what is laughed at. "Le rire c'est le propre de
l'homme," he said—it was his great discovery—and at this
mighty trumpet-sound, the cloister walls trembled and fell,
the fresh air of heaven blew in, and monk and schoolman,
hidden vice and religious terror, fled before the daylight.

Rabelais may be said to be the apostle of modern humour;

the humour which means deep insight into the incongruities of life, and a compassionate knowledge of human foibles. He who has it has found the key to "le profond cabinet de nos cœurs," to borrow the words of Pantagruel. It is the humour of a fellow-traveller, who is laughing at his own discomforts by the road when he laughs at those of other people. This kind of fun cannot belong to primitive times; it is not possible till society has grown complicated enough to deal in contrasts—contrasts of something subtler than those of mere sensation. The laughter of Heroes, including the Homeric, though very wholesome to hear, was always about something that would not move a muscle of our sympathies; and the jokes of the first comedies, French and English, would not now amuse the smallest schoolboy. There is plenty of this archaic mirth, besides the newer sort, in Rabelais; he is Jan Steen as well as Michael Angelo; but his antics were for the crowd—his laughing philosophy for all time.

If it is rare for a prophet to be recognized in his own country, it is rarer still that the recognition should come while he is still prophesying. Yet when Rabelais' book appeared, the Court of Francis I immediately hailed it as "The new Gospel." The work itself and its reception are a conscious welcome to the New Ideas. The birth of the Giant, Prince Gargantua, who is born in the open air, in the midst of a jolly festival, and wakes to life parched with thirst and calling loudly for drink, seems like a gorgeous, intended symbol of the Renaissance: a description of the birth of the young world, a world courting the sunshine, thirsty for knowledge, drinking its fill. Gargantua was not tied up in swaddling clothes, but kicked and danced as he liked, intoxicated by his first sensation of movement. How far motion would carry the giant, Rabelais did not foresee; he realized that a new order had begun, but he did not know all that it meant. Omniscience alone could have gauged the force that was let loose.

Whatever the opinion his contemporaries had of him, Rabelais himself had no notion of playing the oracle. "It is not vouchsafed to every man to inhabit Corinth," he said, and he squared his practice with his precept. There was nobody so little self-conscious. He would have laughed at the theory of art for art's sake, and he thought that his chance of fame lay in his medical treatises. A great creator, he was seldom a great artist, unless it was by chance; and he had no idea of selection. He composed his book while he was eating his dinner, probably for no graver reason than that amusement was good for the digestion. Human before all things, he despised any kind of affected superiority, whether of rank or intellect. He prided himself on being a provincial, and Paris meant no more to him than other places. When Pantagruel met a Limousin who talked to him in the French and Latin jargon of the Schoolmen, the Prince thrashed him into honest French again; and when Gargantua wrote to his son at Paris, he bade him frequent men of letters, who, he said, were there *as much as in any other town.*

François Rabelais was born in Touraine, in the steep grey town of Chinon: "Chinon, ville insigne, ville noble, ville antique, voire première du monde"—so he called it in the fulness of his heart. He saw the broad river Vienne as we see it, and the castle cliff rising out of it. He saw the castle itself as we no longer see it : one of the chief feudal palaces of France. Now pink valerian fills every crumbling crevice, and massive ivy throws a mantle over the fragments of the once huge building. The boy, Rabelais, played in the flagged and tortuous streets which climb arduously up to it; the streets through which Joan of Arc, travel-stained and weary, had ridden, near a hundred years before, to her first interview with the King : streets of crooked silver slate houses, leaning here and there and almost meeting across the black shadows of the footway. He may have turned, as we do, when he had toiled to the top of the hill, and paused awhile to look down on the wavy sea of close-packed roofs, cut by the piercing spires of church and convent. And, perhaps, could his ghost return there, he would laugh to see his own modern statue, standing —surrounded by the old world—opposite the river below.

It was in one of these hill-side streets that Rabelais first saw the day-light that he loved. All that we can tell is that his father was probably a vintner; that he possessed a vineyard and a farm, " La Devinière," just out of Chinon and kept a tavern in the town, hard by a pastry-cook's shop. " Plût à la digne vertue de Dieu," wrote his son, " qu'à l'heure présente je fusse .... chez Innocent le Patissier, devant la cave peinte, à Chinon, sus peine de me mettre en pourpoint pour cuire les petits pâtés." The Painted Cellar was most likely his home, and the jolly vision that he conjures up of himself baking little cakes in a white "pourpoint," doubtless explains his succulent lists of pastries and sweetmeats, which tempt our appetites as we read them in his book. He went to school at the neighbouring village of

Seuillé, then at Les Baumettes, where he found playmates in the rich du Bellays and in Geoffroi d'Etissac, afterwards Bishop of Maillezais, all of them destined to be his faithful friends through life. They were better-born than he, but in those robust days, once away from their homes, little boys of fortune and little boys of no fortune learned their declensions together.

When he had left school, he went to the Monastery of Fontenay, in the Vendée, and, in 1511, took up his abode there. The only chance then for a book-loving lad of scant means was to become a monk and use the library of his Order. This was what Rabelais did, and the step decided his destiny. He had not known what a cloister really meant; the grossness and ignorance of his fellow-monks shocked and disgusted him. There was only one of them, Pierre Lamy, in whom he found a fellow-spirit. Together they read all the theological works in the Library shelves—and their Order did not benefit by the reading. Rabelais enlivened the dulness by his pen. Like all enterprising scholars, he began a correspondence and pursued an abstract friendship with the great Budé. Lamy, we may hope, shared in the learned results. As time went on, the two rebels became more daring and mastered the art of smuggling. They got books from the outside. Geoffroi d'Etissac sent them to Rabelais, so did his new friend, "le bon, le docte, le sage, le tout humain, tout débonnaire et équitable André Tiraqueau"—a lawyer, famous in his own day for his brilliant talk and humour— almost as famous in society as Rabelais was soon to become. These presents of mundane literature wiled away the tedium of many monastic hours. But Rabelais was not destined to remain within four walls. The Abbot at last discovered his

books and seized them—Rabelais demanded them back—the
Abbot refused his demand—and Rabelais took French leave
of the Abbot. Still in his monk's dress, which he wore for
the rest of his days, he grasped his scrip and staff and
wandered forth into the open—Nature's pilgrim, bound for
the shrine of Truth. This was in 1524. He had spent
thirteen years in the cloister. Along the highways of France
he pursued his unshackled course. At first he did not go
far afield. Etissac, now a Bishop, lived close by in Poitou,
and he went to stay with him in his palace at Ligugé.
Here he had his first experience of freedom. We seem to
savour his enjoyment of every day as it passed, in a rhymed
letter (or rather its ending), which he wrote thence to a
friend:

> " A Ligugé ce matin de Septembre,
>   Sixième jour, en ma petite chambre,
>   Que de mon lit je me renouvellais,
>   Ton serviteur et amy, Rabelais."

The Bishop would have liked to keep his guest longer,
but Rabelais did not remain. He wanted to quench his
thirst for travel, and "the world was all before him where
to choose." He took the road to Poitiers where he made
a long halt, drinking full draughts of life : the life of roads
and streets, birds and beasts, hostels and taverns. Thence
he wandered all over France—to La Rochelle, to Normandy,
wherever the spirit took him. He stayed at some time
with his other school-friends, the great du Bellays, Guillaume
and his younger brother, Jean, in the family Castle at Langeais. They were keen patrons of letters besides being good

comrades. Guillaume, Sieur de Langeais, gave Rabelais a cottage opposite the Château. He must have dined often at their table and kept the best society; he must have heard free discussion of every theme that interested his busy brain. But his hunger for experience remained still unsatisfied. Living in other men's houses meant a certain amount of restraint. The desire to wander again possessed him; he bade farewell to his hosts and resumed his journey. [1]

The first sensation of liberty over, he began to shape his plans. The Universities—centres of good company as well as of learning—attracted him. His first experiences were not particularly edifying. At the College of Bordeaux, with which he began, "ne trouva grand exercise," either for his mind or his body; and he carried away little more than a jovial memory of the boatmen playing at dice on the shore. At Toulouse "he learned dancing thoroughly and became well-skilled in sword-play with both hands: such as is ever the fashion among the Students of that University." It was wise of him to try nothing more heretical than dancing, in the town of bigots. But like the less prudent Dolet, he found he could not abide in a place which, as he said, burned its thinkers "like salted herrings." He was not anxious for the stake. "I am thirsty enough by nature," he remarked, "without heating myself any more," and he lost no time in departing. A leisurely journey to Bourges was his next move. At Nîmes he saw the Pont du Gard and the

---

[1] There is a story that the du Bellays made him a Curé of a neighbouring village, Sonday, where he first practised medicine and where he remained a long time. But there is no credible evidence to give stability to so improbable a legend.

Amphitheatre, "œuvre plus divin qu' humain." At Angers
"il se trouva fort bien." At Bourges he studied law, to
good purpose, as the poor lawyers found out when "Pantagruel" covered them with ridicule. His next University
was that of Orleans—the object of his good-humoured contempt. Nothing did he learn there, he said, excepting the
game of tennis; and as for the examinations, they were
mere child's play, invented for great lords. He found a
longer resting-place at the University of Paris. He came
just about the time that Ignatius Loyola was leaving it.
Middle-aged though he was, the founder of the Jesuits had,
after his conversion, humbly put himself to college to fit
himself at all points for his great task of proselytising. Rabelais declared himself not too much edified by the scholarship that he found within the academic walls; but he pursued
the study of medicine and definitely adopted a doctor's
profession.

When he left Paris for Montpellier, the fame of his
medical knowledge had preceded him. He arrived there in
1530, after six years of pilgrimage, and became physician
to the Hospital of the city. There is a story that directly
he had entered the town, he gave a public lecture—with a
dissertation on Botany—at which all the Faculty was
present: a lecture so learned and eloquent that he took
his audience by storm and earned the title of "Doctor".
It is more probable that he was only said to deserve it.
At all events, Montpellier thronged to his lectures and he
gave a course upon the Aphorisms of Hippocrates. Perhaps
it is more important that while he was there he made essential progress in his science, and exchanged the unscientific

theories of Galen and his fellows for more modern ideas. They took a more tangible form after he had left Montpellier for Lyons.

In that favoured city he took up his abode in 1532. He made his home in the Grand Hôpital and lectured to the medical students. [1] The enlightenment of his fellow-citizens emboldened him, and he did not let time stand still. He surprised and delighted his pupils by an exploit even more daring than his dissertations at Montpellier: the dissection of a man's corpse, for the first time in France. An action so destructive was supposed to interfere with the Resurrection of the body at the Last Day; and before venturing upon it, it had hitherto been necessary to get the Pope's permission—the only means of avoiding the evil consequences. Rabelais, however, did without a Papal passport, and Lyons, the freethinking, only applauded his courage. Dolet wrote him a sonnet: "On the body of a hanged man" (Rabelais used the body of a criminal), and other local poets were doubtless not wanting in a store of weighty Latin compliments.

Rabelais' lavish good humour added to his popularity. There was a sweet reasonableness, a magnetic quality about the man, which won all sorts and conditions to him. He must have been like morning sunshine in the Hospital wards and at the bedsides of his richer patients. "A sad or surly-faced Physician is bad for an invalid," he wrote; "but one

---

[1] He remained physician of the Hospital for two years, but was then dismissed from his post, because he too often absented himself.

of a glad countenance, open and serene, maketh a sick man
happy.... As for the speech of a Doctor, it should have
but one end: without offence to God, to rejoice the heart
of the sufferer." He said he should like to cure men's souls
as well as their bodies, and he often succeeded in doing
something like it. "I am not well," his friend, Sussanneau,
writes to him from a sick-bed—"drugs do me no good;
I do not know what is the matter with me.... Au
fonds" (he concludes) "je me languis de toi; viens donc
me reconforter avec ta bonne figure et cette langueur sou-
daine disparaîtra."

Meanwhile Rabelais, physician and philosopher, had been
using his odd moments for writing his book. He had already
published a learned edition of Galen and Hippocrates, and
a few of the "Almanachs" then popular: promiscuous col-
lections of grotesque prophecies and fables, eagerly read by
the public. Claude Nourry, the printer, was the man chosen
to bring out his new work—the first part of "Pantagruel."
"Gargantua," which now precedes it, was really written later.
"Pantagruel" appeared in 1533 and made a sensation at once.
Rabelais and Shakspeare were alike in meeting with immediate appreciation, though not with so empyrean a fame as
afterwards awaited them. The Court hailed the "New
Gospel"; Francis read it with avidity and turned a deaf ear
to the Sorbonne. Pantagruelism became a recognized term
for laughing philosophy. More copies were sold in two
months than copies of the Bible in nine years. Rabelais'
fame rose and brought about a change in his fortunes.

In 1534, Jean du Bellay, afterwards a Cardinal and the
Bishop of Paris, came to Lyons, on his way to Rome. He

was bound thither on business connected with Henry VIII's divorce—that capacious State-pie, in which every potentate in Europe had a finger. He knew Rabelais. He wanted a secretary ; Rabelais wanted a change. There was little difficulty in striking the bargain, and, before long, the doctor had changed into the diplomat and Rabelais was on his way to Rome—one in the retinue of the cleverest prelate in France.

II

THE DU BELLAYS AND RABELAIS

The du Bellays were among the remarkable families of the Renaissance. We become almost bewildered by the number of striking figures that crowd every corner of the sixteenth century. It seems as if we stood before a great fresco, thronged with figures, each one new, each one so interesting that we wish to know it separately from the rest. And yet as we look at the many heads in the picture, we almost turn away in despair of accomplishing our wish.

There were three du Bellays, brothers : Guillaume, Jean, and Martin, all men of repute. The most renowned was Guillaume, Sieur de Langeais, "soldier, diplomat, writer. An indifferent courtier, he was the person in Europe best-informed as to the Court intrigues, and the most absent-minded at the 'lever du roi.' Charged with all the most delicate missions.... considered better than an army by the Emperor, never an advocate of unreasoned conquest, he was, in short, the best politician of this reign." Rabelais, whose first visit to him must have been often repeated,

was enthusiastic for his host. At Langeais he learned, so
he said, "le culte des armes héroïqes," and the Lord of
Langeais was his ideal of a gentleman. Rabelais must have
been in the house when its master died, and it was he who
penned the noblest panegyric on him; "Le preux et docte
chevalier," as he calls him, "in whose lifetime France enjoyed such great felicity that all the world envied and respected her. But of a sudden, on his death, the world
began to despise her and has done so this long while. . . .
And after that he had died, his friends, his servants and
his servitors . . . . (among whom I count myself) looked at
one another in silence, all affrighted, without saying a word
with their lips. But each man thought the more in his
heart, knowing full well that France was bereft of an excellent and very needful knight, whom the gods had recalled
to themselves as their right and natural property."

The writings of this great man-of-all-work were chiefly
historical, but here he had a rival. His youngest brother
Martin, otherwise the least significant of the three, was the
historian of the family, and he has left us a chronicle of
his age, quaint, shrewd and lucid. About the second brother,
Jean, the patron of Rabelais, there is more to be said.
"Less universal than Guillaume, but quite as full of perspicacity," he also played a leading part on the diplomatic
stage. He was a person of distinct political aims. His
main object was to counterbalance the power of the Emperor
and, for this end, to ensure the alliance of France and
England, under the ægis of the Pope. He showed infinite
resource in maintaining a hold on Henry VIII and keeping
him in good humour—bestirring himself about the divorce

with an energy that left no stone unturned: "For that he knew full well that the true office of friends sometimes lieth in bearing each the other's anxieties, without looking at them too closely." This rather elastic creed was calculated to ingratiate him with monarchs. He was, in truth, a favourite with Henry and had long been concerned in his domestic affairs. In 1532, a year before the death of Catherine of Aragon, the King had been anxious to bring Anne Boleyn to meet the French Court at Calais. Anne was not yet recognized as his wife and the scheme offered obvious difficulties. Jean du Bellay was sent to England to arrange matters. Diplomacy is a pleasant profession, and enjoyment a dutiful means of pursuing its purposes. Du Bellay sent the Constable Montmorency a buoyant account of his doings pending the conclusion of his business. The letter gives us an idea of his familiar relations with Henry.

"Monseigneur," it runs, "Meseemeth that I should not be acting like a gentleman if I hid from you the good cheer which the King and all the company are making for me; or the intimacy with which he honoureth me. The livelong day I am quite alone with him. We go a-hunting and he telleth me all his private affairs, taking as much pains to give me pleasure in the Chase as if I were a very great personage. Sometimes he placeth us, Madame Anne and myself, each with our bow and arrows, to await the first passing of the deer—a fashion in hunting that you will understand. At other times she and I are left tête-à-tête, to watch the flight of the deer. When the hunt is over and we arrive at one of the King's royal houses, he is

no sooner dismounted than he desireth to show me everything he has on the estate, and everything he meaneth to
do. The Lady Anne hath made me a present of a hunting
suit, a hat, a horn and a hound. This that I write, Monseigneur, is not to try and persuade you that I am so likely
a man as to make all ladies love me; but to let you know
how quickly groweth the friendship of this King and our
King; for all that the Lady Anne doth, she doth it by
commandment of her liege Lord, his Majesty of England."

No junketings, however, caused him to lose sight of the
work he had in hand: "I know as a fact and on good
authority," he wrote, "that the greatest pleasure the King
can give to the King, his brother, and to Madam Anne,
is to write bidding me invite him to bring her with him
to Calais, to be seen and feasted by everyone. But they
must not come without the company of ladies, since good
cheer is ever the better for their presence." This was wily
of him, as he knew the ladies of France had refused to meet
Anne Boleyn. He added a more daring suggestion: the
presence of the French King's sister would, he said, be held
a *sine quâ non*, although he was sworn not to reveal the
source of his knowledge. Margaret solved the problem by
feigning illness; Anne Boleyn by never stirring from the
town of Calais, where she duly arrived. The fêtes—planned
for the fields round the town—thus became impossible; the
Kings met; and Henry and Anne returned home with their
train.

Jean du Bellay only went on working the harder at
cementing the English alliance. He found it no easy task
to make two such slippery monarchs keep their word—the

one political duty, or shall we say moral convenience?—
recognized by the easy-going Envoy. "The first rule of
friendship," he said, "even among great princes, is to keep
faith with honour. Where that is wanting, the holy name
of friendship must not be spoken." "Holy," has a great
many meanings in the diplomatic code. His interpretation
involved renewed efforts to procure Henry's divorce. To
gain his end he travelled in midwinter from Paris to
London, and from London to Rome. He went to Rome
twice between 1533 and '37, and thought that the Pope
would be swayed by him. Clement VII admired his eloquence, but that was all. He was a weak creature and the
Emperor's threats and promises went farther with him.
Charles V won the race, and the Pope lost England for ever.

It was on the earlier of du Bellay's two embassies to
Rome—the occasion of his being made a Cardinal—
that Rabelais first went with him as his secretary. The
nobleman was charmed with the "docte et réjouissante compagnie" of his fellow-traveller: "l'homme toujours prêt," as
he called him. He valued Rabelais' equable humour, his
supple mind and just views. No less did du Bellay suit
Rabelais. Machiavellism implies shrewd powers of observation, and du Bellay was a generous Machiavelli, free from
malice. Their tastes were in agreement. Rabelais, when he
crossed the Alps, said that he had three wishes: to see the
Italian Scholars, to collect plants, and to excavate ancient
busts. In the first and last of these his patron could doubtless furnish him with ample information. It is a pleasant
picture, the Ecclesiastic and the Doctor, side by side on Italian
high-roads, or taking their ease at their inn, talking of life

and science, discussing the last Venus dug up on the Palatine, laughing at life and its follies—perhaps a little at its wisdom.

Rabelais' main business at Rome was neither botany nor excavations, though the Cardinal gave him a vineyard to dig in. His work was, as usual, the observation of men. He could not have been in Rome at a more interesting time, and du Bellay's confidence in him provided him with rare opportunities, both on this and on his second visit, for his patron brought him there again in 1535. He was allowed to be present at the most intimate conferences. He heard the Cardinal of Trent discuss the famous Council which was to bring concord to Christendom. "I was there," he wrote to the Bishop of Maillezais, "when he said to M. le Cardinal du Bellay: 'The Holy Father, the Cardinals, Bishops and prelates of the Church recoil from the Council and will not have it mentioned. But I see the time coming—and close upon us—when the prelates of the Church will be forced to ask for it, and the laymen will refuse to hear them.'"

Rabelais also witnessed the humiliation of Florence and of its sad Duke, Alexander de' Medici. And he saw the Rome which the Emperor had sacked in 1527 making ready nine years later for his triumphal entry as a visitor to the Pope. Two hundred and four buildings were demolished in his honour. "It is piteous," writes Rabelais, "to see the ruins of the houses, churches and palaces which the Pope has had pulled down and destroyed to prepare the way for the Emperor.... and no compensation at all has been offered to the owners." He must have laughed in his sleeve when he beheld Charles prostrating himself in public at the feet of the Pontiff whom he had made into his vassal.

All round him Rabelais found intrigue, time-serving, petty quarrels and false reconciliations—food enough for his stringent irony. Little did the scarlet-hatted plotters know whom they had among them; not, at all events, till they had read their "Pantagruel." The Island of the Papo-manes, the parrot prelates in cages, the sacred and wordy Decretals which meant nothing, must have given them surprises not altogether agreeable. For the Pope himself, whether Clement VII or Paul III, Rabelais maintained a respect half cautious, half decorous. He took the trouble to get Absolution from Paul III[1] for his old offence of leaving the monastery without permission. It is difficult to believe that the sin weighed upon his conscience. Very likely the Cardinal urged the step as good for his career. However this may be, Rabelais' compliance does not show his character in its noblest aspect. He was not born to be either a fighter or a martyr. He despised forms and did not despise expediency. Perhaps it was this creed which made him dedicate to the Pope the second Book of his work. The farcical allegory disguising the meaning of his words protected him from dangerous consequences.

Meanwhile he writes the most varied letters from Rome. He gossips about the doings of the Sophi and the Sultan with as much easy familiarity as if he were talking of his next-door neighbour. Or leaving public events, he rambles on to his friend, the Bishop, about garden matters—sowings and seasons—a new-found herb to sweeten Madame

---

[1] Clement VII died, and Paul III succeeded him, between Rabelais' first and second visits to Rome.

d'Etissac's bedroom—or seeds for salads. Pimpernel, which
he looks for everywhere, is not to be had, but he sends
every other sort: even some of that which the Holy Father
has sown in his secret garden of Belvedere.

He describes the Venetian Ambassadors as "four good old
men, all grey-headed," and dwells on the magnificence of
the Cardinal of Trent's suite: robed in red, and bearing on
their right shoulders an embroidered wheat-sheaf, closely-
bound, with "Unitas" written round it. Rome is expensive.
He writes Monseigneur d'Etissac the most light-hearted of
begging letters. His pocket-money has vanished—"and yet,"
says he, "I have spent nothing on naughtiness, or even on
tit-bits for my palate.... But all my coins go on these
scrawls of letters; and on hiring my furniture and getting
decent clothes, even though I try to manage as thriftily as
I can."

On his second visit he sends a book of prophecies, picked
up in Rome, to the Bishop. The place, he says, is abandoned
to such follies. He has not the slightest faith in them,
"but," he adds, "I have never before seen Rome so much
given up to vanities and divinations. The cause, I think,
must be: 'mobile mutatur semper, cum Principe vulgus.'"

Had Rabelais but written more letters, we might have
had his portrait of the people whom he met. It is interesting to think of the men he may have talked with. He
must have seen, if not spoken to, Galileo and Giordano
Bruno; and perhaps Michael Angelo also, who was living
between Rome and Florence.

Rabelais made a third stay in Rome, when Jean du Bellay retired there after the death of King Francis. He was

there when the Dauphin was born, and helped at the Fête given by the French Cardinals in honour of the event. The triumph of the evening was of his design : a firework panorama of Rome, crowned by the Pope on the top of the Vatican— an olive-branch in one hand, a thunderbolt in the other.

But that was towards the end of his life. The interval was full of experience. Much happened, much also was supposed to happen, to him. A whole Apocrypha has gathered round his name. It is to the time which followed his second stay in Rome that the famous legend of Rabelais' "Quart d'heure" belongs. Improbable though it is, it is worth the telling. There is no smoke without fire, and traditions prove character when they do not prove fact. Rabelais, so runs the story, left Rome in 1537, and arrived, travel-stained and penniless, at the gate of Lyons. He was anxious to reach Paris, but had not the means to do so. The ancestor of Scapin, of Figaro, was not to be daunted. He got some motley rags, put them in a small trunk and made for an inn in the town. His looks were those of a tramp, but his manner was such that mine Host believed in his promises of payment and gave him the "very private room" he asked for. He also demanded bread and wine and a little boy who could read and write. While he was waiting he took some cinders, sealed them up in several packets and, when the child came, bade him write as he dictated. On one was inscribed "Poison for the King of France," on another "Poison for the Queen," and so on through all the royal family. This done, he dismissed his scribe, bidding him on no account reveal what he had been doing. The boy went straight home and told his mother,

who dutifully hurried to the Mayor. The Mayor arrived
at the inn and verified the report. Rabelais' appearance,
his luggage, his answers to the Mayor's questions, confirmed
his worst suspicions. The Poisoner only said he must get
to Paris: he had things of the highest importance to tell
the King. No time was lost; a good horse was brought;
he was mounted upon it and, under a stout guard, was
taken to the capital. He entered Paris as he intended,
without spending a farthing. Once in the presence of the
King, Francis recognized him and asked him in some surprise why he arrived in such a plight. Rabelais' answer—
his straits—his strategy—more than satisfied his sovereign;
and the jolly King and the jolly philosopher closed the
episode with laughter. The whole tale is so improbable
that it needs little comment. It is inconceivable that the
Cardinal should not have given his secretary money to return with; still more inconceivable that the well-known
physician should not have been recognized at Lyons. But
the exploit was in character and, as likely as not, Rabelais
invented it to amuse his cronies at dinner.

At all events he went that year to Paris, and we hear
of his being present at the dinner that was given in Dolet's
honour. Thence he returned for two more years to Montpellier, to delight the town with fresh lectures and take
his final medical degree. Soon after, his faithful friend,
the Cardinal, made him Secular Canon of St. Maur, where
du Bellay himself had a palace. Here Rabelais lived, off
and on—working at his Third Book, till 1545, when it
appeared. After that, he led a strange vagabond existence
about which we know few details. He lectured at Angers,

he bought a property at Chinon. When his faithful admirer, Francis, died, in 1547, and the new reign opened with religious persecution, the author of "Pantagruel" was obliged to flee to Metz. He earned his living as a doctor there, but was so poor that he had to appeal to the Cardinal du Bellay for money. It was from Metz that he went for the third time to Rome. Later on, he was allowed to return to France; was, indeed, discharged from the ranks of the heretics and made into a parish-priest. In 1550, the Cardinal du Bellay presented him with the living of Meudon.

His capacity for compromise came again into play. Heroics and rashness offended his good sense. Ease he must have for the pursuit of knowledge, and he held that the end justified the means. The friends at his back went for much, but his caution was his best friend at court.

There are a good many uncanonical stories about his pious fulfilment of his parish duties. Thrashing the children was one of them; teaching them to read was another. He gave lessons in plain-song to the young clerks. He received visits from prelates who came long distances for his counsel. They asked his advice about very odd matters, and it is hard to discover whether they consulted him as a clergyman or a Pantagruelist. The Bishop of Narbonne, so says legend, came from afar to Meudon, on purpose to get his opinion about the legitimacy of an infant, born in his diocese. It is like one of the knotty points Rabelais invented for his Pedants in "Gargantua", and is probably quite as fabulous. The truth is that his priestly avocations did not take up too much of his time. Nature had made him a better traveller than a Curé, and he went on rather frequent trips during the period of his ministry.   For all that, he seems as usual to have gained the love of the country-side.   "Allons à Meudon," runs a saying of a hundred years later, "nous y verrons le Château, la Terrasse, les Grottes et M. le Curé: homme du monde le plus revenant en figure, de la plus belle humeur, qui reçoit le mieux ses amis et tous les honnêtes gens, et du meilleur en-tretien."

The Castle of Meudon belonged to the Catholic Guises. During the time of Rabelais' ministry, their protégé Ronsard lodged in one of its towers, known as the Tour de Ronsard. There Joachim du Bellay sometimes joined him, and the two poets met the Curé.   It is strange that the men who transformed French poetry should have lived side by side with the man who transformed French prose.   Stranger still, that writers who were making for the same end—the suppression of pedantry—the creation of a real French lit-erature—should have felt such antipathy for one another. For Ronsard's dislike to Rabelais was hardly to be equalled, even by du Bellay's.   Aesthetes and Realists are not made to get on with one another.   The fastidious and patrician art which chiselled verse to the minutest perfection did not suit Rabelais' exuberant genius.   Both poets wrote epitaphs upon him which do not redound to their credit.   Ronsard's is too cruel to be remembered: du Bellay's is bad enough. "In this tomb, lies a tomb"—it ran—"I am Pamphagus, annihilated here by the crushing mass of my body . . . . I exercised the art of healing; but the art of rousing laughter was my only care.   Therefore, traveller, shed no tears, but laugh, if you wish to give pleasure to my shade."

Jealousy had something to say to this, but natural hostility had more.

Their intercourse, however, was not long. In 1552, Rabelais resigned his living. Soon after, in the same year, his Fourth Book came out. The two incidents were presumably connected. His writings, loved by the Court and the public, were not loved by any theologian. Though caution had enabled him to escape persecution, Catholic and Protestant were equally strong against him. Calvin condemned him from the pulpit; and the Huguenot, Estienne, no less than the Sorbonne, would have liked Rabelais to be burned. He probably heard from high places that he must choose between his parsonage and his book, and true to his flag, he chose his book. He had, it is true, applied to the new King for permission to print his work. The permission was retarded, and only arrived after his resignation. It was the last permission that he asked for. His last and Fifth Book, parts of which are generally accepted as spurious, did not appear till 1562, nine years after his death.

Rabelais did not dare the stake—he courted no pain or peril. But his final action had been one of moral courage. It was a fitting close to life. He turned his steps towards Paris and there, in the Rue Des Jardins, the end came. He died in 1553,[1] at fifty-eight years of age—twelve years before the birth of Shakspeare, five years after the birth of Cervantes, nineteen after that of Montaigne. "Je vais cherchez le grand Peut-être": these, says tradition, were his

[1] The exact date of his death is uncertain; it may have been a few months earlier, in 1552. But various facts point to 1553 as the most probable date.

parting words to the world. They may well have been so :
he believed in the immortality, in the endless vitality of
the soul. His warrant for belief was in his own breast. It
is fitting to imagine that great spirit, full of insatiable
curiosity, ranging, free from its bonds, through vast new
worlds: enjoying the fulfilment of its possibilities as gaily
and courageously as it had done upon the earth. He had
loved the body, but never to the detriment of the soul—
"l'âme intellective", as he himself named it. "L'âme intellective" gave him his reward.

While he was alive, the pageant of his century absorbed
him. Nothing of experience came amiss : it was his natural
element. We may not make assertions about the unknown ;
and yet there is one thing we feel sure of—wherever his
spirit may now be, it is taking an immense interest in life.

CHAPTER XVII

(1533—1552)

I

GARGANTUA AND PANTAGRUEL

THERE are many aspects under which we can regard the New Gospel of the Renaissance—Rabelais' great book—full of "the caprices of his strength," full of "huge fantasies of the debonnair giants, whom he served in all humility." He wrote at a time when men and women still delighted in fairy-tales; and he used them with childish enjoyment, as a means of conveying realities. His fiction pleased him almost as much as his irony. His first book tells the experiences of the Giant Gargantua, son of the Giant Grandgousier; the other four recount the education and adventures of Gargantua's son, Prince Pantagruel—also a giant—who, in his manhood, sets forth in his ship to seek "the Temple of the divine Bacbuc"—the well-head of the Fountain of magic wine—the distant shrine of knowledge. Gargantua is less primitive than Grandgousier. Pantagruel is more intellectual than Gargantua; his outlook is larger, his aims are more spiritual. Grandgousier was said to be the likeness of Louis XII. Gargantua and Pantagruel together are supposed to give a picture of Francis. The portraits are rather indefinite, but the whole book is full of undercurrents and fables. Sometimes Rabelais is conscious of his allegory, sometimes he is not. Often, like all great creators, he writes truths the full significance of which he does not know. Truth has an organic power of growth which time alone develops; and every seer of Truth lets loose a force which has a life apart from him: which acquires new meanings with new centuries.

In approaching such a mass,—an almost inchoate mass— of literature as these five " Books " represent, it is well to decide at the outset what we are going to seek there, or at least what we are going to discard. There is, to begin with, the expert's point of view. Learned disputes have raged over the fifth Book, the greater part of which is evidently not by Rabelais. It is written by an author of Protestant convictions, and Rabelais had no more taste for definite Protestantism than he had for hierarchical Catholic- ism. The satire is cruder, the style heavier, and it is only in the last chapters which describe the Temple of Bacbuc, that we again recognize the master-hand. He had evidently left Part V unfinished at his death, excepting for the last few chapters—the climax of the whole—which he had written with all the force and all the fancy of his genius. The rest he had probably sketched out ; and some admiring disciple, in possession of the fragments, filled in the outlines and, twelve years after he died, published the result.

But the province of the expert is a world in itself, which it is not our task to enter.

There is also the historical aspect of the work. It is both easy and repaying to regard it as the mirror of the times, the epitome of Rabelais' existence. It is full of colour and movement; it will yield us every scene of that rich and stirring generation.

"As one who dreams waking, he saw before him the motley pictures of his life. First the narrow horizon of the valley where he was born; its 'prentices' gossip—its peasant's brawls. Next his profound reading in the Cloister, with its one little window open on the outer world.... Then the lawyers of Poitiers and the easy-going days of a vagabond-student.... Or the country gentleman thrashing the police; or the old towns on the Loire, in all their picturesque disorder.... At last the studious peace of Montpellier and the comparative security of a science which the Church allowed." [1] All this and a great deal more besides, till the number of impressions grows bewildering.

But vivid though they are, and amply repaying, there are still better things to be found in the overflowing pages. Rabelais the man, Rabelais the thinker, stands revealed to us, erect, there. As we turn the leaves, we get to know his dealings both with men and with ideas. His attitude towards Nature, towards man, towards God, becomes clear to us. And it is to discover his thoughts as far as we are able, that we now approach his writings.

"Every genius," says a French writer, "has one face turned towards time and another towards eternity." "Rabelais," he adds, "in his own day was first and foremost a physician." It told in his dealings with people. He had the doctor's merciful view of poor broken humanity. He knew that bodily misery had a great deal to do with sin. He had the most modern notions about nerves and tempera-

[1] Vie de Rabelais: René Millet.

ment. He believed in sympathies and antipathies. Ill-health, he said, was "une farce à trois personnages: le malade, le médecin, la maladie." He saw that the mind reacted on the body and the body on the mind. A doctor must not only be gay of speech; he must be smart and beautifully dressed. Fasting he condemns, "since it is a hard matter to keep the spirit kind and serene when the body suffereth from inanition." Too much food is bad, "for to him that surfeiteth it is hard to conceive things spiritual." Such sayings may not seem of great weight, but they sound the humane note of compassion, and that was the note of Rabelais.

His humour, however caustic, was full of this quality. Much of this humour is, unfortunately, outside the pale of discussion. Rabelais' chaotic coarseness cannot be denied. It is inconceivable that so noble a mind could so debase itself: that the philosopher, the star-lover, should, in a moment, turn into a pot-house boor. There is no explanation, saving that his prodigal vitality carried him he knew not whither. But his indecence never injured his kindness. His humour was always that of a man who loved his fellowmen. He did not know what the word "cynicism" meant. His formless grossness was at least less harmful than the cruel grossness of Dean Swift, whose laugh was not "le propre de l'homme." The dregs of the wine might be sickening, but the vintage was good.

Rabelais' Muscadel came fresh and bubbling from the spring: "la fontaine de mes esprits animaux," as he called it. Panurge, the prince of rascals, is the mouthpiece of much of his humour: Panurge, the Falstaff of France, whom Pantagruel picks up in rags and makes into his boon-

companion. If much that Panurge uttered does not bear
quotation, Rabelais has put into his lips many of his wisest
and merriest sayings. He was a thief, a coward and a
braggart; he could also babble o' green fields. And, like
Sir John, he was at no time without the human touch—
the love of good fellowship. Rabelais' mirth is never directed
at what is really sacred. His irony is content with the
things that are held so, and his laugh succeeds where sermons and legislation are impotent. He runs full tilt against
the abuses in the world. Hypocrite priests, fashionable
doctors, grabbing attorneys, unjust judges in fur-lined coats,
all have to take their share of his satire. "The law's delays,"
"the insolence of office," come in for their turn. The futile
pedantries and puerilities of the law-courts roused him even
more than its shams, and he is always at his best when he is
making game of legal language. Fools he divided into "the
metaphysical, the predestined, the fools elect and the fools
imperial." He believed that folly had done more harm on
the earth than sin and he plied its endless etiquettes with
ridicule. Like all true humourists, he revelled in incongruities; and his Hades, where Cleopatra sells onions, adjusts
most of the world's inequalities. Other pens have been subtler,
none more generous than his. And he is not only compassionate: he asserts the dignity of mankind. He causes
it to emerge fresh and strong from its rags and its dust-
heaps. He knows it was made to be happy. Wherever he
turns, he holds a brief for humanity in the immemorial lawsuit against humbug and corruption.

Rabelais stands out finely as a humourist. Yet, for posterity, there are wider and nobler sides of him. The "face"

which he turns to eternity is one of ever-ranging expression.
His attitude towards Nature gives the key to his whole
character. In one of his fables—the sumptuous fables of
Rabelais—he makes her the mother of Harmony and Beauty,
and "Contre-Nature" of Hatred and Discord, the harsh
children of a deformed parent. He worshipped Nature, and
to learn her secrets was his panacea for the stricken world.
"Give thyself up with all thy soul to the search after
Nature's secrets"—so wrote Gargantua in his famous letter
of advice to his son Pantagruel—"Let there be no sea, no
river, no fountain, the fish of the which thou dost not know;
and make thyself acquainted with all the birds of the air,
the trees, the bushes, the fruits of the forest, every sort of
grass on the earth—every metal hidden in the bowels thereof.... Thou shouldst, in faith, read the books of the scholars,
but, above all, have constant recourse to experience. And
by patient study get thyself a perfect knowledge of that
other world which is man.... What an abyss of knowledge there lieth under my feet!"

Rabelais had the courage to descend into the abyss. Yet
he had measured its depth; he was no cocksure explorer.
He was one of those rare men of science who combine
minute observation with rich imagination. Goethe was another, but he lived in the dawn of a scientific age. What
was remarkable about Rabelais was his *enjoyment* of the
universe. He loved and watched Nature at a time when
men had no eyes for her—when rivers still meant elaborate
river-gods, and groves were the only acknowledged sort of
woodland. In the past, the poet, Charles d'Orléans, had
shown a faithful feeling for the earth and her seasons; but

he was alone of his kind. In Rabelais' own day Ronsard and du Bellay, for a few years his contemporaries, were creating a new world of poetry in which Nature had a place. But it was, with few exceptions, still a classic nature, and Ronsard's delicious forest fountains are usually mere adjuncts of light love.

Rabelais was a born naturalist. His experiments only made him more reverent. He tried them in almost every direction. Botany was his best-loved study: a garden his unfailing resource. He was always practical. Tradition says that he brought melons, and violets of Alexandria from Italy into France. He knew intimately all the insects that are hostile to the various crops. He gave fascinating instructions about the growth of hemp. In his part of the world it was called Pantagruélion—and one wonders whether this was the humble source of the great name of his Prince. "This same Pantagruélion," he says, "should be sown at the coming of the swallows, and taken up when the grasshoppers begin to grow hoarse." Knowledge of herbs and flowers was in his eyes an essential part of education. Ponocrates and his pupil have delightful days "herborisant," and return home at evening time with their hands chock-full of plants.

If they had the eyes of their creator, they could tell every bird by its flight. His shrewd mind had made many modern observations. Song and movement among beasts and birds were, he discovered, often the result of natural appetites. Hunger was a potent magician. "It teacheth the brutes arts of which Nature knows nothing. It maketh poets of ravens and jays, parrots and starlings.... and teacheth them to speak and to sing. . . . Other birds it subjugateth in such manner that even when they mount up in the full liberty of heaven, now fluttering, now flying away, now making love to one another, it causeth them suddenly to descend to the earth. And this same hunger maketh the elephant to dance, the lion and rhinoceros to twirl and to leap, according to its commandment." Perhaps Nature alone can provide a parallel for his own promiscuous prodigality which seemed to pour out good and evil indifferently. Wherever he turned he found fresh food for admiration. "The industry of Nature," he says, "appeareth marvellously in the frolic she seemeth to have held in forming her sea-shells. So rich are they in variety, so countless in colour and design, so fanciful in their shapes and markings, that art can never imitate them."

When he looks at the stars he speaks in a higher strain. Every evening, when the Prince Pantagruel has done his lessons, his tutor takes him to the place in the house which is most open to the sky and shows him the face of the heavens and makes him watch the aspects of the stars. Then, "full of adoration, they pray to God, the Creator, ratifying their faith towards him and glorifying Him for His immense goodness."

The God revealed by Nature was the God whom Rabelais worshipped. The new discovery of natural law filled him with a sort of ecstasy. He hated asceticism. He hated it worse than death — far worse than the sins it was meant to suppress. To him it meant falsehood and immorality. He never tired of waging war against it with all the weapons in his armoury—his deepest thought, his barbed irony, his

irresistible laughter.   None had had better opportunities of
judging it.   His years in the cloister had shown him not
only its gross evils, but the stubborn ignorance that it
fostered.   He pursued it with equal vigour in all its forms
—intellectual as well as moral.   The Schoolmen he detested
as cordially as the monks, and their system was the object
of his mirth.   "Why should you not believe this?" he says
of an incredible fact—"Because, you say, it is absolutely
improbable.   I tell you that just for this reason you ought to
believe it with perfect faith.   For the Sorbonnists say that
Faith is an argument about things of no sort of probability."

Upon the monks he poured his contempt.   At best they
were gluttons and drunkards, like his own Friar Jean
l'Entommeur.   They worked havoc, they made mischief, they
heaped humbug upon the world.

"They mutter," he wrote, "a vast number of psalms and
Aves which they do not understand in the least.   The
which I call a 'moque-Dieu' and not a prayer to the
Almighty. . . .   Every Christian, of any class, in any place
and at any time, can pray to God; and His Spirit prays
and intercedes for men and God receives them into Grace."

As for pontiffs and prelates, they get no better treatment
than their humbler brethren at his hands.   In his picture
of Hades, Pope Julius II is a pieman who charges too
highly for his pies and is soundly thrashed for his fraudu-
lence.   And if we want thorough-going satire, we need only
travel with Pantagruel to the Island of the Papomanes,
where Cardinals are kept in gilt cages, like parrots, and
the mythology of mediæval Papacy is scattered by a blast
of ridicule.

But Rabelais was no mere destroyer; he had something
to build up in the place of what he pulled down. He was
that rare creature—a critic with an ideal. He embodied
his ideal in the Abbey of Thelema—the Utopian Cloister—
which is the fulfilment of all his dreams for the world.

Over its carven portal stood written, "Fais ce que
voudras." Renaissance and Evangel were side by side, for a
second motto was emblazoned there. "Enter here," it ran,
"all ye who in your lives proclaim the Gospel, fearless of
men's hatred. Here shall ye find a refuge and a fortress
against hostile error.... which poisons the world. Enter,
I say, and found a deeper faith." There were many who
responded to the call. Men and women alike retired there
to study in one another's company. They were men and
women fresh from the brush of Titian. Their raiment was
of silver and rose-coloured tissue, and in their golden hair
the ladies wore "papillettes" of gold and precious stones.
Their staircases were of porphyry; they had galleries and
libraries; gardens and courts with fountains. Their guardian angels were the three Graces, with water flowing from
their breasts. All the sculptures, all the beauty, of the
Châteaux of Touraine encompassed them. Rabelais enjoyed
endowing them with the splendour that he loved. With
intellectual splendour also; they read together devoutly—
philosophy and science were their daily bread. None of
their faculties rusted for want of use. They lived fully and
nobly, because, says Rabelais:

"Free people, well-born and gently nurtured, talking together in goodly companies, have a natural instinct, a spur,
which pricketh them on to virtuous deeds and withdraweth

them from vice; and this spur is named Honour. These
same people, when by vile subjection and constraint they
are deformed and enslaved, divert from its true course
the noble affection by the which they are willingly impelled
unto goodness, and use it to remove and circumvent this
yoke of servitude. For we always set forth on forbidden
enterprises and covet that which is denied us."

And as the Thelemites "proved all things," they also
made experiments in marriage. The monks of the happy
Abbey were often claimed by the world's affairs. Each one,
when he left, singled out his lady and took her with him
as his bride. And "the husbands and wives who chose each
other freely at Thelema loved each other at the end of
their lives as dearly as on the first day of their marriage."

Goethe would have delighted in Thelema. His attitude
towards science is not his only point of resemblance to
Pantagruel. Both believed in self-development. But Rabelais' creed, if less lofty, is warmer and more human than
Goethe's. It certainly leaves little room for sacrifice or for
heroism, but he thought that people found ample discipline
in the humble charities of daily life. "Men," he said, "were
born for the aid and succour of men." Nature herself sets
the example. The stars lend us their light; the earth her
sweetness, and they ask for nothing in return. "We establish
sovereign good, not by grasping and taking, but by opening
our hands and scattering bounty. And we deem ourselves
happy, not if we receive much from others, as the sects of
your world prescribe, but if we give largely unto them."

He paid little heed to the rivers of Parpha and he loved
to bathe in Jordan. The one thing that he condemned was

scorn of the obvious—a refusal to walk in the ordinary ways of life. "Nothing," he wrote, "displeaseth me excepting a search after novelty and a contempt for common usage." Family-life, he believed, with its plain duties, offered a field wide enough for most people.

"Depart, poor folk, in the name of God, the Creator," so says Grandgousier to the pilgrims, "and may He be your constant guide. But henceforth take care how ye undertake these idle and useless journeys. Maintain your families; work, each man, at his own business; teach your children; and live as the Apostle, St. Paul, teacheth you. If you do this, God and the Angels will have you in their keeping, and the Saints will be with you."

The consecration of humdrum is, after all, no unnecessary creed. It has not been hackneyed, nor has it been beautified, because it is so needful that men forget to preach it. Rabelais set his feet firmly in the Via Media. There is always the element of caution in such a choice and he was not the man to despise it. "Oh," cries the coward, Panurge, "how small is the number of those whom Jupiter hath so much favoured as to predestine them to cabbage-planting! For they always have one foot on the earth and the other is not far from it. Let who will talk high about happiness and sovereign good. *I* decree that whoever planteth cabbages hath attained to happiness at once."

This is one point of view; but Rabelais had another and a finer. However keenly we demand the absolute, we have to discover that we are mortal. Asceticism seemed to him not only false, but presumptuous. The Middle Way, resignation to matter-of-fact, besides prudence needs humility and a profound patience. "I have this hope in God," he wrote, "that He will hear our prayers, seeing the firm faith in which we proffer them; that He will fulfil our wishes, provided they are lowly. The Mean, say the ancient sages, is golden.... and you will find that the prayers of such as have asked for what is moderate have never gone astray. Wish then for what is moderate. It will surely come to you, and with all the better cheer, if you toil and work while you are waiting. 'All very well,' you will say, 'but God might just as well have given me sixty or eighty thousand as the thirteenth part of a fraction. For He is omnipotent. A million from Him is as little as a farthing.' Ah, but who has taught you, poor people, thus to discourse and to prate of the power and predestination of God? Peace! Humble yourselves before His Holy Face and recognize your imperfections. This is the Truth on which I found my hope."

Rabelais was confident in his creed, and his creed went farther than his definition of it. "Pantagruelism," he says, "consists in a certain quality of mind—gracious and robust—conceived in scorn of accident and fortune. Do ye ask me why, good people? I will give you an unanswerable answer: such is the Will of the all-good, the almighty God, in the which I acquiesce. And I reverence that holiest Word of good tidings, the Gospel, as first it stood written."

The last phrase is suggestive. Rabelais believed in the Gospel. He took no care to hide the nature of that faith, or his views concerning the mystery of Spirit. They stand revealed in his book, bold and clear in the full light of day.

II

THE FAITH OF RABELAIS

Pantagruel's sunny acceptance of common life, his sancti-fication of the Via Media, mean, it may be urged, nothing more than the religion of the Frenchman—on an Olympian scale—the religion of good sense and good humour: the cheerful scepticism, which sees and accepts things just as they are and does not aim too high for success.

Had Rabelais stopped here, he would have remained a philosopher and made no more exalted flight than Montaigne. His deep insight into human nature led him farther and he believed in the permanence of soul. The interdependence of body and soul was one of his dogmas, and Descartes' theory that soul was an essence apart, complete in itself, would never have appealed to him. Thank the good God, he says, when you eat and drink, "for by this sweet bread and wine He cures you of all your perturbations, whether of body or of soul." But, for all his naturalism, he declared the supremacy of spirit. When Gargantua writes to his son, he tells him how he should mourn if the boy were only to resemble him in "the lesser part of me, the body, if the better part, the soul, which makes men bless your name, were to prove degenerate and debased." In the infinite powers of that "better part" he had a strong faith. The soul brings forth good and evil, he said, and they have no existence apart from it. Things are bad, or the contrary, "because they proceed from the heart and the thought of man. The spirit is the workshop where good and ill are created."

Tradition has it that Rabelais died saying, "Je vais chercher le grand Peut-etre." Another story (which was known soon after his death) tells how the Bishop of Evreux possessed a Galen, annotated by Rabelais. By the side of a passage in which the elder doctor denied the immortality of the soul, the younger and greater had written, "Hic vero se Galenus plumbeum ostendit." The Bishop, according to report, made use of the note to undeceive Henri IV, who had always looked upon Rabelais as an atheist. But quite apart from these tales, true or apocryphal, we have, in his great book, his own testimony as to his creed.

"I believe," says Pantagruel, "that all thinking souls (*toutes âmes intellectives*) are beyond the power of Fate's scissors. All are alike immortal; whether they belong to angels, demons, or human beings." And elsewhere he bids them await death, like the good poet, Rominagrobis, "with joyful bearing, frank countenance, and radiant looks," that we may here have a foretaste of "the sweet felicity that the good God hath prepared for His faithful, his chosen servants, in the life beyond—the Life of Immortality." What the nature of a future life might be Rabelais did not try to define; the hair-splittings of theology were the object of his greatest scorn, and he had no wish to belittle infinity by formulæ. When his company of pilgrims, led by Prince Pantagruel, enter the great Temple of Bacbuc, the priestess gives to every man wine from the same cup and the same fountain; but in each one's mouth it tastes differently and becomes another wine. This allegory represents Rabelais' whole attitude towards Truth; to him it was an absolute reality, taking a million forms in a million minds. Yet no one could find such words as he with which to blazon forth the Infinite; they seem the very emblems of Truth.

"Go, my friends," says the priestess, when she has given the wine, "go, in the keeping of that Intellectual Sphere whose centre is everywhere, whose circumference is nowhere, and whom we call God. The Egyptians hail their sovereign Deity as the Abstruse—the Hidden One. And because they invoked Him by this name, entreating Him to reveal Himself to them, He widened their knowledge of Himself and His creatures, guiding them by His bright lantern."

Christianity, expressed in action, seemed to him the clearest ray which the lantern had hitherto vouchsafed. For him Christ was "the Saviour King, in whom all oracles, all prophecies found an end: just as the skulking shadows vanish at the light of the clear sun." And later he embroiders his thought with that strange mixture of noble religion and Renaissance adornment, so often seen in the Church sculpture of his day.

"Pan is dead!" cries a voice only heard by Pantagruel's pilot, as he steers the ship amid the Grecian isles. "All the same," says Pantagruel, "I interpret this to mean that great Saviour of the faithful, who was slain shamefully in Judea through the envy of the Pontiffs, the Doctors, and the Monks. And the interpretation seemeth to me in no wise repellent; for He can well be called Pan according to the Greek tongue, seeing that He is our all. And all that we are, all that we live, all that we have, all that we hope, is Him, in Him, from Him, by Him. He is the good Pan, the great Shepherd, who, as the passionate Corydon attesteth, loveth not only His sheep but His shepherds."

Rabelais was a Modern. He was a great Reconciler. He tried to make peace between faith and science, imagination and reason, the natural and the supernatural. "If," he says, "we would achieve a sure and satisfying knowledge of the divine, two things are necessary—God's guidance and man's company." With us of to-day any reconciliation of the spiritual and the material has been a conscious struggle, a gradual adjustment of facts; but with Rabelais it was a spontaneous expression of views which he never took to be conflicting. Our creeds may be the more experienced; but his are the more vivifying—rich as they are in the splendour and robustness of youth.

His colossal genius sets him apart in his age, but he was not alone in his ideas. Many of them, as we know, were shared by other thinkers—a handful of men scattered over Europe, who formed the Broad Church party of the day. Erasmus, Sir Thomas More and their school, were the best known among them, and much that they wrote would have pleased Prince Pantagruel. Zwinglius, the Swiss Reformer, although a confessed Protestant divided from them in creed, belonged to them by his thought. He loved Socrates and gave him a place between David and St. Paul. "Religion," he wrote, "was not confined within the boundaries of Palestine; for God, the Spirit, did not only create Palestine, but the whole Universe. He feeds the souls of all His chosen, wherever they be—and His choice is hidden from us. Hath He, indeed, called us into His secret counsels?"

Or there was Conrad Mutian, a disciple of Erasmus. "There

is only one God"—he said—"it is the names we give Him
that differ. But let us not name Him; these are mysteries which should be wrapped in silence, like the mysteries
of Eleusis. Scorn inferior gods and hold thy peace." "Religion," he writes elsewhere, "should be the doctrine of pure
humanity." The works of Erasmus supply a harvest of
such sayings. "If," he says in one place, "you would gain
the peace which is the ideal of your religion, you must
speak as little as possible of dogmatic definitions, and on a
great many points allow everybody a free and personal
judgment." Christian myths, he tells us, would hardly be
better than Pagan, if they were not taken allegorically. It
is the business of the sage to liberate the meaning from
the symbol; he must leave the dogma to the mob.

Sir Thomas More was haunted by the same ideas. He
pursues them among his Utopians who "define virtue to be
life ordered according to nature. . . . Their churches be very
gorgeous, not only of fine and curious workmanship, but
also . . . . very wide and large, and able to receive a great
company of people . . . . Religion is not there of one sort
among all men, and yet all the kinds and fashions of it,
though they be sundry and manifold, agree together in the
honour of the Divine Nature, as going divers ways to one
end: therefore nothing is seen or heard in the churches
but that seemeth to agree indifferently with them all. If
there be a distinct kind of sacrifice peculiar to any several
sect, *that* they execute at home in their own houses. . . .
They call on no peculiar name of God, but only Mythra;
in which word they all agree together in one nature of the
divine Majesty whatsoever it be."

These men, in spite of their liberalism, were not conscious innovators. They were deeply attached to the old bottles and did not see that their new wine was likely to burst them. Rabelais, in the prologue to his fourth book, addressed to the Cardinal de Châtillon, says that he would certainly light his own funeral-pyre—" a l'exemple du phénix," —if one word of heresy were found in his pages. He disliked Luther as much as did Erasmus, and Sir Thomas More went to the scaffold in the cause of Papal supremacy.

Rabelais stands apart from his comrades for more reasons than one; and it is not only his mighty genius which carries him past them. The warmth of his beliefs distinguished him from the rest. Erasmus and his intellectual followers were cold towards humanity, except as an idea; they loved learning and refinement, despised fools, and hated ignorance and the mob. Sir Thomas More was, it is true, full of benevolence; but the masses, for him, were still the lower classes, and it was more as a thinker that he benefited them in his distant Utopia than by any active intercourse. Rabelais alone loved them, not as objects of philanthropy, but because he loved his kind, and because good nature and honesty, the virtues he most cared for, were oftenest found among the people. His best fables are about peasants, and cabbage-planters were his heroes. Probably his very faults, his natural coarseness and unbridled jollity, had a good deal to do with his sympathies; but for all that, they were grounded upon a generous love. There was no scorn in Rabelais' large and sunny nature. He did not even despise fools; the worst he did was to laugh at them and put them into particular pigeon-holes. There are, he says, several sorts of fool, "the metaphysical fool, the predestined fool, the fool elect, and the fool imperial." Shakespeare himself could not show a greater amenity."

The thought of Rabelais bore blossom in his own times and in those immediately after him, but it did not bear fruit till a much later day. It is difficult, perhaps impossible, to gauge his work or determine who are his spiritual descendants, and yet it is hard to refrain from casting a glance in that direction. He belonged, as we have said, to the Reconcilers: to those who wished to combine the old with the new, and knowledge with religion. But it is not too much to say that the modern school of science— the lovers of Nature and Reason, the students of their laws—are descended in direct line from Rabelais, though king and dynasty are alike unconscious of one another. Newton and Locke, Darwin and Huxley, Herschel and Pasteur, would all have delighted him. When we come to the unscientific, we do not trace his lineage so clearly. In France, as M. Brunetière has pointed out, Gargantua's naturalism too easily turned into other *isms*—materialism, individualism, and what not, leading men far enough from Rabelais' noble beliefs. Even his philosophy of cabbage-planting and the value of the obvious turned to cynicism in the mouth of Voltaire, who was his fellow in irony as well as in his hatred of shams. Perhaps it needed the heart of the giant, Gargantua, to ennoble the creed of common sense. He and his "esprit Gaulois" grew, as it were, to be part of the French soil and, while they enriched it, became undistinguishable from it.

Far different is it with Rousseau. He and Rabelais—the

first apostles of Nature—may be said to represent the two
great natural schools of thought; those who with Rabelais
look at Nature from the outside; those who with Rousseau
look at her through the medium of their own souls. Rousseau formed a larger number of writers by his direct influence: the Romantic school and its followers—Châteaubriand,
George Sand, De Musset, Victor Hugo—but Rabelais will
probably have more effect on thought in the long run.

So much for France. It is curious that it should be in
England that his most recognisable descendants can be found.
Charles Kingsley, his eager admirer, is one of them: Kingsley
with his "consecration of things secular" and his reverence
for every form of life. Robert Browning is another—he
who loved the light and fought asceticism as the Devil;
he who reverenced the "poor coarse hand" and said that
"All good things are ours, nor soul helps flesh more, now,
than flesh helps soul." Browning's orthodoxy heightens the
resemblance; like Rabelais, he was content to let things
alone and accept the old forms, provided he might fill them
with a new meaning. Among earlier authors there are none
so closely related as these two to the Prince Pantagruel.
Sir Thomas Browne, it is true, also doctor and philosopher,
bears some resemblance to the Renaissance thinker; but the
"Religio Medici" is made for the by-ways of wisdom—for
the intimate firelight of the study—and has little to do
with the great high-roads of thought.

Love—extended to our fellows—is to Rabelais, as to
Browning and Kingsley, the only solution of human ills.
If men would help one another there would be "peace
among mortals, love and delight, good faith, repose and

feasting. No lawsuit, no war, no disputing." And without this large charity, intellect, which he so much valued, seemed to him worthless. "Wisdom," he says, "cannot enter an unkind spirit, and knowledge without conscience is the ruin of the soul." No better words could be found with which to close a chapter on Rabelais: words, like himself, strong, generous, serene.

BOOK IV
THE END OF THE REIGN

AUTHORITIES CONSULTED FOR CHAPTER XVIII.

Lettres de Catherine de Médicis.

Lettres de Diane de Poitiers: edited by GUIFFRY.

Lettres de Marguerite d'Angoulême.

Etudes sur François I: PAULIN PARIS ("Rélations des Ambassadeurs Vénétiens sur les affaires de France," as quoted in this work).

l'Heptaméron: MARGUERITE D'ANGOULÊME.

Récit d'un Bourgeois de Paris.

Mémoires de Benvenuto Cellini.

Works of Brantôme: Vol. VII.

Margaret of Angoulême: MARY ROBINSON.

Livre d'Etat de Marguerite d'Angoulême:

LE COMTE DE LA FERRIÈRE.

Histoire de France (Vol. VIII): MARTIN.

La Renaissance ⎱ MICHELET.
La Réforme ⎰

CHAPTER XVIII

(1540—1546)

THE King of France was no longer young; he had reached the period of middle-age—a period ill-suited to his nature. But he never ceased to make the same splendid impression on all who beheld him. The Venetian Ambassadors at the French Court, contemporaries of Tintoret and Titian, painted vivid portraits with their pens. In one of his despatches Giustiniani gave us Margaret's picture; another man, Cavalli, presents us with that of Francis, when he was about fifty years old. "He is," runs the account, "of a presence so royal, that without knowing him or ever having seen his portrait, there is not one stranger who would not say when he saw him: 'That is the King.' There is in all his movements a gravity and a grandeur which, to my thinking, no prince can hope to emulate. He has a fresh colour.... eats and drinks well, and no one could sleep better. What is more important is that he insists on living gaily, without too many cares. He loves distinction in apparel. His clothes are braided and slashed and sprinkled with precious stones. His waistcoats are of most excellent workmanship and his pleated chemise shows through the opening, in true French fashion. His *body* enjoys the endurance of every sort of fatigue, but he does not like to fatigue his *mind* by more thought than is needful. . . ." Secondary decisions, the narrative continues, he left to his ministers; big issues, such as war and peace, he settled himself—but in no matter would he brook any resistance. He was an excellent talker when the talk demanded wide rather than profound knowledge. . . . "And, to come to another order of ideas, he speaks passing well on the chase and on all bodily exercise; of painting also, and of letters, and of languages, dead or living. Perhaps the world has the right to ask a greater activity of him: an attention better sustained in the enterprises he begins; but it cannot ask for more knowledge or for a finer perspicacity."

His fresh colour was deceptive; his vigour fictitious. He suffered from a painful illness which told upon his temper. Society always revived him for the moment, but depression returned with solitude. He was growing tired of the Duchesse d'Etampes—another way of saying that she was growing old. He was more than tired, he was mistrustful of her. He believed that she was plotting with the Protestants and had sold her faith to Charles V. The suspicion, which probably had grounds, was sadly embittering to their relations. "Souvent femme varie, fol qui s'y fie," he wrote with his diamond ring upon the window-pane at Chambord, one day when he was alone with his sister; and the couplet is thought to allude to Madame d'Etampes. Margaret, his faithful confidante, shared his feelings. The poor Duchess was not so willing to leave him as he was to leave her. The sister, as usual, thought that everything should bow to her brother's will and Madame d'Etampes' obstinacy

irritated her. She wrote of it with temper, in verses that
are better turned to prose. "To still care at forty," they
run, "to feign a malady which age should restrain, and
then to rush to religion in a pet—this is a consummation
more to be dreaded than desired."

Matters were not improved by the state of things at the
Court. There was a new world there. The theatre had
changed its drama; there were fresh combinations and a
shifting of old parts. Two women had appeared on the
stage, each as important as the other. The one was the
Dauphine, Catherine de Médicis, a mere girl when she married; by now a force in the kingdom. She was at her best
in her early days, before her position as Queen gave her
room to develop her vices. She never committed an action,
even a sin, to no purpose. She was excellent company and
the King took to her at once. She became his favourite
companion out hunting (when she rode astride like a man);
and he soon found himself consulting her about public
affairs. Nor did he find any cause to repent of his
confidence.

The second star on the horizon was Diane de Poitiers,
Henri the Dauphin's mistress, and the widow of the Sénéchal de Brézé. The domestic life of those days defies explanation. Its politeness was at all events in advance of
its delicacy. If the King was hand and glove with his son's
wife, he was equally intimate with his son's mistress. It
was he who arranged this liaison with a view to the prince's
education. Diane was a widow of thirty-seven, Henri but
a boy, gloomy, awkward, and inarticulate. His father had
never cared for him. "Je n'aime pas," he said, "les enfants

songeards, sourdauds et endormis." Diane was to form him —make a man of him.

No one has been more misrepresented than she. Of the popular legends about her, hardly one is true: unless it be that of the ice-cold bath which, Diana-like, she took daily to preserve her beautiful complexion. Primaticcio's famous portrait of her as Artemis was a purely fancy affair and he had probably never set eyes upon her. She has enjoyed a reputation for beauty: she was, as the one authentic portrait shows her, a plain woman with a face full of intelligence. She evidently aged early, "for," says de Méze-ray quaintly, "it was a grievous thing to see a young prince adore a faded face, covered with wrinkles, and a head fast turning grey, and eyes which had grown dim and were sometimes red." She must have had something better than beauty to hold the Dauphin as she did; but it was not the charm that history has supposed. The part of the heroine of romance has always been allotted to her; in reality she was a downright practical woman of affairs, with a capacity for large views and a talent for education. If it is not paradoxical to say so, she was full of convention and propriety: an improper propriety, starting from an unsound basis. She had no other love-affair besides this with her pupil. [1] She was

[1] A story has long obtained that Diane de Poitiers was the mistress of Francis as well as of his son. M. Guiffry, in his preface to her letters, has shown how improbable it is. It rests mainly on a tradition. Her father, M. de la Vallière, was implicated in the Constable Bourbon's plot against the King, and consequently arrested. It is said that his daughter pleaded for his life, that Francis demanded her love as the price of a pardon, and that she gave it. La Vallière's sentence was in fact commuted—at the eleventh hour—

Diane de Poitiers, 2ᵉ femme de Louis de Brézé Grand Sénéchal de
Normandie, créée Duchesse de Valentinois par Henri II en 1548

LA·GRANT·SENECHALLE

Diane de Poitiers, la Grande Sénéchale.
Cabinet des Estampes de la Bibliothèque Nationale ;
d'après Jean Clouet.

F. p. 312.

no coquette. She always dressed as a widow—in black and white—and the Dauphin and his Court wore the same colours, out of compliment to her husband. She never indulged in petty vanities. Her letters show her just as she was, hearty, heartless, beneficent. One is written in thanks for some Mayence hams—"les très bien-venus, pour être une viande que j'aime fort." Another begs a "bonne amie˙ to come and be "régaillardée" by her; a third condoles with a friend for the loss of his child, and frankly bids him "not to vex himself as he is sure to have many more." For the death of Lady Jane Grey, whom she had met, she feels some slight regret; " the sweetest and cleverest princess ever seen," she calls her, and this is, perhaps, her nearest approach to sentiment.

She did very well by her charge, the prince, who remained in love with her all his life. What powers there were in him he owed to her. The Dauphine naturally hated her, and bored holes in the ceiling of her room that she might watch her doings with Henri below. But she was far too clever and unprincipled not to see that if she wanted power herself she must keep good friends with her rival. So she made a Mentor of her; and when, ten years after her marriage, she at last had a child, it was Diane who presided at its birth and gave advice about its health and bringing up.

from death to lifelong imprisonment, but there is no valid basis for the rest of the legend. And the love-letters, evidently to the King, which have always been supposed to be hers, are now practically proved by M. Champollion Figeac to have come from Madame de Châteaubriand.

Catherine found means, however, to show her dislike of her councillor. She opposed her in minor ways. The Court had split up into two camps, constantly at war. Diane, the Dauphin and their party, growing in power as the King grew weaker; the Duchesse d'Etampes and her followers, who were generally worsted in the fight. Diane's group, including the two Guises, Duke and Cardinal, represented strict Catholicism; the Duchess, whose convictions formed a ready channel for her jealousy, espoused the cause of the Protestants. Catherine, in her fear of popular revolution, was a bigot at heart, yet she openly made friends with Madame d'Etampes by virtue of their common enmity. The King's sympathies were with Diane. Resolved on salvation, he tried to obtain it in his last years by his persecution of the new faith. The terrible massacre of the Vaudois—a blot that nothing could efface—took place in 1545; and the following year the poor weavers of Meaux suffered for their faith. Francis had much to answer for.

At home he did his best to drown disagreeable memories and to forget advancing years in distraction. He consoled himself with his Petite Bande, a troop of ladies chosen for their wit and beauty, who accompanied him wherever he went. They talked, they hunted, they dined with him; they were dressed in his colours. Catherine led them; the two little princesses, Madeleine and Marguerite, were of them. This is perhaps a sufficient proof that the "Bande" was not so black as it was painted. Even Kings have scruples, and Francis would hardly have allowed his little girls to consort with improper women. But their gaiety was rather artificial, and the whole affair was operatic—a feat of elderly flirtation. Sorrow broke in on his frivolities, and over-shadowed the last seven years of his existence. In 1545, his son, Charles, Duke of Orleans, died of the Plague, and soon after, he lost his daughter, Madeleine, married to the King of Scotland. Francis, who loved his children, was hit very hard.

His public life too had been troublous. There had been eight years of almost continuous fighting, for the war had hardly ceased since 1536, when the Emperor had resumed hostilities. Francis had occupied Savoy and Piedmont; Charles V had ravaged Provence. At last he was compelled to retreat and, in 1538, a truce was patched up at Nice. The next year he visited the French King at Paris. There were pageants; there were feasts and junketings; but they had no effect on Charles. A new war broke out in 1541. Francis, at the end of his tether and with all the world against him, cast about for allies. He degraded France by accepting the help of Soliman the Magnificent, Sultan of Turkey—an alliance which excited indignation in the Em-peror and in England. Soliman, however, helped Francis by diverting the Imperial troops, and in 1544 the French gained a brilliant victory over the Allied forces at Cérisole, in Piedmont. The same year Charles and Henry, who had planned a joint invasion, descended upon France. Charles went to Champagne; Henry lay before Boulogne. But they did not work well together; the scheme was unsuccessful and the Emperor made peace with Francis at Crépy, in the autumn of 1544. The war with England went on smoulder-ing until 1546—the year before Henry's death.

Through all his anxieties the King found his best support

in his sister. He used to send her to church to pray for
his success against the Emperor. "Ma Mignonne," he said,
"allez vous en à l'Eglise, à Complies, et là pour moi faites
prière à Dieu." He summoned her to his bedside when he
was ill, and it was most likely to amuse him that she wrote
her book of Stories, the half-merry, half-poetic "Heptameron." She jotted them down while she was travelling
about the country in her litter, probably on her journeys
to and from her brother. The Sénéchale de Poitou, her
duenna and Brantôme's grandmother, was with her to hold
the silken inkstand steady for her pen, as they jolted along
the roads. We can imagine Francis laughing at the strange
adventures of the Friars, as he lay on his sick couch. When
he was convalescent, he wandered in her company from château
to château and showed her his latest improvements. For
his great resource besides Margaret was still his passion for
building. He was completing Chambord and Fontainebleau;
he was ornamenting his Château of Madrid, built directly
after his captivity; he was still re-constructing the Louvre
(the work was begun in 1528), and turning it from a
prison-fortress into a "logis de plaisance pour soi y loger."

Margaret admired them all because they were his handi-
work. "I should have started sooner," she writes in 1542,
"had it not been for the great wish I felt to see Chambord.
I found it of so great beauty that none but its creator is
worthy to sing its praises." The King was at Paris. She
humbly thanked him for promising to show her Fontainebleau. "To see your buildings without you," she says, "is
to see a lifeless body; and looking at the work without
hearing your intentions concerning it, is like reading in

Hebrew." Three years later she was again at Chambord—
this time with her brother; and to cheer his ailing spirits
they went on together to Fontainebleau. They sauntered
in the stately gardens, they talked of old days. Margaret
wrote poems on their conversations; Francis, no doubt,
responded. It was one of their happiest times together and
almost the last.

On Fontainebleau most of his energies were centered. It
had been a mere hunting-box, "une âpre solitude," and in
past times he used to date his letters from "My Desert of
Fontainebleau." Now he had turned it into a fairy palace,
with gardens cut out of the surrounding forest. It was the
home of his heart and he was bent on making it a masterpiece of magnificence. Francis was the patron of both
schools, French and Italian, but for the moment he was
possessed by Italy. He summoned Italian workmen to Fontainebleau—an Italian was master of the works there. Painters, Venetian and Tuscan, came over at his bidding. Dramas
and poems have been written about them. We know how
Leonardo died in his arms; how Titian worked for him;
how Andrea del Sarto lived at his court for French gold.
Primaticcio, taught by Romanino, and Il Rosso, the pupil
of Michael Angelo, both of them prodigies rather in their
time than ours, decorated Fontainebleau with big frescoes
in the decadent style. Il Rosso had a suite of apartments
there; but he usually painted in the rooms of "Madame
Temp"—his rendering of Madame d'Etampes—or he worked
in Paris where Francis had given him an Hôtel.

But the Italian who enjoyed the most intimate relations
with the King was Benvenuto Cellini; his memoirs, at all

events, lead us to think so. Whatever their exaggerations, it
was true that Francis delighted in him : "a man after his own
heart", he called him. Benvenuto was just the short of showy,
resourceful person to take his fancy; and the ingenious caprices
of the Italian sculptor's art, sometimes delicate, always effective,
appealed to his kingly taste. The first time that he saw his
work—a silver jug and basin—he declared it was finer than
any antique. According to Benvenuto, they were on the most
familiar terms. "'My friend,' (so he writes) 'said the King
to me one day, smiling the while in his beard and slapping me
on the shoulder, 'I don't know which is the greater pleasure :
that of a King who finds an artist to his mind, or that of
an artist who finds a King to understand him.' 'Sire,' I
replied, 'if I am the man you speak of, my happiness is doubtless the greatest that any man can feel.' 'Let us say,' the King
answered laughing, 'that both our pleasures are equal.'" He
gave him a lodging in the Petite Tour de Nesle in Paris, and
constantly visited his studio. Sometimes he came unaccom-
panied—sometimes he brought a whole party. The Dauphine,
the King and Queen of Navarre, all appeared with him one
day to look at the great silver Jupiter—the first of an Olympian series, never completed, which he was making for the
gallery at Fontainebleau. Now and then Margaret came alone,
when she happened to be staying at the Court, and her admiration for him was unbounded.

Benvenuto would have invented quarrels, had he not found
them ready to his hand. But he had no difficulty in falling
out with Madame d'Etampes. She ordered a silver salt-cellar
from him—she kept him waiting in her ante-room—he went
off in a huff and let someone else have it. Then she sent one

of her household to lodge in Bevenuto's Tour de Nesle. He
turned the intruder out and was only saved from the consequences by the intercession of Margaret and the Dauphin.
Not content to rest there, he repeated the offence with another
of the Duchess' protégés. This time she complained more
loudly. "Sire," she said to Francis, "I verily believe that this
lunatic will sack the whole of your Paris." "Eh! Madame!"
replied her Sovereign, "ought he not by rights to get the
best of these scoundrels who come and disturb him in the
excellent work he is doing for me?" Madame had gained
nothing by her anger; her reign was indeed at an end. She
took up the cause of Primaticcio, and Diane adopted Benvenuto. The Duchess meditated vengeance. There was to be
a show at Fontainebleau. The long gold and brown gallery,
its gilt wood panels and golden ceiling, were completed. Primaticcio was to display some antiquities he had brought from
Italy : Benvenuto his masterpiece—the silver Jupiter. He
never doubted its surpassing any ancient statue, nor, to do
him justice, did any of his friends or his enemies. It is
almost a comfort to find that bad taste is not confined to
modern days, that it even pervaded a century famed for
the beauty it produced. Madame d'Etampes was so sure of
Cellini's superiority that she tried to persuade the King not
to come. When this failed, she arranged the exhibition for
the evening, when the Jupiter would not be well seen.
She had met with her match. The dexterous Benvenuto
fixed a torch in the hand of his statue, and when it was
lighted, it showed his Jove to perfection. The King was
enchanted—the antiques were nowhere—the Duchess and
Primaticcio were discomfited.

The only hitch in Cellini's intercourse with Francis was due to money. The King had offered him too mean a salary and had ignominiously to yield to the sculptor's demand for more.

The fact was that Francis was growing stingy—another sign of advancing years. Curiously enough, lavish though he was in personal display, he had always been close-handed about giving presents, excepting to the ladies of his Court. On them he spent a fortune—they counted among his private vanities. So did his Fool, Triboulet, on whom he showered suits of motley, Pierrots' caps, and the like. But as for other people, entries of gifts are of rare occurrence in his ledger. One such there is which moves us: the entry of "some red dolls, a cradle, a toy tournament, a tiny ivory box, and a doll's kitchen in silver"— all for a child of unknown name. To charm his heart thus she must often have sat upon his jewelled knee and prattled in his royal ear. It is the most winning picture that we have of him. There is another mention—generous enough in sound—of a present to Bayard: a white satin garment lined with marten; but the glamour rather wanes when we find that it was made from the remnants of an outworn suit of his own. Parsimony never decreases. His building grew more extensive, his charities less so. But it must in justice be said that Cellini was the only artist who complained of him. He probably exaggerated his grievance to make a good story of it—whether in France or in Italy, whither he finally returned.

There were shows of wit as well as art in the long gallery at Fontainebleau. Every man of note was entertained there:

weighty poets, Greek scholars, Hebrew pundits—the whole
Collége de France, including Postel on his return from the
Holy Land. It is a fantastic picture, that of the King and
the traveller: Postel, bronzed by the sun, telling his tale
with dignity; Francis, with that lively curiosity, that naïf
belief in all that he heard, which belonged to the listeners
of his day; a map stretched out between them, one of those
vague old maps, mixtures of fact and fancy, which still hang
for our confusion in the desolate corridors of palaces. To
see the King thus is to see him at his best. The worthiest
moments of his later days were spent within the frescoed
walls of Fontainebleau.

AUTHORITIES CONSULTED FOR CHAPTER XIX

L'Architecture: PHILIBERT DE L'ORME.
Vie de Philibert de l'Orme: VACHON.
The French Renaissance: MRS. PATTISON.

CHAPTER XIX

(1540—1550)

THE FRENCH ARTISTS

IN spite of his love for Italy, Francis was true to French art. At Blois, at Chambord, at Azay, he employed Frenchmen. And the art of France in his reign had made an immense stride. It had assimilated foreign influence—had come to itself. It was conscious of its forms and its purposes. The old artist, Michel Colombe, brought up in half Flemish traditions, open to suggestions from Italy, fusing the two elements in a new mould, had stood at the parting of the ways. Philibert de l'Orme and Pierre Lescot completed his task and crystallized his tendencies. Their work was colder and less poetic, for crystallizing is a cooling process; but the result was a national art, independent and self-possessed. The name of Philibert de l'Orme is inseparable from the Tuileries, built in the next reign but one; that of Pierre Lescot is identified with the Louvre, begun under the ægis of Francis. De l'Orme, the aristocrat, full of a polished elegance, seems the counterpart of Ronsard; Lescot, refined and subtle, the pendant of du Bellay.

Philibert de l'Orme was born of noble parents, in 1518. His genius, always constructive, showed itself from his earliest years. At twelve or thirteen he was sent to Rome; at fifteen he already had two hundred workmen under him. In his "Architecture" he describes how one day he was measuring and excavating, with all the ardour of youth, near the Arch of Santa Maria Novella. A Roman Bishop came by with a friend; the two men stopped to question the boy and were so struck by him that they invited him to the palace where they lodged. It was the beginning of his success. Cardinals took him up; Paul III made much of him and commissioned him to build in Calabria. In 1536, Jean du Bellay persuaded him to return to France and enter his service at Lyons. The Cardinal was the focussing point of very divers rays. Probably de l'Orme knew Rabelais besides the poets of the Pleïade. He left little in Lyons except the unfinished church of St. Nizier. Later he went to Paris, and it was not long before he entered the King's service. In 1545, he was made Architect of the Fortifications—an honourable post, more military than artistic. Like contemporary poets, de l'Orme over-valued conceits; he revelled in ingenuity. He tells us with pride how he routed the besiegers of Brest by painting wooden cannons which they took for real ones; and by posting men without pikes to look like serried rows. Henri II made him Court Architect and Superintendent of the Works at Fontainebleau. It was not till then—until Catherine de Médicis adopted him—that his real career began. It reached its climax when she gave him the commission to build the Tuileries, but that was only in 1564. This carries us far beyond our period, and it is not for us to write his record—more of it, at least, than affects the reign of Francis.

From first to last de l'Orme showed the same qualities.

He belonged to the intellectual school; perhaps he was the first architect who did so. He liked to make form express definite thoughts: thoughts that were elaborate, and sometimes artificial. He chose the Ionic style for Catherine's palace, because the Ancients had used it for the temples of their goddesses. It was, he said, "invented to suit the proportions of ladies"—an elegant compliment in masonry. But he was no mere maker of compliments. His real value lay in the fact that he was typically French. France, from his day to that of Racine, and beyond it, has demanded the confining limits of the classical; has asked for a classical vessel to hold her native ideas. Philibert, engineer, writer, draughtsman, architect, was, above all things, the artist of his nation— lucid, conscientious, a firm opponent of the Italian camp.

"The French," he said, "are so constituted that they think nothing good that doth not come from a foreign land and cost a high price. There you have the French temperament .... mobile-minded and mercurial .... For, in sooth, the architect who hath true knowledge of his art .... can by his good wits and godlike understanding discover an infinity of noble conceptions, in whatever kingdom he may be. And the best inspiration cometh from the things that are natural to the country where they live: by imitating and interpreting the nature which God hath created: whether His trees, His birds, or His beasts .... and thereto must they add the knowledge of the properties and differences of all things. I will show you the French column that I have designed .... the which can be carved and enriched as I have told you—by the reproduction of all things natural to French soil and to the inclination of Frenchmen."

Rabelais and de l'Orme would have been happy walking in the fields together. To him that hath, more shall be given; creation is for the creator—this is the burden of Philibert's teaching. He has left us a delicious woodcut of "Le bon et le mauvais Architecte." The bad one has nothing but a mouth for babbling, and the cap and cloak of a philosopher, "pour contrefaire un grand docteur et faire bonne mine." The good architect stands, "un homme sage en son jardin," in front of the Temple of Prayer. Before him lie the skulls of some oxen, "the which signify the coarse and heavy minds that impede him." His secrets he shows to all comers, and he does not hide his "beautiful treasure of virtue, his cornucopias of sweet fruit.... his brooks and fountains of knowledge." He has wings on his feet for diligence; four hands "to handle many things;" four ears, "since he heareth more than he speaketh." "Three eyes hath he: one to adore the holy divinity of God, to contemplate the beauty of His works and to consider the Past. The second to observe and measure the Present—to order and to direct whatsoever the moment offers. The third to foresee the future, that so he may guard against the assaults of fortune and the great miseries of this miserable life." As Philibert continues, his own feet get wings and he mounts to higher regions. His conclusions are strangely modern. Self-knowledge, he says, is the true secret of art: his words seem the conclusion of the whole matter.

"Let the architect," he writes, "learn to know himself and find out his gifts and capacities; and if he is conscious that aught in him is wanting, I counsel him to be diligent in asking it of God. But when he has set in order all that

is needful for the accomplishment of the task committed to
him, then let him withdraw into himself and remain alone
in his study.... or his garden.... For there is neither
art nor science, whatsoever it be, in which there is not
always more to learn than has been learned; and only the
Lord God is perfect in all wisdom.... to Whom nothing
can be added—from Whom nothing can be taken away.
We.... being mortal, can only know by fragments.... and
our knowledge will always be apprenticeship without end."

In later life, after her plans for the Tuileries, Catherine,
as became a Médicis, gave herself up to Italian influence and
led the Italian faction. Diane had ever been the patroness of
the French School and she was not sorry to steal de l'Orme
from Catherine on the strength of it. The Art feud was
only one of many that went on between the crowned, and
the uncrowned Queen. De l'Orme built Anet for Diane, and
took as his crest the moon shining on an elm. The lumi-
nary he had chosen had brought him luck. He must, indeed,
have had a good horoscope. His rewards were almost equal
to his merits and his fortunes knew few variations.

Pierre Lescot, the creator of the Louvre, was eight years
older than Philibert. He also went to Rome in his youth,
though he did not make nearly so brilliant an impression as de
l'Orme. Like him, too, he entered the King's service. Francis,
always good at appreciating, recognised his gift and made much
of him. He seems to have relished Lescot's company, for he
allowed him to stand by him at dinner and watch him appease
his kingly appetite. It may seem a questionable privilege, but
he backed it by more solid benefits. One of these was an
order to rebuild the Louvre and to turn it from a fortress

into a palace. It was to be the rival of Ecouen; for Montmorency's boastful magnificence was vexing to the King's
eyes. But the project was only begun; the volatile monarch
forgot it in dreams of Chambord and Fontainebleau, and
only took it up again just before his death. Lescot continued it in the next reign. He was always a prosperous
artist; money came to him and abbeys were bestowed on
him. Ronsard—who quarrelled with Philibert—wrote a poem
to him. Little, however, is known of him, and his fame,
whether then or now, is in no wise equal to that of de l'Orme.

Under him there worked a genius greater than himself.
This was Jean Goujon, sculptor and decorator. Decorators
in those days were counted as mere subordinates to architects, and Goujon was Lescot's servitor, ornamenting where
his Chief built. Lescot was not slow to find out that he
had a past-master as craftsman, and the public soon made
the same discovery.

Some writer has said that Goujon had a "fluid genius."
He seemed to possess a subtle sympathy with water—to
know its delicious secrets of coolness and undulation. He
watched the waves till they became dancing Naiads; he
watched the figures of maidens till they turned into rip-
pling waves. And his chisel, recreating them with an inde-
finable magic, conveyed a salutation both to wave and to
maiden. Those who have stood before the Fontaine des
Innocents—the public fountain which he sculptured for
Paris—have felt the watery enchantment. They have seen
his rhythmic figures—bending here, curving there, haunting
but elusive, floating on aerial draperies. He worked, too,
under Lescot, on the Louvre. His "Glory" still holds her

palm on its walls; his Fame—an elegant Fame—still blows
her trumpet. She was busy, he said, in proclaiming the triumph
of Ronsard's verse. [1] Later it was Diane who employed him
at Anet. He presented her with the necessary trope: his
famous statue of Diana, long—and erroneously—supposed
to be her portrait. Perhaps he should never have ventured
on so definite a subject. Exquisite and reposeful as the
figure is, she is not a goddess: she remains a light woman
whom he adorned as Diana.

De l'Orme and Lescot, we have said, were the counter-
parts of the Pleïade. The Muse of Ronsard whispered also
to Jean Goujon. His work was Ronsard translated into
marble, and he alone could have conjured the Nymph of
the Poet's Fontaine de Bellerie—the spring that was buried
in the forest.

It was strange that this Pagan in imagination should
have had Protestant beliefs: should have died in the cause
of his faith as well as of his art. Legend says that he was
killed on St. Bartholomew's Eve, while he was working on
the Louvre, or else on the Fountain of the Innocents. But
legend, as usual, stops short at the point where we most
wish to hear more, and this is all that we know either of
his death or his religion.

A colleague he had who was a fervent Huguenot. Goujon
was working at Ecouen while one, Bernard Palissy, was also
embellishing it: Palissy, the indomitable artist and Calvinist,
who spent eighteen years of his life in a search for the

---

[1] He has also left us his Seasons, serene and victorious, on
the front of the Hôtel Carnavalet, afterwards Madame de
Sevigné's, then a new building.

secret of making white enamel. His search was crowned by his finding what he sought; but the discovery only came in the reign of Henri II, and it does not fall to us to describe it. A history so concentrated as his will not bear abbreviation; and so, though his struggles belong to the reign of Francis, they cannot be told apart from his success. How single-handed he fought with adversity; how he built his furnaces with bleeding hands; how he toiled and starved and froze and suffered; how he sacrificed his family to his quest; how victory came at last and fame also for a space; and how he finally perished for his Protestant faith, in a dungeon of the Bastille—all this' is material for other biographers.

The same may be said of lesser artists whose youth, but not their maturity, belongs to our period. There is Germain Pilon with his sculptured Graces; or Barthelmy Prieur, maker of busts. They, with a throng of smaller men, rank as Henri II's subjects. Their work is no longer fresh: it shows the first signs of decadence. Artificialness can have a naïveté of its own. A people like the French, whose nature it is to be unnatural, make the paradox possible. In the second half of the century the naïveté disappeared, the artificialness remained. Elegance began to pose and simper; sentiment grew sickly; compliment turned into hyperbole. The earlier art of France, if it had not a soul, was at least inspired by mind and quickened by intellectual grace. Now it became materialized and the senses came into play. Architecture kept its promise longest, but after de l'Orme's generation, it also exchanged its simple dignity for ornate pomp—its eloquence for grandiloquence. The morning was over; the sweet coolness, the limpid light, were gone, never to return. The afternoon that was coming was not a time of progress. It mistook heaviness for sincerity, masked vice for virtue, scrolls and flourishes for the truth. It worked without an ideal, or rather for a false one. When that ideal was realised, it assumed the form and features of Louis XIV of France.

AUTHORITIES CONSULTED FOR CHAPTER XX

Vie de Ronsard: CLAUDE BINET.

Œuvres de Ronsard.

Œuvres Choisies de Ronsard: SAINTE-BEUVE.

Vie de Joachim du Bellay (preface to Œuvres Choisies):
BECQ DE FOUQUIÈRES.

Œuvres poétiques de Joachim du Bellay.

Défense de la Poésie: JOACHIM DU BELLAY.

Tableau du Seizième Siècle: SAINTE-BEUVE.

Causeries de Lundi; SAINTE-BEUVE.

Histoire de la Littérature française: RENÉ DOUMIC.

Dames Illustres: BRANTÔME.

Dames Illustres: HILARION DE LA COSTE.

Vie de Clouet: BOUCHOT.

CHAPTER XX

(1548—1550)

THE RISE OF THE PLEÏADE

In the year of grace, 1548, a young man with golden hair stopped his horse before an inn, on the road from Poitiers to Paris. He paused at the vine-wreathed door and called for refreshment. In the tavern guest-room he found another traveller, a nobleman to judge by his appearance, handsome, richly dressed, of about the same age as himself. They greeted—they spoke—they drank together. They found they had both come from Poitiers. It may have been some traveller's remark about sky or road that first drew them together; that made each aware of the note of distinction in the other. Before the meal was over, they had struck on the theme of Poetry; of its past and the classics; on the golden theme of its future. On and on they sat, talking and glowing, striking out sparks from each other. The new arrival listened intently as his companion poured forth his eloquence; showed him a vision of what poetry might be—of what he himself meant to make it. When they rose they had resolved not to separate.

The men of those, days had impulses worth having; they trusted the flash of insight—leaped, not in the dark, but in the daylight. The youth with the golden hair was poor;

he had come from studying law at Poitiers; yet he had not
a moment's hesitation in throwing up his career then and
there and sharing his new friend's fortune. That friend
was a poet. He lived in a College for Poetry—an experiment of yesterday—where he and a few choice spirits were
brooding over Greek tragedians and dreaming poetic dreams.
His tongue was potent to persuade; his name was Ronsard.

Thus did Pierre de Ronsard and Joachim du Bellay meet
with one another and lay the foundations of a new poetry
in France: a poetry that was to kill the versifying of
mediæval schoolmen and abolish the ancient conventions;
to do away with treatises in rhyme and establish a fresh
and living lyric. Before or since there has been no such
coming together of two poets, except perhaps the greater
and more gradual one of Wordsworth and Coleridge, who
destroyed the neat couplets of the eighteenth century and
brought the world back to Nature. It was not Nature
which the Pleïade re-vindicated: the time had not come for
that. They were not a spontaneous school; but they aimed
at purity—at classic simplicity; they were decorous, not
pedantic. Before turning to the personal history of their
leaders it may be well to enquire what their aims were—
even though the result of those aims does not come within
our period.

The idea of the School originated with Ronsard, but he
could hardly have carried it out without the collaboration
of du Bellay. Both men were—spiritually speaking—the
children of the Pedagogues. Ronsard was educated by one;
but, like other children, they turned out very different from
their parents. And yet it was to these faithful if stubborn

guardians that they owed their knowledge of Greek and
Latin authors, their reverent acceptance of the classics as
their model and their standard. Ronsard studied Roman
and Athenian—studied and adored. He saw that their
strength lay in their being the voice of their country and
their age. He saw that his own country should seek such
expression of its personality, but he wished to keep the
classical form. Then, by a flash of genius, the central truth,
the secret of all progress, was borne in upon him. He com-
prehended that the old was capable of development—the
classical of fresh adaptation; that the new should not be
in opposition to the old, but a re-adjustment of its qualities. Affectation is a sign of decay; French literature had
grown affected, had imported euphuistic words, was divorced
from the language of the people. The French tongue had
become poor: it sadly needed enriching. It was, after all,
a Latin tongue and could without effort assimilate many
Latin elements. The Pleïade borrowed a store of words
both from Latin and from Greek and boldly naturalized
them in France; it banished a number of others which
should not have found their way there. Ronsard, we know,
was an impassioned gardener. He carried the art into
letters, and spent long days in grafting fresh buds upon
ancient stems.

He was born in 1524, in the Vendômois. His blood was
noble, even remotely royal. He was seventeenth cousin to
Queen Elizabeth, and in later years, she sent him a diamond
ring as a symbol of his poetry—a fit symbol of enduring
brilliance. When he was nine years old he was sent to
school, but he did not like it and only stayed for a year.

At the ripe age of ten ' he became page to the Duke of
Orleans and, at twelve, he transferred his services to James
Stuart of Scotland. With him he went for three years to
Great Britain, two and a half of which he spent in Scotland,
the remainder in England. He was too young to be talked
to by people of interest; but he must have seen the great
Catholic nobles—must have loved the beauty of Westminster
and the golden barges on the Thames. At fifteen, he returned to France and the household of the Duke of Orleans.
It was not long after this that occurred one of the decisive
events of his life. He met with Virgil. A groom of the
Duke's, impassioned for the Mantuan, first revealed his
beauties to Ronsard. Thenceforward he was hardly seen
without a Virgil in his hand. He knew the more modern
poets too, and had Marot at his finger-ends. The world of
books allured him more and more, but it was not for want
of experience. He returned to Scotland a year after he left
it, and was nearly shipwrecked before he came home again.
He was sent by France on diplomatic jobs to Flanders; he
accompanied Baïf to the Diet of Speier and Guillaume du
Bellay to Piedmont. But no amount of adventure com-
pensated for the charms of literature. In his own mind he
had resolved to retire from Court and to make a profession
of Letters.

At first his father would not hear of it, but the boy was
not to be daunted. His spirit, says his old historian, "was
one which from its birth had received that infusion, that
fatal impression of poetry, which none can injure; nor could
he bind himself by other laws than his own." So manfully
did he persist that his parent at last gave in, on condition

that he should never become a poet, or hold a French book
in his hand. Happily, schoolman though he was, he did
not make Pierre promise not to write one. Perhaps it was
the sad fact of his son's growing deafness—a bar to aristo-
cratic professions—which helped him to yield to his wishes.
The poet of seventeen withdrew to solitude at Blois, where
he dreamed and read, and read and dreamed again. He
also fell in love—with "Cassandre"—the first of a varied
dynasty; and he sent her sweet songs, light sighs in verse,
all the pretty wares that a Cassandre could ask for. It was
but a passing sentiment. His real emotions were his long
hours with Virgil and Plato in the Forest of Gastine—
where he wandered "par les taillis: verte maison des
cerfs".... "often alone, but always in the company of the
Muses." He lingered whole days in grassy places, or sat by
the mossy rim of his favourite Fontaine de Bellerie. Later,
when he had another love, he found another fountain—la
Fontaine d'Helène, which had power to quench the thirst of
poets. But there is no need to use any words except his
own—instinct with the freshness of the woods.

> "Car je vis; et c'est grand bien
> De vivre, et de vivre bien....
> Ayant toujours en mains pour me servir de guide,
> Aristote, ou Platon, ou le docte Euripide:
> Les bon hôtes muets qui ne fâchent jamais.
>
> .... O douce compagnie, douce et honnête,
> Un autre en caquetant m'étourdirait la tête.
> Puis du livre ennuyé, je regardais les fleurs....
> .... Et l'entrecoupement de leurs formes diverses
> Peintes de cent façons, jaunes, rouges et perses,

Ne me pouvant saouler, ainsi qu'en un tableau,
D'admirer la Nature, et ce qu'elle a de beau,
Et de dire, en parlant aux fleurettes écloses,
'Celui est presque Dieu qui connait toutes choses.'"

When he was rather older and more famous he had a
lackey of his own who used to spread picnics for him. He
was very particular in his orders and has left them behind
him in verse.

A SON LAQUAIS

Achète des abricots,
Des pompons, [1] des artichauds,
Des fraises, et de la crême.
C'est en été ce que j'aime:
Quand sur le bord d'un ruisseau,
Je la mange au bruit de l'eau,
Etendu sur le rivage.

Strawberries and cream still exist at Blois, an inviolate
link with the Past; and the stranger who eats them beneath
the beech-trees by the Loire may feel himself the nearer to
Ronsard.

When he left Blois it was for Paris, but here he changed
his abode. He crossed the water from Les Tournelles to
the house of Lazare Baïf, Maître des Requêtes, and a faithful scholar of the old school: a long-tried family friend, and
his Chief when he went to Speier. Baïf had great expectations of Ronsard. He had interesting theories about the
education of youth, which he was trying on his son, Jean
Antoine. He now invited Ronsard—Jean's elder by four

---

[1] Water-melons.

THE RISE OF THE PLEÏADE 339

years—to live with them. Another and an older poet already lodged beneath their roof and helped them with their work. This was Jean Dorat—also of the Schools, but fired with enthusiasm for classical poetry. Baïf poured forth his learning upon Ronsard. The young men heard lectures in Paris on philosophy and on science, but it was Dorat who charmed him "du phyltre des bonnes lettres." After a little while he (Dorat) resolved to set up a College of his own— the famous Collége de Coqueret. He carried off Ronsard, and young Baïf was not long before he followed them. Other rising men, eager for study and seclusion, gradually joined the group and formed, little as they knew it, the kernel of a new movement.

Ronsard was ignorant of Greek. Not so young Baïf who had learned it for years with his father. He was only too proud to serve as a master, and Ronsard picked it up easily, with "l'aimable conférence" of Jean Antoine, who, at all hours of the day or night, unravelled for him the grievous beginnings of the Greek language. Ronsard taught him his metrical science in exchange. Meanwhile he learned Latin with Dorat by a new method; he plunged into the deeps of philosophy; his tutor initiated him in the classic art of Anagrams. Ronsard began imitations of Pindar and Horace. He was overtaken by an insatiable thirst for knowledge. "He—who had been trained at the Court and accustomed to sit up late—now continued his studies till two or three in the morning; and when he went to bed he woke up Baïf, who got up and took the candle—unwilling to let Ronsard's place at the study-desk grow cold." There is something infinitely touching about these penniless young poets, who could not afford two candles, hearing the chimes at midnight and sowing their wild oats over books.

With Ronsard the creative work soon produced fruit. "He began to brood on great designs for the bringing of our language forth from childhood." He tried to enrich it in every way. He even went to work with the various artisans so that he might learn the terms of their trades : "prenant garde aux moindres choses.... faisant son profit de toutes." When he first wrote some small poems, they showed, says the old biographer, "je ne sais quoi du magnanime caractère de son Virgile." Dorat, with rash hyperbole, prophesied he would be the Homer of France, and spent his time pondering what books he should choose to nourish the genius under his care.

Virgil had made one epoch in Ronsard's life. Now there came another. Dorat read aloud to him Aeschylus' "Prometheus." At first he was struck dumb. "When he had tasted the flavour of it—'Why,' he exclaimed, 'oh why, my master, have you hidden these riches all this time from me?'" This new inspiration kindled his energies; he translated the "Plutus" of Aristophanes into French and, with Baïf to help him, had it acted in the theatre of the College. His schemes for French poetry grew maturer, the company at Coqueret was increasing, and a fresh arrival, Rémy Belleau, proved a sympathetic comrade in his plans.

It was at this point that he and du Bellay met in the tavern by the roadside. "Fine minds," says his historian, "can hide themselves no more than the light of Phœbus, their guide." It is well when they find one another.

Du Bellay's life had not been as happy as Ronsard's. A

year younger than the latter, he was born at Liré, in Anjou, in 1525. His parents were of gentle blood—relations of the great du Bellays. They died early and Joachim was brought up by his brother, a stern man who spoiled the boy's youth by his severity. When he too died, he left his son in the tutelage of Joachim. The post involved endless worries. There was not enough money; want was at the door. The guardian, little more than a lad, broke down under the strain. His strength gave way and he was laid by for two years. What Ronsard's deafness did for Ronsard, du Bellay's illness did for du Bellay. It turned him to the study of the classics. He had always had a longing for learning and no opportunity of satisfying it. His brother had not given him any real education, and since he became his own master, means and leisure had both failed him. Unlike Ronsard, he was alone and unaided; but, like him, he was a poet. In his solitude he, too, developed the conception of the New Poetry; of adopting the classic forms and filling them with modern ideas. Exact imitation of the Ancients he thought a false and foolish standard; he saw, like his unknown colleague, that the feeling of French poets must be their own.

He was by way of being under the protection of Guillaume du Bellay, and was vaguely destined for the military profession. But when, in 1543, the Sieur de Langeais died, his plans changed. Perhaps he was not sorry to renounce the glory of arms: the Cardinal could get him preferment in other directions. But the short way to the Cardinal was through the Church, and the short way to the Church was through the Law. So Joachim became a law-student at Poitiers, and it was on his return thence that he fell in with Ronsard.

The two men were made to collaborate. Their very infirmities bound them together. Strange to say, du Bellay too was deaf. He wrote Ronsard a "Hymn to Deafness", and Ronsard wrote him a sonnet on the same theme. Their talents suited admirably. Ronsard, the more illustrious, was also the more exquisite in form; du Bellay, not so perfect in shape, had a subtler and a deeper note. Readers of Beaumont and Fletcher may observe the same difference in their qualities. Ronsard, who was born to sing, needed a man who could speak : du Bellay had the gift of eloquence—in prose as well as in verse. They retired together to work out their schemes at leisure in the College of Coqueret.

Under the spell of Ronsard, Joachim's writing changed its character. He had composed verses at Liré which, in spite of his theories, kept something of the old-fashioned stiffness. But now his hand became freer, his fancy richer. His fellow-poet applauded him. They both rhymed about sparkling wines—about quaffing them with their heads crowned with roses; but, in reality, their fare was of the plainest. They wrote like Epicures and lived like Anchorites. However light their songs, their idea of their art was a solemn one and, in their eyes, fame was a sacred charge. "Whoso desireth to fly over the world"—wrote du Bellay—"through the lips and the hands of men, should long dwell apart in his chamber; and he who wisheth to live in the memory of posterity should, like one dead in himself, oftentimes sweat and tremble. While our courtier-poets eat, drink, and sleep at their ease, he should endure hunger and thirst and hard vigils. Those are the wings on which the writings of men

fly to heaven.... Glory is the only ladder by the steps of
the which mortals mount with light feet to the sky, and
make themselves companions of the gods."

And Ronsard sounds the same strain. " Prose," he says,
" is the language of men ; but poetry is the tongue of the
gods. No man should be its interpreter, if he be not anointed
thereunto from his birth and dedicated to its ministry."
Art was the only religion of either poet. Ronsard was a
Pagan through and through, though he lived and died
a Catholic : a Pagan of the most graceful and orthodox
refinement, who liked courtly manners, even in a wood.

> Je n'ai souci que d'aimer
> Moi-même, et me parfumer
> D'odeurs, et qu'une couronne
> De fleurs le chef m'environne.
> Je suis, mon Belleau, celui
> Qui veux vivre ce jour'd'hui :
> L'homme ne saurait connaître
> Si un lendemain doit être.

These are hardly Christian sentiments, and Ronsard's attendance at Mass does not alter their nature.

Du Bellay was also a Pagan, but he was not so light-
hearted as Ronsard ; his views of life were sadder and
profounder. Ronsard is like a ̓swift and gleaming swallow
who skims the waters without cleaving them ; du Bellay is
like a sea-bird, grey and white, who loves the deeps and
hovers over them, though he does no more than touch them
with his wings.

A School was by now gathering round them—a galaxy of
small stars ; and they gave it the name of the Pleïade, after

a circle of Greek poets. Their disciples are little remembered: Dorat and Baïf and Belleau; Amadis Jamyn, Ronsard's page; Estienne Jodelle, the playwright. There were others who joined the group, but their names were of little significance. The two leaders were meantime busy at Coqueret, preparing their verses for the press. Du Bellay was perfecting the Sonnet, which might be called his gift to his country. Melin Saint-Gelais, it is true, had already written poems in that form; but they had not been many or beautiful and it was Joachim who established them in France. Great ladies, in later days, paid him back in his own coin. Margaret of Savoy, his Duchess, sent him her gracious attempts. Even the stern Jeanne d'Albret unbent and tried her Protestant hand at them. But before he reached these honours there were bad times to be gone through. In 1549, he brought out his first book of poems, "Olive"—not among his best— and dedicated it to the Duchess Margaret. Ronsard's "Cassandre" followed in 1550. In the same year the poets blew their trumpet-blast and threw down the gauntlet to the public. Du Bellay's "Défense de Poésie" appeared in print. It was a full statement of their views, expressed with an orator's eloquence and in prose that seems embroidered with words: and yet each one is essential and the effect of the whole is simple. The best parts reach the level of poetry— they recall Sir Philip Sidney's "Apology". But the French work is greater—is a challenge: there is something heroic about it.

The challenge was not allowed to pass unheeded. No sooner was it read than it brought a swarm of hornets round the ears of the Pleïade. It was natural that the

Pedants should detest them; they had taken the Academic vessels and used them for their own purpose. But the followers of Marot, who had hitherto represented the National School, disliked them even more bitterly. Their distaste is harder to account for. They were jealous for their Maître Clément's fame: they were also sincerely outraged by the new words that the Pleïade imported. Marot himself would have thought the words absurd, but he would have done justice to the poets' imagination. He would have enjoyed their grace and relished the choiceness of their metres. His disciples were obtuser. Led by Melin Saint-Gelais and Fontaine, they poured contempt on Ronsard and his comrade. They spouted their lines in ranting tones; they mispronounced the hated terms; they cut out whole passages at will, to cover the authors with ridicule; they made fun of them to the King. No wonder that Ronsard longed for the reign of Francis I.

It needed all the skill of the Duchess Margaret—Ronsard's friend as well as du Bellay's—to change public opinion concerning them. She did much to smooth matters over and the disputants themselves grew tired of quarrels. Melin Saint-Gelais made the first overtures. He wrote a complimentary poem to Ronsard. Ronsard put it in the front of his next volume and sent a *tu quoque* to Saint-Gelais. Du Bellay followed his example and the feud, for the moment, was made up.

It is difficult for us of to-day to understand why it arose. The irritations of yesterday are as bewildering as its jokes—they belong to the atmosphere that created them. The words once gibed at are no longer novelties: they have

become embodied in the language. The poems seem to us
little gems—intaglios of fantastic workmanship. They are
not of a great order, but Apollo might have worn them in
his signet-ring and each is lovely of its kind. What can be
more musical, for instance, than Ronsard's farewell to his
love who died young?

> En ton âge le plus gaillard,
> Tu as seul laissé ton Ronsard,
> Dans le Ciel trop tôt retournée,
> Perdant beauté, grace et couleur,
> Tout ainsi qu'une belle fleur
> Qui ne vit qu'une matinée....
>
> . . . .
>
> ....Soit que tu vives près de Dieu,
> Ou aux Champs Elysées, Adieu,
> Adieu cent fois, adieu, Marie;
> Jamais mon cœur ne t'oublira,
> Jamais la Mort ne délira
> Le nœud dont ta beauté me lie.

Or take these lines from his salute to the lark.

> Sitot que tu es arrosée
> Au point du jour, de la rosée,
> Tu fais en l'air mille discours:
> En l'air des ailes tu frétilles
> Et penduës au Ciel tu babilles
> Et contes aux vents tes amours.
>
> Puis du Ciel tu te laisses fondre
> Dans un sillon vert, soit pour pondre,
> Soit pour éclore ou pour couver,
> Soit pour apporter la béchée
> A tes petits, ou d'une achée, [1]
> Ou d'une chenille, ou d'un ver.

[1] Lobworm.

Or take his benediction on the Spring.

> Dieu vous gard, messagers fidèles
> Du printemps, vites Hirondelles,
> Huppes,[1] Cocus, Rossignolets,
> Tourtres, et vous oiseaux sauvages,
> Qui de cent sortes de ramage
> Aimez les bois verdelets.
>
> Dieu vous gard, belles Pâquerettes,
> Belles Roses, belles fleurettes,
> Et vous, boutons jadis connus,
> Du sang d'Ajax et de Narcisse :
> Et vous Thym, Anis, et Mélisse,
> Vous soyez les bien revenus.
>
> Dieu vous gard, troupe diàprée
> De papillons, qui par la pré
> Les douces herbes suçotez :
> Et vous nouvel essaim d'Abeilles,
> Qui les fleurs jaunes et vermeilles,
> De votre bouche baisotez.
>
> Cent mille fois je resaluë
> Votre belle et douce venuë.
> O ! que j'aime cette saison
> Et ce doux caquet des rivages,
> Au prix des vents et des orages
> Qui m'enfermaient en la maison.

And while we seek for a last quotation, we light upon his Sonnet to Helène, which falls from his lyre as if it were already an echo—the ghost of a song : a harmony dying slowly, like the flickering candle-flame he sings of.

[1] Lapwings.

Quand vous serez bien vieille, au soir, à la chandelle
Assise auprès du feu, devisant et filant,
Direz chantant mes vers, en vous émerveillant:
Ronsard me célébrait du temps que j'étais belle.
Lors vous n'aurez servante ayant telle nouvelle,
Desia [1] sous le labeur à demi sommeillant,
Qui au bruit de son nom ne s'aille reveillant,
Bénissant votre nom de louange immortelle.
Je serai sous la terre et, fantôme sans os,
Par les ombres myrteux je prendrai mon repos:
Vous serez au foyer une vieille accroupie,
Regrettant mon amour et votre fier dédain.
Vivez, si m'en croyez, n'attendez à demain:
Cueillez, dès aujourd'hui les roses de la vie.

Ronsard knew where to find the roses and he gathered them with both hands.

When we turn to du Bellay's works we find nothing more perfect than the lines called "A Sower of Corn, to the winds"—and we follow Mr. Pater's example in citing it in the poet's honour.

A vous troupe légère
Qui d'aile passagère
Par le monde volez,
Et d'un sifflant murmure
L'ombrageuse verdure
Doucement ébranlez—
J'offre les violettes,
Les lys, et ces fleurettes,
Et ces roses ici:

Ces vermeillettes roses
Tout fraichement écloses,

[1] Déja.

Et ces oeillets aussi.
De votre douce haleine
Eventez cette plaine,
Eventez ce séjour !
Cependant que j'ahanne [1]
A mon blé que je vanne
A la chaleur du jour.

Du Bellay has an aroma of his own: delicate, discreet, compact of rare essences. Like Ronsard, he is delicious in April and loves to describe "la grande naïve beauté" of Spring-time. He was not made to be popular: no one more despised the public.

Mais moi que les Grâces chérissent,
Je haïs les biens que l'on adore,
Je haïs les honneurs qui périssent,
Et le soin qui les cœurs dévore.
Rien ne me plaît, fors ce qui peut déplaire
Au jugement du rude populaire....

De mourir ne suis en émoi [2]
Selon la loi du sort humain,
Car la meilleure part de moi
Ne craint point la fatale main.
Craigne la mort, la fortune, et l'envie,
A qui les dieux n'ont donné qu'une vie. [3]

And he sounds the same note in the "Discours au Roi":

Ce généreux désir de l'immortalité
Tous l'apportent ici dès leur nativité...
Ce qui nous montre bien que tout on ne meurt pas,
Mais qu'il reste de nous après notre trépas,
Je ne sais quoi plus grand et plus divin encore
Que ce que nous voyons et que la mort dévore.

[1] Que je m'essouffle. [2] Panic. [3] " De l'immortalité des poëtes."

Why, he asks passionately, should the imprisoned soul remain here and not make its own escape to heaven?

> Là est le bien que tout esprit désire,
> Là le repos où tout le monde aspire...
> Là, oh mon âme, au plus haut ciel guidée,
> Tu y pourras reconnaître l'idée
> De la beauté qu'en ce monde j'adore.

His comfort in life was friendship, and there seems no better expression of it than one of his many sonnets to Ronsard.

A PIERRE DE RONSARD.

Si quelquefois de Pétrarque et d'Horace
J'ai contrefait les sons mélodieux,
Oh saint troupeau! Oh mignonnes des dieux!
Cette faveur me vient de votre grâce.
Mais ce grand bien un plus grand bien efface,
M'ayant acquis un ami que les cieux
Guident si haut au sentier des plus vieux
Que son savoir le vôtre même passe.
Donc, Ronsard, un vulgaire lien
N'enchaine pas ton cœur avec le mien;
Des Grâces fut telle amour commencée:
Amour vraiement ouvrage de Pallas,
Et du héraut, facond neveu d'Atlas,
Qui tient mon âme en la tienne enlacée.

It was verses such as these [1] that caused so much disturbance among the poets. But the disturbance did no lasting

[1] The verses chosen are taken from later volumes than those of 1549 and 1550. But the earlier work is no more eccentric than these poems and gives no better pretext for enemies to lay hold of.

harm, and the Pleïade was strong enough to withstand it. They had quick sap in their veins and real life cannot be destroyed. For good or bad, the Movement was launched; it could safely be left to itself. And here, at the outset of its journey, we must stop. Its history, and the further history of its chiefs, goes beyond our limits. Of Ronsard's friendship with Mary Queen of Scots; of Catherine de Médicis' favours; of his brilliant existence at Court, far from the greenswards of Gastine; of his death in the midst of prosperity—it is not our place to speak. Nor is it for us to dwell on the end of Joachim du Bellay, who could never have lived at Court, and died in poverty and suffering, at thirty-five years of age. The record of their maturer days belongs, like those of de l'Orme and Lescot, to the times of the later Valois monarchs. We must leave them on the threshold of fame—in the early dawn of their prime. But the birds sing most sweetly in the dawn, and these had but just awakened.

AUTHORITIES CONSULTED FOR CHAPTER XXI

Lettres de Marguerite d'Angoulême.

Nouvelle lettres de Marguerite d'Angoulême.

Nouvelles Poésies de Marguerite d'Angoulême.

La Coche.

Le Miroir de l'Ame Pècheresse: MARGUERITE D'ANGOULÊME.

Les Marguerites de la Marguerite des Princesses: MARGUERITE D'ANGOULÊME.

Le Tombeau de la Reine de Navarre.

Oraison Funèbre sur Marguerite d'Angoulème: SAINTE-MARTHE.

Histoire de Béarn et de Foix: OLHAGARAY.

Histoire Catholique: HILARION DE LA COSTE.

Dames Illustres: BRANTÔME.

Dames Illustres: HILARION DE LA COSTE.

Poésies de Ronsard.

Livre d'Etat de Marguerite d'Angoulême: LE COMTE DE LA FERRIÈRE.

Le Château de Pau: LAGIÈZE.

Vie de Marguerite de Valois: LA COMTESSE D'HAUSSONVILLE.

Conférences sur Marguerite d'Angoulême: LURO.

Biographical Preface to Les Marguerites etc.: FRANCK.

  „   „ „ Lettres de Marguerite d'Angoulême: GÉNIN.

Preface to Nouvelle Lettres: GÉNIN.

Les Femmes des Valois: SAINT-AMAND.

Dictionnaire Historique de Bayle.

Life of Margaret of Angoulême: MARY ROBINSON.

Causeries de Lundi: SAINTE-BEUVE.

Histoire de France (Vol. VIII): HENRI MARTIN.

La Renaissance: MICHELET.

Marguerite de Valois, Reine de Navarre.
Cabinet des Estampes de la Bibliothèque Nationale ;
d'après Jean Clouet.

CHAPTER XXI

(1547—1549)

THE LAST DAYS OF MARGARET OF NAVARRE

In the last year of the King's life there was peace in his kingdom. After the battle of Cérisole, Charles V and Henri VIII had invaded France, but, as might have been expected, they could not hold together and, in 1546, each separately made peace with Francis. At home also there was quiet. The Duchesse d'Etampes had retired from Court to the house of her husband. There is a tradition that he shut her up and starved her to death for her sins, but there is small likelihood of its truth. Obscurity was punishment enough for her—domestic life an adequate purgatory. We can, without reluctance, leave her to a natural death.

It is to be hoped that Francis had pangs of remorse, but the hope is rather sanguine. He was now a prey to a depression which sprang from bodily causes. The attacks of his painful illness recurred; his sufferings grew greater, his power of resistance less.

In March, 1547, he was staying at Rambouillet, Margaret at the Convent of Tusson, in the Angoumois. It was one of her favourite retreats—she loved the simple nuns there. One night while she was with them, she had a dream which filled her with terror. The King appeared, pale as death, before her; he called out: "Ma sœur, ma sœur!" and his voice failed him as he spoke.

Margaret, when she woke, could not shake off the impression. She knew no more than that her brother was ailing, and she sent at once to Paris for news. The worst seemed a certainty. "If someone came to my gate to tell me the King had recovered, I would run," she said impetuously, "to kiss him, whoever he might be. Were he dirty, mudstained, haggard, or weary, I would embrace him as if he were the properest gentleman in France. And if he lacked a bed and could not find one to rest upon, I would give him my own, while I myself lay upon the hard ground, to reward him for the tidings he had brought me." Some time after, she had the same dream again, and on the morrow she despatched a second messenger to Paris. He returned with the news that Francis had died two weeks before, on the day of her first dream; but not daring to tell her, he said that her brother was well. She was standing in the Cloisters speaking to her secretary about getting a fresh bulletin, when a sound of sobbing at the other end of the building arrested her. She found that it proceeded from a poor mad nun who lived in the Convent. "Why are you weeping, my sister?" asked the Queen. "Alas, Madam!" said the nun, "it is your fate that I am bewailing." Margaret turned sharply to her attendants. "You are hiding the King's death from me," she cried, "but by the mouth of a fool God has revealed it to me."

Francis had died as she would have wished. He heard Mass; he blessed his son; he advised him to diminish the taxes and to suppress the ambition of the House of Guise; he told his servants "not to be scandalised if, in the vehemence of suffering, his heart should seem disturbed. . . . All that night he travailed, repeating unto himself passages of Scripture." Then he heard Mass again and listened to a homily of Origen's—strange matter for the dying ears of a light King. "When he was very near unto death, he kissed the Cross and held it for a long while in his arms. At last he gave up the ghost; whispering the name of Jesus with a great effort, long after he had lost both sight and speech."

It his hard to know how much of this was sincere, how much a death-bed repentance. The monarchs of those days extended the divine right of kings beyond the grave, and demanded as their right a State-entry into Heaven. The ceremonies and pieties of dying sovereigns were part of the proper preparation for the celestial pageants, and Francis, in this respect, was every inch a King.

Margaret, at all events, was ready to canonize him. Her sorrow was so great that at first it exalted her spirit. For forty days after his death she remained at Tusson, "where all might see her performing the duties of Abbess, singing daily with the Nuns, both at Matins and at Evensong." The heavier days came later, when the excitement of grief was over and the dreary hours had to be lived through without the person who had been the centre of her life. Sometimes her pain found an outlet in verse, and the lyrics she wrote at this time—the cries of a broken heart—are far the most moving of her poems.

> "Qui pleurera François que Marguerite,
> Qui fut liée par enfance en son bers? [1]
> .... Depuis les pieds jusque sus le sommet
> En moi ne sens que désolation."

[1] Berceau.

So she sings and the tears choke her voice. Memory
stabs her; she seeks relief in her Dante.

> "Douleur (il) n'y a qu'au temps de la misère
> Se recorder de l'heureux et prospère: [1]
> Comme autrefois en Dante j'ai trouvé;
> Mais le sais mieux pour avoir éprouvé
> Félicité et infortune austère.
> Prospérité m'a fait trop bonne chère.
> Hélas, mon Dieu! que m'est il arrivé?"

The days of the Heptameron were over, and though she
still wrote Pastorals and Interludes and enjoyed seeing them
acted, they were all grave and allegorical. Spiritual songs,
as she called them, suited best with her mood, and to these
she devoted her Muse. Not so long ago an iron casket
was discovered hidden away in the great Paris Library.
When it was opened it was found to contain the manuscript of the religious poems which Margaret wrote in her
closing years. Her daughter Jeanne had stored them there
and they had never seen the light. They show her as she
was after she lost her brother—as she remained to the last
—sweet, steadfast, unutterably sad.

The King's death was the end of her own life. Marot's
verses to her had been prophetic.

> "O fleur que j'ai la première servie....
> Tout donne peine, hélas! non disservie, [2]
> Bien je le sais."

---

[1] There is no pain like that of remembering past happiness
and past prosperity when one is in misery.

[2] Deserved.

So he had written in days that were happy by comparison. Thenceforth cares and griefs seemed to multiply around her and her good fortune to desert her. Her husband was unfaithful and went more and more away from her, with the one good result that he left the affairs of his kingdom entirely in her hands. It was as much a mark of confidence as of neglect, but not the one she would have chosen. "He does not even care to give the pleasure of a single line of his handwriting to a poor ailing woman," she once wrote. Her daughter was as cold as ever. The new king, Francis' son, disliked his aunt and made difficulties about her pension. She had even to debase herself by writing almost servile letters to beg for a continuance of royal favour, or by asking Diane de Poitiers to intercede in her behalf. "You know," she wrote to a friend, "that without it, it would be impossible for me to keep up my house—that I have only just enough to get through the year—and it may surely be believed that without necessity it is not my habit to be a beggar." She implored Montmorency, who had been recalled to Court, not to work against her, and it was largely due to him that at last she got her pension.

"I see that time has not conquered your memory," she wrote to him, "and has not made you forget the love I have borne you, from your childhood onwards." This was all very well, but his memory could have evoked other impressions besides those of her love, and after the pleasure she showed at his disgrace on Jeanne's wedding-day one cannot but regret that she stooped to become his debtor.

The pension, paltry enough, did not come a moment too

soon. All through the time of her uncertainty about it
she had been obliged to live very austerely—retrenching in
everything except charity. She had rather, she said, sell
all the furniture in her Château than diminish her gifts to
the poor. And when the money came, the two first quarters
had to go in paying her daughter's preposterous bills and
the wages of Jeanne's endless retinue. Economy as well as
sensitiveness made Margaret now shrink from society. She
said she was ill and allowed her husband and her daughter
to go to the King's "Sacre" without her; and when she was
asked to be godmother to the new little princess, Claude,
she begged Henri II to accept Jeanne as a proxy. The end
of her letter is piteous: a humble petition to the King
to keep for her the post of Governess to his children.
"Vous suppliant de m'en garder la place," do not seem
the words for a Queen to utter, or for an aunt to write to
her nephew, but sorrow had brought her very low.

She was, however, forced to be present at Henri II's
entry into Lyons—one of the most gorgeous pageants on
record. The Saône was a fairy-land of ships, tented with
red velvet and manned by sailors in satin—scarlet, or
black and white—the colours of the King. They followed
the Royal Boat as it sailed up the river. There were
allegories of the Rhone and the Saône; there were rocks
and satyrs; Greek temples and centaurs; there were obelisks
and fountains of wine. There was, to crown all, a
vast improvised forest, from which, when Henri appeared,
there emerged to the sound of trumpets Diana and her
nymphs. She was an elegant Court Diana, younger than
her living namesake, with a Turkish bow and crimsom satin

boots. Her dress was of "toile d'or noire, semée d'étoiles d'argent," and her hair was "interlaced with ropes of pearls and jewels." She wore a silver crescent on her brow and, while her Nymphs led hounds in silken leashes, she was followed by a lion, which she brought to the feet of the King. "Cette Diane et ses compagnes," comments Brantôme, "c'étaient les plus belles femmes, les plus belle filles de la ville de Lyon—folâtrement accoutrées et retroussées." They must have been a rather trying spectacle for Catherine de Médicis, who watched the show with Margaret from a window in the Rue St. Jean. The next day the two Queens figured in the grand procession through the town: Catherine and her daughter in the first litter, Margaret and Jeanne in the second.

In this same year, 1548, began negotiations for Jeanne's second marriage—the marriage which disturbed the rest of Margaret's existence. Henri II proposed two suitors for the hand of her daughter: Antoine de Bourbon, and François de Lorraine, son of the Duc de Guise, whose brother had married the daughter of Diane de Poitiers. Henri wished for the Lorraine match and said so, but he condescended to ask Jeanne which man she preferred. The Jeanne of twenty was still the Jeanne of eleven.

"Do you wish, Sire," she replied, "that the woman who ought to be my train-bearer should be my sister-in-law, and that I should hobnob with the daughter of Madame de Valentinois?"

She was not, however, proof against Antoine de Bourbon, and even expressed a wish to become his wife—much to her uncle's satisfaction and to the discomfort of her parents.

They, especially Margaret, hated the marriage from the first. She probably still wanted the Heir of Spain as a son-in-law, and this new plan was the last drop in her cup. Montmorency had returned to his old ways with her and was acting no friendly part. Reinstated in power, he was in the King's counsels, and he persecuted Margaret to make her yield to Henri's wishes. She got no quarter from the King, who did not conceal his distaste for her. "The farther I see," he wrote to Montmorency, "the less goodwill I expect from my aunt and my uncle." Their opposition enraged him, and so suspicious did he grow that he went the length of intercepting all their letters, to make sure they were concocting no scheme that interfered with his own. He summoned the King of Navarre to court, but the wily prince pretended to be ill and did not appear. He was not so firm, though, as Margaret, and after a time, he consented to yield to Jeanne's will. In the end Margaret herself was forced to give in to Montmorency's importunities, but she did so unwillingly and never changed her mind about the marriage. After its celebration her royal nephew, Henri, wrote a description to Montmorency.

"I have never," he said, "seen so joyous a bride. She did nothing but laugh.... This wedding is the best pledge I can have from her parents. Her father pretends to be the happiest creature in the world—you know the man; but from what I can gather about him and several others, he cares for nothing, now that his daughter is married, excepting to live well and to get heaps of money."

And again in another letter—

"The Queen of Navarre is on the worst terms possible with her husband—and all because of her love for her daughter who takes no notice of her mother. You never saw such tears as my aunt shed when they parted, and had it not been for me, she would never have gone home with her husband."

Henri II was certainly not a pleasant relation, though Margaret, who had to keep well with him, pathetically describes his society as "une compagnie tant aisée à vivre." From Catherine, she says, she has "never yet heard a word that one sister should not say to another," which may have been some consolation for the King's indulging in so many. As for Jeanne, except for a triumphal return to Pau, she practically passed out of her mother's life. Her literary respect for Margaret seems to have been her strongest feeling for her, as the storing of her manuscripts implies. But this was cold comfort for a heart like Margaret's, and she did not live to have the warmer one of holding a grandson in her arms. Her chief friends were her faithful maids-of-honour who lived with her and loved her. Their very names—Madame d'Avangour, "qui ne fait qu'écouter;[1] Mademoiselle St. Pather, who made jam; Mademoiselle d'Orsonvillers, sung by Marot—have the fascination of an echo: the echo of a refined splendour, half stately, half intimate.

As time went on, broken though she was, Margaret's interests began to re-assert their claims. Her spirit could not bear confinement to one chamber, even when it was that of

[1] Margaret's saying about her.

sorrow. Poets and scholars still visited her conrt and dedicated their works to their " Mæcenas", as they called her,
and she still read what they wrote. Books always kept their
hold on her and she spent many hours among her own,
ranged in the shelves of her library, in the binding she had
chosen for them—rich brown leather sprinkled with golden
daisies. All her belongings were decked with devices, many
and various, grave and fantastic, with her Marguerite turning
to the sun and her "Non inferiora secutus"; with her "Plus
vous que moi"; or her lily between two daisies with the
words "Mirandum naturæ opus", and a crown above the
flowers.

There was one marked change in her after her loss. Though
her charity and tolerance remained unshaken, though Reformers still presented her with their tomes, she returned
more and more to the faith of her childhood. With her
we may be sure that it was no fear of death that made her
do so. She had always stopped short at the daring of
Luther. Bruised as she now was by life, the unconsoling
gloom of Calvinism repelled her, while the beauty and emotion of the Catholic ritual drew her irresistibly back to it.
The masses for the dead, the prayers to Virgin and Saints,
suited well with her mood. She was living in the Past
more than in the Present, and the Church of Rome was the
Church of her mother and her brother, the Church of her
own early days. She founded convents—she became strict
about orthodox ceremonial. On her death-bed she told her
Confessor that she had protected the Reformers from pure
compassion and had never separated herself from Catholicism.
This was half true—she had at no time renounced the central

beliefs of the old creed; but it was a reformed Catholicism that she made for, and she certainly protected the Reformers from taste as much as from pity. Those who love her cannot but feel sorry that this should have been her last expression of faith. Her heart ruled her reason in death, as it had done in life, and she was a sweeter, if not a wiser woman for it. She was wide rather than strong, "seeking", as a French critic has it, "to find a footpath in all directions." One must not malign admirable spirits through one's admiration, or ask for more than they can give us. Bayle is cleverer in his surprise that a princess, born a Catholic and im-passioned for a brother who persecuted, should have been able to accomplish what she did.

"I cannot conceive," he says, "how this Queen of Navarre raised herself to such a high point of equity and reason. It was from no indifference to religion, since it is certain that she was very pious and studied the Scriptures with singular concentration. The beauty of her genius and the greatness of her soul must have shown her a by-way which very few people knew of."

Bayle does not exaggerate. If she did not establish a new ideal, or rather an old one reformed, she never sullied either old or new by thought, word, or deed. Unkindness and stu-pidity kept far from her—Christ was more than the Pope to her. She was always true to charity and held it high above dogma.

But La Marguerite des Marguerites was closing her petals. "Cette mère aimable de la Renaissance" was soon to desert her children. A short while before the end she had another dream. It was of a white-robed figure who held a wreath

towards her and said "Bientôt". She took the apparition
as an incontestable sign of her death and began to prepare
for it. She withdrew from public affairs, restored the man-
agement of the kingdom to her husband, wound up all
her business, and retired to the Château of Odos, in Bigorre.
We cannot but hope that he and she had, in these closing
days, some sort of return to the comradeship of early times.
The last sum entered in her account-book was for her New
Year's present to him. We wish it had been his to her.
The manner of her death was strangely like that of her
mother. In December, 1544, a comet had appeared, supposed to be the presage of Paul III's end. Margaret took
it also as an augur of her own. She was anxious to see it,
and, in the contemplation of it, she caught the chill that
was fatal to her.

"Le vrai dormir, le très-doux sommeiller," she had written
of death when it was not near her. When it came, when
she was told that it must be soon, she did not wish to
die. She found, said Brantôme, "ce mot fort amer, disant
quelle n'était point tellement âgée, qu'elle ne put vivre encore
quelques années." But it was not to be. She received Extreme Unction from a simple Franciscan monk, without any
pomp or state. Soon after, her speech failed her and she
lay unconscious for three days. At the supreme moment,
she rallied. Some memory of her brother must have haunted her; like him, she called out "Jesus" three times
and fervently kissed the Cross which had lain all the
time in her arms. The struggle was over—her heart was
at peace. Her own prayer, made in past years, was at last
fulfilled.

Seigneur, quand viendra le jour
    Tant désiré
Que je serai par amour
    A vous tiré?...
Essuyez des tristes yeux
    Le long gémir,
Et me donnez pour le mieux
    Un doux dormir.

Whatever her husband's relations to her in her lifetime, there is no doubt about the sincerity of his sorrow. He was a weak creature and directly he had lost her he became a prey to remorse, perhaps also to the luxury of expressing it. He knew, too, how sorely he needed her at every turn and how ill he should get on without her. There is something touching, even dignified, in the description of his grief.

"What," says the old chronicler, "shall we say of the King, bereft of his Margaret? No longer did he run a strong course. He seemed as one swaying from side to side, wretched and ill at ease, like those, who unaccustomed to the sea, cross from one vessel to another, trying to avoid falling into the water. So this poor prince strayed hither and thither. In vain his people attempted to comfort him. 'Ha! my good subjects,' he cried, 'I know that one must leave off complaining and mend one's ills as one can. I know that this is the lesson which Reason teaches us—that, considering my rank, it is a dishonour to me to shed these womanish tears.'" (Philosophers, he says, may be allowed to weep, since moderation always keeps a dignity of its own.) "But I have come to a resolution, even though I wept as I made it. I am certain that we must all bow to the will

of God Who has wisely ordained this law for Man, only
making him mortal to deliver him from mortality by the
everlasting life of the soul.   And he who does not pay this
debt to God gaily is most miserable, both in life and in
death.   For that man is a bad soldier who follows his Captain reluctantly.   My mourning is deeper for you than for
myself.   She loved you with such a love that she would
have spared nothing for your good . . . . but as all must
suffer death . . . . (which we dread too much as a perilous
cliff in our voyage), I shall obey the great Pilot, even though
I am swallowed up in the hell of my anguish; and I shall
let myself drift with the wind which it pleaseth Him to
send me from heaven." [1]

Henry of Navarre had an eloquent tongue and eloquent
thoughts.   He probably in time persuaded himself that he
had been a good husband.   He had had his tender moments,
and it was easy to dwell upon them.   There is still a book
in the Library of the Arsenal in Paris, a book of Christian
instruction for children, which contains a miniature of them
both.   Henry is in a garden holding a flower towards Margaret,
who is seen behind a grating, robed in cloth of gold, with a
black head-dress and a veil.   Below the Navarre arms stands
written—"I have found a precious Marguerite and gathered
it into my inmost heart."   The portrait is not quite un-
truthful—the grating *is* between them.   It is thus, at all
events, that we like to remember them; thus that, after her
death, he did remember her. [2]

[1] Olhagaray : Histoire de Béarn et de Foix.

[2] His own was not till 1555, when his daughter Jeanne
succeeded him.

Margaret had the funeral that all Queens have. Her wax effigy was laid in the Church at Lescar and watched by three lords, holding the three Royal trophies : the crown, the sceptre, and the "Main de Justice," which was carried with her up to her tomb. All the great nobles of France were present at her funeral—all except Montmorency, who kept a grudge against her even at her death, and made himself conspicuous by his absence.

"The Sister and wife of Kings ; the Queen of the Muses ; the tenth of their band and their dearest care ; the fourth Charity ; the Queen of knowledge—lies beneath this marble." Such was the epitaph which a poetess wrote for her. Showers of funeral tropes followed in due season. Nor were they from France alone. In 1550, there appeared in Paris a volume of a hundred Latin distiches in her honour, composed by the three Seymour sisters, worth y[nieces of Lady Jane Grey and pupils of a French tutor, Nicholas Denisot. He himself, with a crowd of others, Baïf, Dorat and the like, translated these rhapsodies into Greek, French and Italian, and they added poems of their own. Ronsard and du Bellay, who can hardly have known her, followed suit with polished praise.

> Ici la Reine sommeille,
> Des Reines la nonpareille,
> Qui si doucement chanta ;
> C'est la Reine Marguerite,
> La plus belle fleur d'élite
> Qu'oncques l'Aurore enfanta.

So wrote Ronsard, most exquisite of laureates. All the harvest of panegyrics was ultimately gathered into a book,

"Le tombeau de la Reine de Navarre," to which Sainte-Marthe contributed his "Oraison funèbre"—a piece of living prose worth all the verses put together.

The best monument to the Queen's memory was perhaps the life of her niece—her favourite niece and her namesake, Margaret of Berri, Duchess of Savoy, who humbly modelled her life on that of her aunt. "For as the Easter Daisy, or Marguerite, hath the healing virtue and standeth as the symbol of consolation.... so did this princess bring comfort to many." She took the children of the countryside and brought them up. She was tender to the weak; she protected men of letters. Joachim du Bellay was her Marot: he burst into tears when he knew she was leaving France for her new duchy. She wrote passable poems—she cared for all that was beautiful—she refused (so Ronsard told her chronicler) many great suitors for the sake of Duke Emmanuel Philibert of Savoy, the man she loved; and, unlike the first Margaret, she married him in her youth. It was no fault of her aspirations if she did not accomplish so much in Savoy as her aunt had done in Navarre, but the fault of a mind less brilliant, less vigorous, less comprehensive, than that of Margaret of Angoulême.

For Margaret belongs not only to her time and her circle, or to the circumstance of her position. As a woman of letters she belongs to posterity and the world. Her gift, though not of the first order, was enough to entitle her to rank among the creators of literature; and if her personal life was over, her public life lasted on. The "Heptameron" will always be her chief title to fame. It is a collection of Boccaccian stories told by a goodly company of men and

women, full of life and laughter, whom her subtle pen has
painted in vivid colours. Some of them were portraits—
many of their narratives were true. Margaret took little
pains to mask either people or events, even where her own
love-affairs were concerned. And the book holds the memory
of her Pyrenean country. Every description breathes with
personal experience, whether she writes of the storm and
the mountain-torrent which prevented the progress of the
company, or the hillside monastery which sheltered them,
and the green Alpine meadows where they sat to tell their
tales.

She wrote these *Nouvelles* between 1544 and '48. [1] One of
her favourite writers, Antoine Le Maçon, had come back some
time before from Florence, and had, by her orders, published a
volume of Boccaccian romances which he brought with him.
Their success was unheard of. She tells us that the King,
the Dauphin, the Dauphine " made so great a stir about
them, that, could Boccaccio have heard their illustrious
praise, it would have raised him from the dead." Margaret,
Catherine de Médicis, and the great Sénéchale of Poitou agreed
to write a rival book together and took to their pens with
enthusiasm. But events of importance intervening, they had
to let the scheme drop, and Margaret was the only one who
resumed it, just about the time of Francis' illness. The
work was not published till 1558, nineteen years after her
death, by one, Pierre Boaisteau, who altered the whole book,
even to its name, and called it "Histoire des amants fortunés."

[1] See "Life of Margaret of Angoulême" by Miss Mary Robinson, whose argument for the adoption of these dates seems
conclusive.

Jeanne complained of the wrong thus done to her mother, and another publisher brought out a new edition, fairly faithful to the original text [1] and dedicated to the author's daughter. Thus, with many emendations, have the tales come down to us; and as fresh critics have arisen, fresh light has been thrown, thin disguises have been removed, personages identified. As a picture of the morals of the day—of its queer mixture of vices and virtues—of court comedy and court tragedy—it stands alone of its kind. The art that wove the rich tapestry is no small one; an art which, at this moment, startles us by its freedom: at that, charms us by a sweetness and sublety all its own. The hand is the hand of a Princess, but the voice is the voice of a human being; we feel that each word is written by an unworldly woman of the world.

When we come to the poems, praise flows more slowly. The tradition of her day was a dull one—at best a tradition of naïve philosophy—and she was more intellectual than poetic. Her thoughts are often interesting. If she repeats them till we are tired, we must remember that they were fresh discoveries to her. She was full of the new sense of natural law, of harmony in all things.

> "En l'homme et bête; animaux et en plantes,
>   Un seul en tous est être et mouvement,
>   Vie, penser, raison et sentiment."

[1] He was a cautious editor and left out passages, even stories, which he thought too heretical for safety; but he re-established the order in which the Queen of Navarre herself told the tales.

"Le Miroir de l'âme pécheresse," we have already glanced at. It is a long evangelical hymn of conversion and its main interest lies in the risks that she ran for it. Probably the Sorbonne found other reasons for condemning it beside those that it alleged. There are one or two phrases referring to her past life which, however great her repentance, might well cause alarm in the hearts of suspicious old divines. She confesses her former doubts to God; she tells Him she thought Him an immoral Being; she cites the language she once used.

> Vous nous faites de mal-faire défense,
> Et pareil mal faites sans conscience.
> Vous défendez de tuer, à chacun,
> Mais vous tuez sans epargner aucun
> De vingt trois mille que vous faites défaire.

Of the Scriptures she says:

> Las! tous ces mots ne voulais écouter.
> Mais encore je venais à douter
> Si c'était vous, ou si, par aventure,
> Ce n'était rien qu'une simple écriture.

These are strong words for any generation—Voltaire would not have disowned them. But the charm of Margaret was unconsciousness, and when she uttered what was daring, it came as much from her heart as did the romantic mysticism of her later days.

We feel no reluctance in quitting her reflective poems. Yet amid her vast tracts of rhyme, there spring up here and there little flowers of thought and fancy which we should like to gather up in a posy. There are her lines

on Joan of Arc—the flawless crystal lamp—"toute déifiée,"
through which God's light shone clearly. Or her sonnets
on sacred and profane passion, in which the greater Love,
finding the smaller, tears the bandage from its eyes, the light
wings "du corps trop tendre et beau," and then takes the
wounded Cupid in his arms and makes of it a bigger Love
than it has been. Or here, to continue, is her description
of the work of poets :

> De toutes fleurs chacun livre est couvert,
> Faites d'émail sur un fonds de velours vert...
> L'entendement n'en est à nul donné,
> Fors à celui qui est poëte né.

The last two lines are very like an aphorism. So is her :

> "Faits passés sont maîtres des présents."

a foretaste of modern ideas.

Margaret's pen had its sprightly moods and was charming in them—in her recipe for Life, for instance :

> Trois onces faut prendre de patience ;
> Puis de repos et paix de conscience
> Il en faut bien la livre entière...
> ... Pomme d'amour faut prendre, mais bien peu—
> ... De moquerie une once, voire deux...

A grain of the "moquerie" sometimes steals into her
Pastorals and Interludes. The most important among them
is perhaps "La Coche"—the old word for Coach—dedicated,
in the days of their friendship, to the Duchesse d'Etampes.
There is in it a picture which shows Margaret on her knees,
presenting her book to the Duchess. This is the least ab-

stract part of the work; the rest is feminine metaphysics. Three weeping ladies dispute with academic fantasy as to which of them should bear the palm for sorrow. Margaret listens to them in a grove and cheers their occasional swoons. The first loves and is no longer loved; the second has been deserted for another; the third, who is the most highly-strung, has renounced a paragon lover for the sake of her two mournful friends. Nothing short of a storm can check their elegiac prolixities. It breaks; a large, unessential Coach rolls vaguely on to the scene and they are carried off in it by Margaret, who resolves to write down their sad case and bring it before an umpire—the Duchesse d'Etampes. She is a magnificent umpire in cloth of gold and ermine and "force pierreries;" and she is sure to out-Solomon Solomon. So all are content, and the "Coche" bears the lachrymose company into the land of oblivion.

The whole poem is not wanting in a kind of stiff fascination, but it touches no human chord. It was reserved for sorrow to draw real poetry out of Margaret. Her verses about Francis are many, but perhaps the tenderest and most musical of her poems is one that she wrote to a Baby Princess, a child of her brother's who died young. It is an exception among the earlier poems, usually colder and more elaborate: but, again, the inspiration which warms it is drawn from the depths of grief. It takes the form of a dialogue between herself and the little spirit.

(MADAME CHARLOTTE PARLANT A SON AME)

Saillez dehors, mon âme, je vous prie,
Du triste corps tout plein de fascherie—

—Où vous étiez en obscure prison—
Pour parvenir à la belle maison,
Avec les saints et leur confrèrie;
Laissez-le là puisqu'il en est saison;
    Saillez dehors.

(MADAME LA DUCHESSE PARLANT A L'AME DE MADAME CHARLOTTE)

Répondez-moi, ô douce âme vivante,
Qui par la mort, qui les fous épouvante,
Avez été d'un petit corps délivré,
Lequel, huit ans accomplis, n'a su vivre;
Dites comment en la cour triomphante
De votre Roi et Père êtes contente,
En déclarant comme amour vous enivre,
    Répondez-moi !

Las ! mon enfant, parlez à votre tante
Que tant laissez après vous languissante,
. . . .
Pour soulager ma douleur véhémente,
    Répondez-moi !

(RÉPONSE DE L'AME)

Contentez-vous, tante trop ignorante,
Puisqu'ainsi plait à la Bonté puissante
D'avoir voulu la séparation
Du petit corps, duquel l'affection
Vous en rendait la vue trop plaisante.
Je suis ici belle, claire et luysante,
Pleine de Dieu et de lui jouissante;
N'en ayez deuil ni désolation.
    Contentez-vous !

Her own poem is a fitting close to the story of Margaret
of Angoulême—la perle des Valois; of Margaret of Navarre,

the sister, the wife, the friend, the poet. Other words of hers there are—words that she wrote about herself—which seem to us still more fitting: a truer epitaph than those which poetasters composed for her, and yet too simple and unconscious for any sepulchral marble. "Celle," they run, "qui a plus porté que son faix de l'ennui commun à toute créature bien-née."

Queen that she was, she had borne the burden—and she slept in her turn.

Her name is inseparable from her age; inseparable from the brother whom she loved. In some ways they were the complement, in others, the opposite of one another. The contrast they presented in their early days held good at the end of their lives. Both may be said to have fallen short in achievement, if their deeds are compared with the aims with which they set out. Francis failed from too little feeling; Margaret from too much. He lacked the seriousness, the weight and concentration, which are needful to carry out big purposes. Had he boasted these qualities, the fate of Italy would have been different. He would either have never tried to win her, or else he would not have lost her. He would not have betrayed Reform; he would have enlarged the field of the Renaissance. Had he simply been bad, or had he possessed less sensibility, he might have pursued the single-minded policy of a cool nature. But this he could not do, even in matters of detail. Cold and impressionable, choked by his impulses, blown hither and thither by the senses, he did not know what he was making for, and he ruined his own heart as well as the hearts of others.

He caused enough suffering to Margaret. He could not injure a character so rich and so noble as hers. Her personality must have left its trace on everybody who knew her, and, in this way, she accomplished more than she dreamed of. But had it not been for him, she would, we must repeat it, have fulfilled the ideal of Erasmus; she would have created a Broad Church in France. Whether or no it could have taken root in a nation which likes all or nothing—scepticism or Rome—is a very different question. But she would in any case have founded a tradition of enlightenment; she might have softened and widened Catholicism, and curbed its cruelty and intolerance. The period that followed hers was one of the ugliest in history. It was a period of cynical bigotry and coarse persecution; of effeminate corruption, of exhaustion caused by surfeit. The best days of the Pleïade ended with its leaders; those of the Renaissance artists, with Lescot and de l'Orme—with Goujon and with Palissy. Art became impure and decadent, busy with luxury and detail. As for Romance, it was buried beneath Materialism.

This had not been the case in the reign of Francis. Whatever the grossness of his age, it was grossness capable of heroism. It sought no dark corners; it was frank to excess. Whatever the immorality, there was about it a certain naïveté—an effervescence belonging to a day when men had the force to enjoy themselves. The grossness and the vice were alike deplorable, but they were the seamy side of a wholesome-minded time, ignorant of the subterfuges of satiety. It was a time of beliefs and convictions strong enough to make a Rabelais—to create a great and generous art. And Francis I and his sister, apart from their faults or their virtues, were at least faithful to one charge: they were ever the protectors of the Beautiful. Margaret of Angoulême went further—she held out her hand to the thinkers of her generation. Though all else about her be forgotten, this should be remembered: she was, from beginning to end, the loyal servant of knowledge; the friend of the Graces; the guardian-spirit of the French Renaissance.

INDEX

INDEX

A

B

C

R

V

W

Z